A Critique of Fabricated, Discriminatory, Judgmental, and Sexist World Religions

Lifting the Spiritual Self-Esteem of the LGBT Community

Khepra Ka-Re Amente Anu

iUniverse, Inc.
Bloomington

iUniverse books may be ordered through booksellers or by contacting:

iUniverse
1663 Liberty Drive
Bloomington, IN 47403
www.iuniverse.com
1-800-Authors (1-800-288-4677)

Because of the dynamic nature of the Internet, any web addresses or links contained in this book may have changed since publication and may no longer be valid. The views expressed in this work are solely those of the author and do not necessarily reflect the views of the publisher, and the publisher hereby disclaims any responsibility for them.

ISBN: 978-1-4502-9934-3 (sc)
ISBN: 978-1-4502-9935-0 (hc)
ISBN: 978-1-4502-9936-7 (ebook)

Library of Congress Control Number: 2011903164

Printed in the United States of America

iUniverse rev. date: 6/26/2012

Dedicated to Miriam, Lisa, and Gwen

"All national institutions of churches, whether Jewish, Christian, or Turkish, appear to me no other than human inventions, set up to terrify and enslave mankind, and monopolize power and profit."

Thomas Paine 1737–1809

Author, journalist, intellectual, radical, revolutionist, and one of the founding fathers of the United States of America

Contents

PREFACE

The first reason I made the decision to write Lifting the Spiritual Self-Esteem of the LGBT Community: A Critique of Fabricated, Discriminatory, Judgmental, and Sexist World Religions, is to provide support and information to any Lesbian, Gay, Bi-Sexual or Transgender individual who has serious concerns about any world religion that claims to be the word of some God or chosen spiritual one. Secondly, the LGBT community should counter and then ignore the ridiculous religious claims that the LGBT lifestyle is in violation of the word of God and is somehow unnatural and aberrant.

(Note: I do not like using the "H" word; to me, saying someone is homosexual is like using the "N" word.)

Anyone with any level of intelligence, living in this present time and place on Earth, knows that sexual preferences are predetermined at birth. I am a heterosexual African-American male, and it is disturbing to me when I hear people use religion as the basis for their anti-LGBT beliefs.

Would anyone in their right mind base their spiritual self-esteem on Bigfoot, Santa Claus, or Peter Pan? These are fictional stories. Religion is man-made, mythological, discriminatory, judgmental, sexist, ethically divisive, and monetarily driven. Religion is nothing more than a reworking of astronomy and African/Kemetic/Egyptian/Anu/Ethiopian stories, woven into unique ethnic cultural and spiritual myths.

It is my hope that the information in this book will give the LGBT community (or any heterosexual individual) source material to use against any extreme individual, organization, or religious denomination that tries to project and impose their man-made, mythological, judgmental, discriminatory, and narrow-minded religious beliefs onto others.

People who use religion to bully others should be refuted with facts about their own religion and beliefs. None of us is perfect, and until these extreme individuals and religions get their own hypocritical lifestyles together, they need to go sit down in a corner and figure out how to stop their aberrant and immoral behavior.

Religious leaders often engage in deviant behavior, fueled by rampant abuse of authority. They use God as the predatory vehicle to seek sexual gratification from women and inflict sexual abuse on children, women, and men.

They need to take a long hard look at the violence found within their religious texts and examine the psychotic sanctioning of slavery and discrimination found in the scriptures of Christianity, Judaism, Hinduism, and Islam.

Religions like Christianity and Judaism need to do something about their scriptures, which condone the unconscionable enslavement of children and the buying, selling, and owning of slaves; they even go so far as to tell the believers how hard you can beat a slave and how many days are allotted if the slave dies before there are consequences for the slave master.

Scriptures in Christianity even tell slaves how obedient and loyal they should be to their masters. Until religion gets its moral compass aligned, it cannot have an intelligent, credible, or moral position on social, civil, and human rights issues like same sex marriage.

Not everyone has a problem with their spiritual self-esteem. To those who do, my grandmother told me that the only thing for certain is that we are all going to die at some point in time. Only then will we know what comes next: heaven, hell, or a very long restful sleep. It makes no sense worrying about death.

All you can do in life is be a good person: respect others; respect the earth; care for animals—if you can afford to; try to reach your full potential; be the best person you can be; help others; avoid having preconceived beliefs about others; and love and take care of yourself and your loved ones. There may be other things you can do to be a good person, but if you do the above, you would be considered a good spiritual person, in my opinion.

This brings me to the third and main reason I wrote this book. I am part of a large extended family. Two of my cousins, Miriam and Mark, are members of the LGBT community—Miriam is a lesbian and Mark is gay. Our family is very religious (Christian); whenever I would talk to Miriam and Mark the topic of religion would always come up. They are fine with their sexual orientation and know it was predetermined at birth.

My extended family members love and support my two cousins unconditionally; however, they project their judgment day scenario fears onto them. As a result, they were concerned about the negative position religion held regarding Miriam and Mark's LGBT lifestyle. My two cousins are strong-minded, successful people. One day when I was talking to Miriam, she said that she and Mark had come to the conclusion that they would like to go to heaven, but if it meant giving up their lifestyle for religion, they would just as soon go to hell.

Miriam told me that sometimes her spiritual self-esteem was low. I began to share with her the information I had learned about the man-made origins of the world's religions. I also mentioned how they were myths woven into unique ethnic, cultural, and spiritual stories—especially Christianity. I provided Miriam with a list of scholars and authors from many different fields: researchers, historians, scientists, biologists, and anthropologists.

I wanted Miriam and Mark to be able to counter the religious arguments against their LGBT community. Miriam took the time to learn more about what we had talked about and shared the information with Mark and their friends. Months later, when the three of us got together, Miriam and Mark told me how much the information had helped them with their spiritual self-esteem. They suggested that I share the information with others in the LGBT community, as well as people in the heterosexual community who may have a similar problem with religion. This gave me the idea to write this book.

Religion does not have all the answers. Religion is just someone's opinion, and people have the right to believe or disbelieve the message. I am a student of African/Kemetic/Egyptian/Anu/Ethiopian history. I have spent the last twenty-five years studying, researching, and teaching this history. In the writing of this book, I have utilized the knowledge I acquired over those twenty-five years.

Let me make several points before you begin to read this book. First, my name, Khepra Ka-Re Amente Anu, is an East African name. It is not a Muslim name and is not associated in any way with the man-made religion of Islam.

"Khepra" is the name of a mythical African male creation god. "Ka" is the word for the human spirit. "Re" is the name of another mythical African male creation god. "Amente" has the same meaning as the word "Amenta"; according to many Egyptologists, Amente is the place where the departed soul goes on its path to everlastingness and eternity.

When I chose the name Amente, I did so because it is considered by some African historians to also be the female counterpart to the mythical male creator god Amen, and half of my genes come from my mother. "Anu" is the name of the mythical first ethnic group of Ethiopia or East Africa, which includes the mythical characters Osiris, Isis, Heru (Horus), and Tehuti (Thoth). They are referred to by Egyptologists as the Black Anu.

Second, I use the term African/Kemetic/Egyptian/Anu/Ethiopian because both Egypt and Ethiopia are on the continent of Africa. Kemet is an aboriginal name for Egypt and Anu is an aboriginal name for Ethiopia. The mythical religion of Kemet/Egypt originated from East Africa/Ethiopia/Sudan/Kenya, and is a reworking of ancient African religious myths. Throughout the book I will use the term Africa/Kemet/Anu to refer to the regions mythical religion and geographical location.

The oldest near complete fossil skeleton remains of human ancestors —Ardi (4.4 million years old) and Lucy (3.2 million years old)—were found in present-day Ethiopia.

Many of the predynastic mythical gods and goddesses—like Osiris, Isis, Nephthys, Seth (Set), Heru, and Tehuti—are associated with Ethiopia and the East Africa region. Religious and symbolic structures like the Tejen or Tekhen (obelisk) are located in Ethiopia—see chapter 6 for the African/Kemetic/Anu symbolic history and meaning of the Tejen or Tekhen.

People existed in Africa before 3100 BCE and the start of the Egyptian dynasties, with their mythical religious beliefs. The religious beliefs of the Egyptians did not just appear out of nowhere; their religious myths are nothing more than a reworking of other African religious myths.

Third, the scriptures of Islam, Judaism, and Christianity are much younger than the religions claim them to be. I am being kind to these religions when I list the dates of the origin of their beginnings in this book.

I am more concerned in this book with critiquing the similarities between the religions themselves and the way the myths repeat the same mythical concepts and fables.

Astronomy has also influenced the world's main religions—the sun, moon, stars, and constellations play a symbolic role in the representations of religious symbols and myths.

INTRODUCTION

Let me state up front that I believe that man-made religion is not the word of some god or divine prophet of a god, but a reworking of astronomy and mythical African/Kemetic/Anu stories. I also believe that African/Kemetic/Anu religion is based on mythical stories and beliefs of ancient African people. My purpose throughout this book is to critique the religious writings, hymns, texts, spiritual books and mythical stories of all the world's dominant religions. This is to identify their similarity and common origin.

Religion is nothing more than man-made myths; it is not the word of God. When you see the similarities, you can draw your own conclusions.

I have no agenda in writing this book. I am an African-American male who was raised a Christian. When I write about African/Kemetic/Anu history and culture, I am writing about all of our history and culture. I believe that all humans come from a common ancestor in East Africa; we are all related. We are all literally cousins of each other.

It is important to understand how we verify history before we begin to look at how astronomy and African/Kemetic/Anu religious myths and culture have influenced the formation of the world's dominant religions. There are several ways to verify history: cultural anthropology—the study of cultures, societies, and civilizations; social anthropology—the study of people and their interactions; linguistic anthropology—the study of language; biological anthropology—the study of bones, fossils, and stages of development; and archeology—the study of artifacts and structures found in cultures. Through radio carbon dating, we can determine the age of an object by testing its rate of decay.

Historical references are divided into original sources (called a primary source)—looking at someone or something in person; secondary sources—a picture, drawing, recording, or video of something that requires analysis; and tertiary sources—a written summary of some event or people. During the course of this book, you need to be aware of what sources of information I am drawing my conclusions from. The older a source is—it has the potential to be more credible and reliable.

Anthropological research and radio carbon dating tell us that life began in East Africa; there are two theories as to when the migration out of Africa started. Some researchers believe that a type of human ancestor called a hominid began leaving Africa to populate the world about 2.5 million years ago. The dominant theory supported by most scientists, however, is that modern humans left Africa only about 200,000 years ago (some believe it occurred only 40,000 years ago). These people followed coastlines, crossed over land, walked across land bridges, and navigated short waterways by boat to populate the world.

Most anthropologist and scientist now have come to the same conclusion that historians have been saying since the 1800s. Modern humans lived in Africa for a very long time. Evidence now supports the theory that modern humans evolved some 200,000 years ago. These modern humans evolved physically into humans first, but not behaviorally. Some 200,000 years ago, there was an abrupt and dramatic change in subsistence patterns, use of tools, and symbolic expression. The dramatic change in cultural adaptation was not just quantitative but represented a qualitative transformation. We are who we are today because of this creative explosion.

I am interested in this explosion of symbolic expressions, spiritual beliefs, myths, and ritualistic practices. Modern humans lived in one geographical location (Africa) for thousands of years before they began to migrate. This explains why, even though humans moved to different parts of the earth, they still maintain common elements when it comes to religious myths.

When modern humans began to migrate out of Africa, they faced extreme hardships: global freeze-ups, harsh winters, several major and minor ice ages, and catastrophic volcano eruptions. Sometimes almost whole generations were wiped out. The further away form Africa people moved–Europe, Asia, North America, South America, Australia, New Zealand etc.–the more diverse and unique their myths of religion are, even though as mentioned, the religious myths still maintain common similar elements.

People migrated out of Africa to form the many beautiful cultures around the world today. Human beings are of one species; we are all the same on the inside, and our outer physical differences are minor. There is only one human race, with many diverse ethnic groups populating the earth. Race is a sociological term used to divide people; it often makes us lose sight of our common bond. No ethnic group can claim Africa as their exclusive homeland. We are all descended from Africa, and the history of that continent is all of ours—not to steal, plunder, or destroy but to share.

Animals, on the other hand, come in different species. You can take major organs from one human and transplant them into another. You cannot take an organ from an elephant and transplant it into a dolphin, for example.

There are so many religions in the world today that one cannot count all of them. Most religions develop some type of a creation myth. Science, anthropology, and the subdivisions of anthropology mentioned earlier help us understand how we got here, where we came from, and how we are all related.

This book does not address who left Africa first, whether modern humans replaced the hominids who died out after leaving Africa, or which developmental level of humans we are descended from. It does not matter whether it was hominids or modern humans who left Africa first. Anthropology tells us that we are all descended from East Africa, we are one species, and we are distant cousins of each other. When I write about the history of Africa/Kemet/Anu, I am writing about all of our history. I am not promoting some ethnic agenda. The world's history belongs to all of us.

How old are the world's religions? That question is open for debate. The spiritual practices, beliefs, and expression of ancient religions go back 200,000 years in Africa when modern humans developed. To show how advanced humans were during this period, in June of 2010, archeologists discovered a 58,000-year-old ochre powder production site north of Durban in KwaZulu-Natal, South Africa.

Keep in mind that East Africa is where the oldest (near complete) fossil skeletons of human ancestors have been found. Younger, as old, or older (partial fossil) skeletons of human ancestors have also been found in East Africa. Kadanuumuu, a 3.6 million year old Australopithecus afarenis partial skeleton was discovered in Ethiopia in 2005 by a team of anthropologist led by Yohannes Haile-Selassie, Curator and Head of Physical Anthropology at the Cleveland Museum of Natural History located in my hometown of Cleveland, Ohio.

Kadanuumuu was introduced by Haile-Salassie and others including anthropologist Dr. C. Owen Lovejoy of Kent State University my college alma mater located in Kent, Ohio. Dr. Lovejoy worked on the analysis of the fossil findings. Toumai, a history altering six million year old hominid skull was found in the Central African country of Chad in 2002. Three 160,000 year old anatomically modern fossil skulls of Homo sapiens were found in the Afar region of Ethiopia in 2003, two adults and one child.

In 2008 the son of a scientist accidentally discovered the 1.977 million year old partial skeleton remains of an extinct hominid called Australopithecus Sediba in a cave in South Africa. The discovery in the cave included several specimens including the remains of a juvenile male as developed as a 10 to 13 year old and an adult female in her 20's or early 30's.

"Lucy," an Australopithecus afarensis skeleton 3.2 million years old, was found in 1974 near Hadar, Ethiopia, and on October 1, 2009, archeologists announced the discovery of "Ardi," a Ardipithecus ramidus skeleton 4.4 million years old. This skeleton actually discovered 17 years before the announcement in 2009—was also found in Ethiopia, forty-six miles from Lucy. Both Lucy and Ardi are not modern humans (Homo sapiens sapiens), but as mentioned earlier, are near complete fossil skeleton remains of human ancestors. Lucy and Ardi are also referred to as Hominids. Human development and evolution went thru many stages. The names used for the stages of human development and evolution can vary depending on who the scientist, anthropologist, or source is.

Many of the stages have long and confusing names. Examples are (not in any chronological order): Australopithecus ramidus, Australopithecus africanus, Australopithecus afarensis, Australopithecus robustus, Dryopithecus, Ramapithecus, Homo habilis, Homo erectus, Homo neanderthalensis, Hominids, Homo sapiens, Homo sapiens sapiens, etc. Humans were in Africa for a long period of time before the main migration took place; 4.4 million years ago is a long time for the development of humans. But one can ask the question, how far back in Africa does the belief in some mythical religious story go?

The oldest religious/spiritual book is the African/Kemetic/Anu, *Book of Coming Forth by Day* (Book of the Dead), which goes back to the Old Kingdom in Africa/Kemet/Anu, about 2649 BCE to 2184 BCE. (Note: when two dates are used, the dates are an approximate range of years as to when the particular religion began.) Many scholars and researchers think that the Book of Coming Forth by Day is much older, but I am going to go with the origin dates mentioned above.

These are the approximate origin dates of selected religions—for comparison to the approximate origin date of African/Kemetic/Anu religion and the Book of Coming Forth by Day: Hinduism, 2000 BCE (in India); Judaism, 1000 BCE (in Palestine); Zoroastrianism, 628–527 BCE (in Persia); Buddhism, 600–501 BCE (in India); Jainism, 599–527 BCE (in India); Taoism, 580–500 BCE, and Confucianism, 551–469 BCE (both in China); Christianity, 1-325 CE (in Palestine); Shinto, 100 CE (in Japan); Islam, 570–632 CE (the Arabian Peninsula); Sikhism, 1469–1538 CE (in India); Rastafarian, 1920–1930 CE (in Jamaica); Unification Church, 1954 CE (South Korea); Hare Krishna, 1966 CE (roots in fifteenth-century Hinduism in India); and Falun Gong, 1992 CE (in China).

Jainism and Falun Gong both adopted the equilateral cross (aka the swastika) as their spiritual emblem. The equilateral cross without the bent angles can also be found in the Mdw Ntr (hieroglyphics) of Africa/Kemet/Anu. This cross was stolen and forever tarnished by the psychotic and barbaric Nazi regime of World War II. Religions in Asia, India, Europe, and Africa, as well as Native Americans, have used the equilateral cross as their spiritual symbol. Unfortunately, if one were to wear it today in mainstream America or Europe, it would be perceived as offensive to most people and associated with the Nazis or some other extreme hate group. The Nazis perversion of the equilateral cross is similar to the American Ku Klux Klan's perversion of the Christian cross.

The equilateral cross represents affluence, happiness, comfort, safety, and good luck. In the religion of Jainism, the equilateral cross is bent at right angles and is right facing; in the religion of the Falun Gong, it is reversed and left facing (which way it is facing depends on the top horizontal line of the cross).

The Nazis of World War II (and hate groups of today) were and are, ignorant, simple-minded, and bigoted people, who wore and wear this religious ancestral emblem. They hated and hate Jewish-Americans, African-Americans, Latino-Americans, the LGBT community, and anyone who did and does not belong to their ethnic group.

The Nazis (like the hate groups of today) probably did not know about the original meaning of the swastika. The equilateral cross's positive connotations contradict their psychotic beliefs.

African/Kemetic/Anu man-made religious myths are the main source used for the religious myths found within the world's dominant religions of Christianity, Judaism, Islam, and Buddhism. Hinduism is not as old as African/Kemetic/Anu religious myths, but some texts predate some African/Kemetic/Anu religious myths.

Some of the African/Kemetic/Anu scriptures were reworked over the many Egyptian dynasties. The evolution of African/Kemetic/Anu texts started even before the beginning of the Old Kingdom (2649 BCE), and many of the myths were continually revised by men until the last African/Kemetic/Anu dynasties.

The oldest religious myths carved into stone or clay (and also written on paper, papyrus, or scrolls) are from the religions of Africa/Kemet/Anu and Hinduism. Therefore, it is only fair to say that some African/Kemetic/Anu religious myths could be a reworking of Hindu religious myths.

Regardless of which is more ancient, the fact is that all religious myths are similar and not the word of God but the imaginary writings of men.

Something or someone created the universe, stars, planets, and all life on earth. There is too much order for the creation to have happened just by accident. Our ability to use our cognitive/intellectual ability to think in the abstract (i.e. street smart, our true form of intelligence) is what separates us from the animals on the earth.

This is where the science of cosmogony (the study of the origin of the universe) and belief in a creator come together looking for an answer. Scientists have no clue how the Big Bang occurred; they know what happened after the Big Bang but are baffled by what caused it. It is also interesting how similar the creation stories of Africa/Kemet/Anu and the Book of Genesis in the Bible are with the scientific Big Bang theory.

Even though I have strong opinions on religion, I am in no position to judge whether religion is good or bad for a person in their life. People have to decide what helps them deal with the everyday scenario that life presents to us. There are certain facts in life: two of them are life and death. Someone (or something) created us, and only when we pass over will we know for sure what our fate will be.

In making a case for the spiritual self-esteem of individuals and the LGBT community, I find it strange that religion teaches that God created the heavens and the earth and all that inhabit the earth. On the sixth day, God saw everything he had made and decided it was very good. Then on the seventh day, God ended his work, blessed it, and sanctified it. What does this say about the LGBT community (and the animals that are part of the animal LGBT community)?

Any normal thinking person knows that sexual preference is predetermined at birth in both animals and humans. If the LGBT lifestyle is unnatural and aberrant, then why have so many animals been documented exhibiting LGBT behavior?

Zoologists and animal behaviorists claim that over 1,500 species of animals display some form of LGBT behavior. This includes insects, creatures that reside in the water, birds that fly, and animals that walk and reside on land. Whether it is same-sex courtship, displays of affection, sexual activity, long-term pairings, or parenting, the fact that LGBT behavior among animals is so widespread is proof that it is not unnatural or biologically aberrant.

Sexual preference is predetermined at birth by whoever created us, and whether you are LGBT or heterosexual, you should be proud of yourself.

I am also concerned with religion's judgmental, discriminatory, sexist, and monetary-driven beliefs and practices. If you want to believe in a religion that is mythical and fictitious, that is your free choice, but there is no justification for using your religious beliefs to judge and discriminate against the LGBT community, women, or take advantage of people monetarily.

The striking similarities between the world's religions all point to a common source for their creation. The LGBT community and individuals with legitimate concerns should not base their spiritual self-esteem on religions that are nothing more than the opinion of men, who want to tell others how to live their lives.

One way we can see that religion is man-made is by the way women are treated. The Christian church my mother and I attended treated women like second-class members. Women could not be ministers, sit on the deacon board, or hold any leadership position in the church. The only thing I remember women doing were teaching Bible classes, cooking and serving food, or being the secretary.

Why would any god restrict the leadership potential and limit the input of one half of the human creation? Many women in history have been charismatic and transformational leaders. Women have been pharaohs, queens, and CEOs; they have founded history-altering organizations. This institutionalized discrimination against women shows that religion is man-made and is used as a tool to control women.

Even when I was child, I was bothered by the practice of using religion to raise money. You had to give a percentage of your income to the church. There was a building fund, auxiliary fund, church fund, and deacon fund. The minister always drove a new car, lived in a nice home, and wore nice clothes. I used to say to myself, Didn't Jesus have a job as a carpenter? Did

Jesus ever charge anybody for a sermon? (Just kidding!) Despite my views, most religions need these funds to build a place to worship and recruit the best ministers.

However, there are certain financial practices that cannot be condoned: using religion to sanction and promote slavery for economic profit; selling people fake relics or healing items; and telling people the minister can solve their social and economic problems through prayer if they send in money.

Let me state what I hope a reader comes away with after reading *Lifting the Spiritual Self-Esteem of the LGBT Community.* This is not a book on the historical formation and chronology of the world's dominant religions. It is a critique for criticism focusing on man-made fabricated world religions.

This book uses the actual scriptures of the world's dominant religions or summaries of scriptures to show similarities and common origin. The numerous religious excerpts, summaries of texts, and references to astronomy are presented only for comparison, similarities, and man-made origin.

By the end of this book—after reading all the similar beliefs in God, creation myths, divine saviors, religious concepts, and mythical stories—I hope the reader comes to the conclusion that religion is not the word of some god but is instead just the writings of men.

It is my hope that no one after reading *Lifting the Spiritual Self-Esteem of the LGBT Community* will feel they are doomed to go to some mythical hell because of their biologically predetermined LGBT lifestyle. I hope everyone, especially our young LGBT teenagers, can live a happy, secure, and comfortable life with high personal and spiritual self-esteem, while at the same time caring for others, respecting yourself and others, respecting the earth and all life on it, and being the best and most productive person you can be.

Everyone born into this world has something to offer the world and with hard work, determination, and the opportunity can make the world a better place. Hopefully *Lifting the Spiritual Self-Esteem of the LGBT Community* can help in some small way.

Chapter 1

Belief in a God or Gods

How manifold it is, what thou hast made!
They are hidden from the face (of man).
O sole god, like whom there is no other!
Thou didst create the world according to thy desire,
Whilst thou wert alone: All men, cattle, and wild beast,
Whatever is on earth, going upon (its) feet,
And what is on high, flying with its wings.

This first excerpt is a mythical concept of a monotheistic god from the Hymn to Aten in the tomb of Ay. It is attributed to Pharaoh Akhenaten, who ruled Africa/Kemet/Anu from 1353 to 1336 BCE. During his rule, he elevated Aten to supreme god and forbid the worship of all other gods.

God is one and alone, and none other existeth with him—God is the One, the One who hath made all things—God is a spirit, a hidden spirit, the spirit of spirits, the great spirit of the Egyptians, the divine spirit—God is from the beginning, and he hath been from the beginning, he hath existed from old and was when nothing else had being, he existed when nothing else existed, and what existed he created after he had come into being. He is the father of beginnings—God is the eternal One, he is eternal and infinite and endureth for ever and aye—God is hidden and no man knoweth his form. No man hath been able to seek out his likeness; he is hidden to gods and men, and he is a mystery unto his creatures.… He is the king of truth, and he hath stablished the earth thereupon—God is life

1

and through him only man liveth. He giveth life to man. He breatheth the breath of life into his nostrils—God is father and mother, the father of fathers, and the mother of mothers. He begetteth, but was never begotten; he produceth, but was never produced; he begat himself and produced himself, he createth, but was never created.… God is merciful to those who reverence him, and he heareth him that calleth upon him. God knoweth him that acknowledgeth him, he rewardeth him that serveth him, and he protecteth him that followeth him.

The above compilation of attributes and characteristics of a mythical monotheistic god was compiled from ancient African/Kemetic/Anu funerary, pyramid, and coffin texts by Heinrich Karl Brugsch (1827-1894 CE), a German Egyptologist and scholar.

The same characteristics can be found in the *Book of Coming Forth by Day* most commonly known as the *Book of the Dead*. The *Book of Coming Forth by Day* is a compilation of ancient African/Kemetic/Anu funerary, pyramid, and coffin texts.

Brugsch worked on the translation of the Rosetta Stone and was a friend and associate of the French scholar and archeologist Auguste Mariette (1821–1881 CE) in his archeological excavations at Memphis, Egypt. He was director of the School of Egyptology in Cairo, Egypt, and he was the African/Kemetic/Egyptian commissioner at the Philadelphia World Exposition of 1876 CE.

Religion has no moral authority or credibility to judge the LGBT community because there is enough evidence to question its origin. From my research, religions are man-made with a common origin. There are seven common characteristics of most religions: a belief in God; a creation myth; the birth, death, and resurrection of a divine savior; a code of ethics; a philosophy of trying to attain spiritual peace/harmony/salvation; a belief in immortality; and a judgment day resurrection or continuing cycle of reincarnation, regeneration, and rebirth (or an end to that cycle).

I will write about creation gods and myths later in the book, but here is an interesting myth of several gods in the form of a creation myth.

The Creation Myth of the Heliopolis Ennead

In the beginning, there was only Nu (or Nun), the dark, primordial, chaotic, churning, bubbling waters; nothing existed. The waters began to recede, and a small pyramid-shaped hill (Benben) arose, then more. On Benben stood Atum (Atem), the first of the gods. (Note: Atum was first worshipped as an earth/solar god, then in later dynasties exclusively as a solar god.) In one myth, Atum then coughed (or sneezed) up his son Shu, the god of the air, and spat (or vomited) out his daughter Tefnut, the goddess of moisture. The coughing and sneezing represent "air" Shu. The spitting and vomiting represent "moisture" Tefnut.

In other versions of this myth, Atum created Shu and Tefnut by masturbating or having sex with his own shadow, which he gave a female name (see chapter 2). Shu and Tefnut then somehow got lost playing in the chaos of Nu (or Nun). Atum's only eye is removable; it is called the "Udjat Eye" (Eye of Horus). He sends the eye out to find Shu and Tefnut. The Udjat Eye finds them, and they all returned safely. (I will pick this story up again in the next chapter.)

Shu and Tefnut then gave birth to Geb, god of the earth, and Nut, the goddess of the sky. Nut was lifted up so she would be a celestial canopy over Geb. Nut and Geb then gave birth to four children: Osiris, Isis, Seth (Set), and Nephthys. Osiris became ruler of the earth, and Isis became queen of the earth. Seth was jealous of Osiris, so he murdered Osiris and became ruler of the earth.

The Udjat Eye is usually depicted as the right eye. It is a hieroglyphic symbol meaning royal power and protection from evil gods and disease. The epithet "risen one" is associated with the Udjat Eye, symbolized in art by a cobra. The cobra who rises up to protect itself symbolizes royal power and protection.

Seth, Set, or Setan is an African/Kemetic/Anu god who murders his brother to take control of earth. He is related to storms, the desert, and darkness; he is associated with strength and war. He is called the "God of Chaos" and "Evil Incarnate"; his color is red; and he is sometimes shown with red hair and eyes (and sometimes he wears a red crown). He is often depicted as a strange mix of animals (which represent personality attributes, not worshipping animals): a giraffe, camel, anteater, pig, hippopotamus, crocodile, or snake. The animals represent that he can appear in many forms.

Before Seth turned bad, he was a good god who waged war with another god called Apep (or Apepi). This mythical African/Kemetic/Anu god was the original god of evil; he represented destruction and eternal darkness. He is depicted most times as a giant snake and sometimes as a crocodile. He commanded an army of evil cohorts who battled Ra, the good sun god, for the souls of mankind; only by putting faith in the light of the sun god Ra could one defeat Apep and his cohorts.

Apep would fight Ra for the souls of mankind above the horizon; and when the sun sank below the horizon, Apep would continue his fight to destroy Ra and take the souls of mankind. While below the horizon Ra, the good sun god would bring light and comfort to the tortured souls below the horizon. Sound familiar?

Many early religions wrote about gods and goddesses, and believed in monotheistic, dualistic, or polytheistic gods. They believed, like the later dominant religions, in a philosophical approach to the oneness of the universe, god, and man. The man-made mythical stories of Africa/Kemet/Anu reveal several gods like Atum, Khepri, Ra, Aten, Ptah, Khnum, and Tehuti. Ptah created the world by the "word of his mouth," which is similar to the beginning of the Book of Genesis in the Bible. Khnum created the people of the world on a potter's wheel out of the dirt or mud of the Nile River, also similar to the Book of Genesis.

When Pharaoh Akhenaten ruled Kemet/Egypt, he elevated Aten to supreme creator god, and the society became monotheistic. Other gods like Ra and Amun were joined together to form the most famous supreme creator god, Amun-Ra or Amen-Ra, who was worshipped by the people as a monotheistic god, but was really dualistic: two gods combined into one (the same thing occurred when Ra was merged with Khepri, a lesser solar god). Khepri became an aspect of Ra in the form of a singular creator god.

At times, the people worshipped Osiris, Isis, and Horus as a trilogy. There are thousands of African/Kemetic/Anu gods. Many were worshipped as expressions or extensions of the supreme creator god, much like folk deities, devas, celestial beings, gods, goddesses, and angels are by the world's religions today.

Tehuti (Thoth) was a mythical lunar god; some historians have linked the words "thought" and "time" to this "God of the Moon." You could write a whole book on just this one African/Kemetic/Anu god.

Tehuti was a mythical creator god at times. He was also viewed as the heart and mind of the creator. He was also called the "Tongue of the

Creator," voicing the will of the creator. His words brought every person and thing in the heavens and earth into existence. Once he uttered a command, it was final. He was responsible for the laws, order, form, and maintenance of the heavens. Islam is a lunar-based religion; the Islamic calendar is based on the lunar cycle.

Islamic religious observances and holidays are based on the cycles of the moon. Tehuti, a lunar god, is depicted as a man with the head of an ibis bird, with a lunar or solar disk sitting inside a crescent moon atop his head, or as a man with the head of an ibis bird.

The crescent moon and star are the religious symbols or emblems of Islam. The original calendar of Africa/Kemet/Anu was a lunar calendar (which later evolved into a 365-day calendar), and the moon played a major part in many social and cultural observances, as well as religious myths of the African/Kemetic/Anu people.

Tehuti is also associated with writing the Emerald Texts, which discussed concepts of consciousness, spiritual development of the soul, and divine wisdom.

There has always been a misconception about why animals were used atop the heads of gods and goddesses in Africa/Kemet/Anu. They were not worshipping animals; the animals represented personal attributes (they were allegorical). If you see a picture of the Grim Reaper, you think of death. The animals represent the personality attributes of the particular god or goddess. If you see an ibis with its long beak, which looks like a pen, on the head of Tehuti, it is because in myth he was considered to be the writer of sacred books.

From the Papyrus of Ani

A Hymn to Amen-Ra

> A Hymn to Amen-Ra ... president of all the gods. Lord of the heavens, Lord of Truth, maker of men; creator of beasts ... Ra, whose word is truth, the governor of the world, the mighty one of valor, the chief who made the world as he made himself. His forms are more numerous than those of any god ... Adoration be to thee, O maker of the gods, who hast stretched out the heavens and founded the earth ... Lord of eternity, maker of the everlastingness ... creator of light.... He heareth the prayer of the oppressed

5

one, he is kind of heart to him that calleth upon him, he delivereth the timid man from the oppressor.... He is the Lord of knowledge, and wisdom is the utterance of his mouth. He maketh the green herb whereon the cattle live, and the staff of life whereon men live. He maketh the fish to live in the rivers, and the feathered fowl in the sky. He giveth to life to that which is in the egg.... Hail to thee, O thou maker of all these things, thou ONLY ONE. In mightiness he taketh many forms.

The above hymn gives us a third African/Kemetic/Anu reference to the belief in a monotheistic supreme creator god, who is lord and maker of the gods. This mythical concept is the same as the supreme creator Christian God, who is superior to the son of God, Jesus, or the Holy Ghost and celestial beings like angels.

A well-known god of African/Kemetic/Anu mythology is Heru (Horus), "The Divine Child," and son of Isis and Osiris. Some have linked the word "hero" to him because of his battles with Seth over the kingdom of earth. He was suckled by his mother Isis in the "majesty" or "seat of wisdom" position. Isis (who was impregnated by Osiris) is depicted in art sitting on a throne with a low back, holding the baby Horus in her lap, suckling him and looking straight ahead in the original "Madonna" pose. The Virgin Mary and Jesus image is taken from this depiction. In fact, many of the early Coptic (Egyptian) Christian coins, pictures, and statues represented both Jesus and Mary as black.

Black Madonna's are found mostly at Catholic sites. Churches in Belgium, France, Croatia, Spain, Serbia, Russia, Poland, Portugal, Switzerland, Germany, Ireland, Italy, Luxembourg, Lithuania, Macedonia, Malta, Brazil, Trinidad and Tobago, Chile, Costa Rica, the Philippines, and the United States still worship the Black Madonna. France has more Black Madonna shrines than any other country in the world.

Historical Quotes

To end this chapter, here are quotes on religion from different people in history. I found them in books, magazines, the Internet, libraries, research articles, and newspapers. They are very interesting, funny, and reflective to me, so I would like to share some of them with you.

"Oh these foolish men! They could not create so much as a worm, but they create gods by the dozens."—Michel de Montaigne.

"Religion is regarded by the common people as true, by the wise as false, and by rulers as useful."—Edward Gibbon—also attributed to Lucius Annaeus Seneca

"Religion is the fashionable substitute for belief."—Oscar Wilde

"I am quite sure now that often, very often, in matters concerning religion and politics, a man's reasoning powers are not above the monkeys."—Mark Twain

"The day will come when the mystical generation of Jesus, by the Supreme Being as his father, in the womb of a virgin, will be classed with the fable of the generation of Minerva in the brain of Jupiter."—Thomas Jefferson

"Take away from Genesis the belief that Moses was the author, on which only the strange believe that it is the word of God has stood, and there remains nothing of Genesis but an anonymous book of stories, fables, and traditional or invented absurdities, or of downright lies."—Thomas Paine

"Religious men are and must be heretics now—for we must not pray, except in a form of words, made beforehand or think of God but with a prearranged idea."—Florence Nightingale

"I pray every single second of my life, not on my knees but with my work. My prayer is to lift women to equality with men. Work and worship are one with me. I know there is no God of the universe made happy by my getting down on my knees and calling him great."—Susan B. Anthony

"Millions of innocent men, women, and children, since the introduction of Christianity, have been burnt, tortured, fined, and imprisoned: yet we have not advanced one inch towards uniformity."—Thomas Jefferson

"Faith consists in believing when it is beyond the power of reason to believe."—Voltaire

"The Bible is a book that has been read more and examined less than any book that ever existed."—Thomas Paine

"Man is a religious animal. He is the only religious animal. He is the only animal that has the true religion—several of them. He is the only animal that loves his neighbor as himself and cuts his throat if his theology isn't straight."—Mark Twain

"Religion can never reform mankind because religion is slavery."—Robert Ingersol

"Religious controversies are always productive of more acrimony and irreconcilable hatreds than those which spring from any other cause."—George Washington

"When it is a question of money, everybody is of the same religion."—Voltaire

"The endeavor to change universal power by selfish supplication I do not believe in."—Thomas Edison

"Faith is believing what you know ain't so."—Mark Twain

"I prayed for twenty years but received no answer until I prayed with my legs."—Frederick Douglass

"We have men sold to build churches, women sold to support the gospel, and babies sold to purchase Bibles for the poor heathen, all for the glory of God and the good of souls. The slave auctioneer's bell and the church-going bell chime in with each other, and the bitter cries of the heart-broken slave are drowned in the religious shouts of his pious master. Revivals of religion and revivals in the slave trade go hand in hand."—Frederick Douglass

"Those who can make you believe absurdities can make you commit atrocities."—Voltaire

"It is too late in the day for men of sincerity to pretend they believe in the Platonic mysticisms that three are one, and one is three: and yet that the one is not three and the three are not one."—Thomas Jefferson

"One man says with one's lips, 'I believe that god is one, and also three,' but no one can believe it, because the words have no sense."—Leo Tolstoy

Chapter 2

Mythical Creation Gods and Creation Myths
African/Kemetic/Anu Mythical Creator Gods

Atum (Atem or Tem) is a mythical predynastic (before 3100 BCE) creator sun god. He was also associated with the creator sun god Ra (see below). At first Atum was associated with the earth, because he was the first self created god; he was the first god to rise up out of the primordial waters and stand on the Benben (a small pyramid-shaped hill of dirt). Atum had believers in Heliopolis, Egypt, and throughout Africa.

Atum is a unique and interesting creator god. Atum created himself; he rose out of Nu (or Nun), the dark, primordial, chaotic, churning, bubbling waters of chaos. As the waters began to recede, a small pyramid-shaped hill arose. On the first day, as Atum stood on the Benben, this was viewed in later dynasties as Atum bringing light to the world. He coughed (or sneezed) and spat (or vomited) to produce his children Shu and Tefnut, described in chapter one. In other versions of this myth, he produced Shu and Tefnut by masturbating or having sex with his own shadow, which he gave a female name.

This happened because Atum is both male and female. Atum is the perfect vehicle for creation of the other gods: he is functionally and physiologically bisexual. He has the gender of both men and women. "He" can impregnate "Herself." The African/Kemetic/Anu epithet for Atum was "The Great He-She." He is the supreme being, creator of the universe and the master of the elements and forces of the universe. He produced the first nine gods, called the "Heliopolis Ennead" of Africa/Kemet/Anu ("Ennead" means the cardinal number that is the sum of eight and one): Shu, Tefnut, Geb, Nut, Osiris, Isis, Seth, Nephthys, and Horus. They are referred to as the "Black Anu."

He is associated with an end-of-the-world myth in which everything that he created will be destroyed and he will return as a snake (or eel) back to the dark primordial waters of Nun.

Excerpts of Hymn to Atum
Papyrus Bremner-Rhind

> At the moment of creation, Atum spoke; I alone am the creator. When I came into being all life began to develop. When the almighty speaks, all else comes to life. There were no heavens and no earth, there was no dry land and there were no reptiles in the land.
>
> When I first began to create; when I alone was planning and designing many creatures, I had not sneezed Shu the wind; I had not spat Tefnut the rain; there was not a single living creature; I planned many living creatures; all were in my heart, and their children and their grandchildren.
>
> Then I copulated with my own fist; I masturbated with my own hand; I ejaculated into my own mouth.
>
> I sneezed to create Shu the wind; I spat to create Tefnut the rain … in the beginning I was alone; then there were three more; I dawned over the land of Egypt; Shu the wind and Tefnut the rain played on the sea.

I talked about this part of the creation myth in chapter one. After the Udjat Eye finds the two missing children, they return safely to Atum, who is so overjoyed at their safe return that he weeps tears of joy. We pick up the rest of the myth here.

Excerpts of Hymn to Atum
Papyrus Bremner-Rhind

> With tears from my eye; I wept and human beings appeared [Note: some scholars say "as his tears hit the ground"]; I created the reptiles and their companions; Shu and Tefnut gave birth to Geb the earth and Nut the

sky; Geb and Nut gave birth to Osiris and Isis, Seth and Nephthys; Osiris and Isis gave birth to Horus; one was born right after another; these nine gave birth to all the multitude of the land.

Ptah was a predynastic (older than 3100 BCE) god worshipped throughout Kemet/Egypt but mainly in Memphis and Heliopolis; the Apis bull was used in art to represent his soul on earth. He was a god who gave fertility and rebirth to the people. He represented the three aspects of the universe: creation, stability, and death. He was known as an intellectual god using thought, harmonics, and words to bring about the creation of the universe, the earth, and all that are in it. He was self-created but not created.

He is portrayed as a man with a punt beard (a thin, braided beard about six inches long), wearing a skull cap, wrapped like a mummy with his hands free. He is holding a was-scepter, a sacred staff that is a symbol of power, dominion, and royal authority. Connected to the was-scepter is a djed, a pillar-like symbol representing stability; it resembled the base of the bull's spine. On top of the was-scepter and djed is an ankh, the symbol of life.

Amen-Ra (Amun-Ra) was an aspect of Ra—Amen (Amun) was a minor god associated with the wind and air; his myth became connected with the creator sun god Ra. A combination of two gods Amen and Ra (see Ra below), he was the most complex and widely worshipped of the African/Kemetic/Anu creator gods.

Man-made mythical writings about this creator god go back to the pyramid texts, making his mythical story predynastic (older than 3100 BCE). Worshipped by the Berber (present-day Morocco, Libya, Algeria, and Tunisia), this god also had followers in Kemet/Egypt to Nubia (present-day Sudan).

Amen's name has been used and reworked into several world religions; it is used to end prayers in Christianity and Judaism, as well as affirmations during sermons. These religions are paying homage to an African/Kemetic/Anu god, but most followers of these religions are unaware of it. You also find his name in spiritual writings like the Christian and Hebrew Bibles. Islam uses "Amin," "Ameen," or some variation of Amen as an affirmation in their prayers and the Koran.

Amen was also widely used in the names of pharaohs and gods in African/Kemetic/Anu history: pharaohs Amenhotep I, II, III, and IV; Amenemhet I, II, III, and IV; Tutankhamen (King Tut); Amenmesses;

Usermare-Meryamen Ramses III; Usermare Amenemope; Neferkare Amenemnisu; and others. Amen can also be found among the names of wives of pharaohs and others in military or government positions. It is a very common name, which comes from the creator god Amen-Ra.

Amen-Ra, a combining of two gods (Amen and Ra), is depicted in art in several ways. One is a man standing with a punt beard (described previously) holding a was-scepter in one hand and an ankh in the other hand. On the top of his head is a tall, double-plumed feathered crown. If you want to know what this crown looks like think of, Tablets of Stone, Stone Tablets, or Tablets of Testimony, the tablets Moses supposedly received the Ten Commandments on. This double-plumed crown was also worn by other African/Kemetic/Anu gods and goddesses.

Many African/Kemetic/Anu hieroglyphics and sacred religious texts are engraved on single plume-shaped stone or clay tablets, while the double plume was associated with the gods of Kemet/Anu.

Not only are the tablets that the Ten Commandments were supposedly written on suspect, but the Ten Commandments themselves. Declarations of Innocence, containing Negative Confessions found in the *Book of Coming Forth by Day* are strikingly similar to the Ten Commandments (see chapter 4 for more detail on Moses and the Ten Commandments).

Amen-Ra was the personification of hidden and unknown creative power. Amen-Ra was worshipped as a god who could not be seen or imagined; he was invisible to all; he was neither a part of creation nor was creation a part of him; he created himself; he was eternal; he was the god of the gods who expressed and represented themselves through him. Amen-Ra, also spelled Amen-Re, Amun Re or Amon-Re represented the people believing in him and was the way a person reached their full spiritual development and measured their devotion; he existed outside of nature and was worshipped as a monotheistic god.

In science, he could be the unknown force that caused the Big Bang. In religion, he could be the invisible supreme being that one must measure their devotion and spirituality to by having blind faith. In the Heliopolis Ennead creation myth, he was the unknown entity that creates Nu (or Nun), the dark, primordial, chaotic, churning, bubbling waters of chaos that the Benben mound sprang up from. His story was the most complex of all the creation gods.

Khnum was a very ancient predynastic (older than 3100 BCE) creator god. Khnum was worshipped mostly in the island cities of Philae and Elephantine in Africa/Kemet/Egypt, on the southern border of Kemet/

Egypt. He was worshipped as a water god and considered to be the source of the Nile River. Khnum was also associated with pottery and art (the Nile River would deposit black silt onto the river banks; the silt was used to make clay, which in turn was used to make pottery). He was self-created and was the creator of all things and all things that will be. He was known as "Father of Fathers" and the "Mother of Mothers."

He is depicted as a man with the head of a ram, sitting at his potter's wheel, creating all of mankind out of clay with his hands. He created children on his potter's wheel and breathed life into them, giving them "ka" (spirit). Words associated with his name include "create," "join," "unite," and "build." He is depicted as a ram, the sign of Aries (Fire). A symbol of fertility, he is also depicted as a man with the horns of a ram. He was also worshipped during the New Kingdom (1550 –1070 BCE) as the head of the "Triad of Elephantine" with his wife Satet and his daughter Anuket.

Khepri was another aspect of Ra; he was a minor god whose myth became associated with Ra and became a creator god and manifestation of Ra. His name was spelled several ways, including Khepra, Khepera, and Kehperi. The name Khepri means "he who comes into existence"; he was another predynastic creator sun god (older than 3100 BCE). The symbolism connected to Khepri is interesting. He was a self-creating god, associated with self-renewal and self-generation. He is depicted in art as a scarab, a man wearing a scarab crown, or a man with the head of a scarab. The scarab was viewed as a spiritual symbol in Africa/Kemet/Anu by the masses, like Christians view the cross today.

The scarab amulet was one of the most important and widely worn pieces of jewelry in Africa/Kemet/Anu. The scarab was associated with death, regeneration, metamorphosis, birth, rebirth, and resurrection. Education and knowledge of the behavioral and mating habits of the scarab helps with understanding why the scarab was used as a religious symbol. The scarab (or dung beetle) follows animals around, waiting for them to defecate (they prefer the dung of vegetarian animals). When the animal finally produces feces, the scarab collects the dung and rolls it up into a round ball. They can roll up to fifty times their weight and pull over one thousand times their weight; that would be like a human pulling close to a ton around.

The scarab then rolls the dung to a secure place and buries it for food (or places eggs inside it after copulating with its partner). The eggs then go through a metamorphosis: they turn to larvae, feed on the dung, and new scarab beetles are born coming out of the decaying dung. The people in

Africa/Kemet/Anu were not worshipping a dung beetle; the scarab beetle was used to symbolize the creation of humans on earth. We know from science as well as religion that humans came from the earth, and when we die we go back into the earth. Life on earth went through millions of years of metamorphosis and stages of development to get to life as it is today.

The decaying dung represented death; the eggs and larvae inside the dung represented metamorphosis and regeneration; the newborn scarab beetles coming out of the dung represented birth and rebirth. Resurrection is symbolized in the myth of Khepri, the creator sun god, as a scarab rolling the sun around in the sky.

He would roll the sun into the Underworld (below the horizon in the west, where the sun sets) and finally to the eastern horizon, where the sun rises every morning. The mythical story symbolizes everyone's victory over death and an eternal life through resurrection. The myth of Khepri is derived from funerary papyri, pyramid texts, coffin texts, and the *Book of Coming Forth by Day.*

In art on painted papyrus, Khepri the sun god is often depicted as a scarab beetle in a boat with a sun disk over his head being lifted up by Nu (or Nun) in the form of a man, representing the dark, primordial, chaotic, churning, bubbling waters of chaos.

Whoever in Africa/Kemet/Anu came up with the solar and scarab myths regarding Khepri had to have had access to information on the behavior and mating habits of scarab beetles. This is something that requires hours of observation and study. The scarabs hide their dung in secure places by burying the ball of dung. African/Kemetic/Anu knowledge of the behavior habits of animals; as well as their metaphoric and allegorical use of animals, is also shown in the use of the falcon, hawk, jackal, cobra, hippopotamus, and other animals.

I will explain the metaphoric and allegorical use of the falcon, hawk, jackal, cobra, hippopotamus, and other animals in forthcoming chapters of this book. In order to use the different animals as representations of their mythical god's personalities, one must have knowledge of the animals in question.

The solar myth of the creator god Khepri also shows that the culture of Africa/Kemet/Anu knew that the earth was round and revolving, symbolized by the scarab rolling a round ball of dung around on the ground. Some Egyptologists and historians claim, the basic dimensions of the Great Pyramid at Giza, Egypt incorporates measurements from which the earth's size and shape can be calculated. They were aware of the importance of the sun to our survival on earth.

Without the sun there would be no life on earth and many of the African/Kemetic/Anu solar gods were associated with being the life giving force on earth. The myth about an African/Kemetic/Anu supreme solar god like Ra (Re), was based on the symbolic concept of Ra, sinking beneath the horizon to die, and then rising above the horizon—symbolizing birth, re-birth, and resurrection. Someone had to be observing and recording the repetitious cycle of the earth revolving, and the sun appearing to rise in the east at sunrise, then moving overhead at midday, and setting in the west at sunset.

The celestial bas-relief of the Zodiac found in the Temple of Hathor at Dendera, Egypt, shows that the African/Kemetic/Anu culture was aware of the twelve constellations that make up the "Great Year." This too required observing and recording the different parts of the heavens as they change over thousands of years. (See chapter 6.)

Ra or Re, from early times was represented as a creator sun god; he was considered to be the creator of everything and every living soul. He was worshipped all over Africa/Kemet/Anu; his main center of adoration was Heliopolis, Egypt. He is depicted in art as a man with the head of a hawk or falcon, holding an ankh, the symbol of life, in one hand and a was-scepter, a symbol of dominion, royal power, and authority, in the other hand. On top of the hawk or falcon's head is either a solar disk encircled by a cobra or the Atef crown.

The hawk and falcon represented Ra as the sun god sailing high in the sky on his flight across the horizon. The cobra can be seen on the crown of King Tutankhamen and as mentioned earlier, symbolizes risen one, rising up, royal power, and protection. Ra was believed to be a conqueror of evil, destruction, and death; he sailed through the sky in a boat. The Barque of a Million Years tells the story of how Ra would sail above the horizon through the twelve provinces of daylight; and below the horizon through the twelve provinces of night while he battled and defeated the evil serpent Apep and his cohorts. While sailing through the twelve provinces of night, he would bring light and comfort to the tortured souls and then be reborn and reappear above the horizon in the east.

Over time, Ra was combined with other gods to form one god. Ra was combined with the god Horus (mentioned in chapter 1; more detail in chapter 4) to form Ra-Harmachis, which means "Horus of the Horizon" or "Horus of the Two Horizons." In this form Horus would travel with Ra as one to battle Apep above the horizon.

Ra was also combined with the god Amen, becoming Amen-Ra (mentioned earlier). In a later variation of this myth, Ra was combined with Atum and became Atum-Ra, the first god standing on the pyramid-shaped hill called Benben during creation, bringing light to the world. The man-made mythical solar creator god Khepri was also an aspect of Ra, (mentioned earlier).

The creation myths of the world's religions are similar when you read and compare them to African/Kemetic/Anu creation myths. Mainstream religions use the same attributes to describe creation gods and myths, and they use a similar writing style as well.

Here is an excerpt from a creation myth that uses similar attributes and writing styles.

From the Papyrus of Ani
A Hymn to Amen-Ra

Hail to thee, Ra, Lord of Truth whose shrine is hidden, thou Master of the gods, thou god Khepera [Khepri] in thy boat; at the going forth of thy word the gods sprang into being. Hail Atem [Atum] maker of mortals. However many be their forms he nourisheth them, he maketh the colour of one to be different from the other. He heareth the prayer of the oppressed one, he is kind of heart to him that calleth upon him, he delivereth the timid man from the oppressor, he judgeth between the mighty and the weak.... At his will the Nile appeareth, when the greatly beloved Lord of the palm-tree cometh he maketh mortals to live. He furthereth every work, he worketh in heaven, he produceth the beneficent light; the gods rejoice in his beautiful deeds, and their hearts live when they see him.... His name is hidden from his children. In his name AMEN.

O Form, One, creator of all things, O One, Only, maker of things which are. Men came forth from his eyes; the gods sprang into being at the utterance of his mouth. He maketh the green herb whereon the cattle live, and the staff of life [wheat or barley] whereon men live. He maketh the fish to live in the rivers, and the feathered fowl in the sky. He giveth life to that which is in the egg; he maketh birds of all kinds to live, and the reptiles which crawl and spring. He maketh the rats [or mice] in the holes to live and the birds which are on every green twig. Hail to thee, O thou maker of all these things, thou Only one.

This hymn is to Amen-Ra, who is an aspect of Ra; it is about the mysterious supreme god unknown to gods and mortals. Amen-Ra's creation is manifested through Atum and Khepri in this hymn. The African/Kemetic/Anu writers of this myth were making a clear distinction between humans, gods, goddesses, and a supreme (monotheistic) creation god.

Aten was a mythical creator sun god (who initially was a minor god). Aten's biggest claim to fame was the controversy and chaos surrounding his worship as a monotheistic god. His place of devotion was the city of Akhenaten in present day Tell el-Amarna in the province of Minya, Kemet/Egypt. Located on the east bank of the Nile River, where the sun rises and is reborn every morning, the city Akhenaten was built by Pharaoh Akhenaten and called the "Horizon of Aten." Aten was considered to be the creative force within the universe and the source of the life-giving force on earth.

Aten was a monotheistic god; he is depicted in art as a solar orb—a sun globe with long rays. The rays point downward, looking like long thin arms coming out from the sun. The arms end as human hands offering an ankh (the symbol of life), hanging from the base of the sun disk, or the hands are held out open to all of humanity. Before Aten, Amen-Ra was worshipped as the supreme solar creator god. This all changed when Amenhotep IV became pharaoh.

Amenhotep IV was a teenager when he became pharaoh. First he changed his name to Akhenaten and declared himself the son of Aten, then he replaced Amen-Ra with Aten as the sole monotheistic god. Akhenaten eliminated the worship of any other gods or goddesses, closed the temples, removed inscriptions of Amen-Ra from areas of worship, and imposed a strict monotheistic religion based on Aten. New temples were built, new inscriptions written, and new hymns were written and put to music for Aten.

These changes did not go over well with the people who favored Amen-Ra. They also did not go over well with the priests who were elected by the masses and derived their political power and financial wealth from the following of Amen-Ra, a popular monotheistic god manifested through multiple popular gods and goddesses. When Akhenaten died, his son Tutankhamen restored Amen-Ra as the supreme god and returned Aten back to a role as a minor god.

Before I move on to a critique of creation myths, here is more on the family of Akhenaten: because of the controversy and conflict between Akhenaten and the priests over Amen-Ra or Aten as the supreme monotheistic god, and other social issues, some scholars believe that this royal family met with foul play. They point to the fact that four of the family members died within a seventeen year period of time. Queen Tiye, Akhenaten's mother, died in 1340 BCE at the age of sixty; Akhenaten, who ruled from 1353 to 1336 BCE, died four years later, in 1336 BCE at the age of thirty-six. Nefertiti, his wife, died in 1330 BCE at age forty, and Tutankhamen, his son, died in 1323 BCE at the age of eighteen.

Some scholars have claimed that Akhenaten's spiritual fascination with Aten caused him to neglect domestic, military, and diplomatic concerns. This caused hardship for himself and his family. Because he held religious beliefs in conflict with the priests in Africa/Kemet/Anu, he is referred to by some scholars as "The Heretic King." Akhenaten is said to have been of Hebrew lineage. His father, Amenhotep III, ruled for thirty-nine years before he died; Akhenaten replaced him after his death.

His mother was known for her beauty and for her use of cosmetics. Queen Tiye was known for using creams, lotions, powders, perfumes, lipstick, fingernail polish, eye and facial make-up, even different colored wigs. Nefertiti was one of the most well-known queens of African/Kemetic/Anu history and was known for her beauty as well. According to some scholars, she became pharaoh for a short period of time following the death of her husband, before her son Tutankhamen (who was only about five or six years old) became pharaoh. Her iconic bust, which is on display at the Egyptian Museum of Berlin, is one of the most copied pieces of art in the world.

Tutankhamen was the most famous member of this family; at first, he was thought to be Akhenaten's brother, but DNA testing has confirmed that he was Akhenaten's son. King Tut became pharaoh at age eight or nine. Tutankhamen reinstated Amen-Ra as the supreme creator god and allowed the people to worship the other gods and goddesses. Tutankhamen's sarcophagus (coffin), death mask, jewelry, and other artifacts are on exhibit in the Egyptian Museum in Cairo, Egypt. These items are one of the most widely toured exhibits in world history.

There are four coffins in total, one inside the other in decreasing size, with all of them designed and crafted in the image of King Tut. The outer sarcophagus is a protective red quartzite coffin; the next two sarcophagi are made of gilded wood (having the deep, slightly brownish color of gold), consisting of cedar and oak covered with a thin sheet of gold decorated with faience (glass-like material to give a glossy effect). The fourth sarcophagus includes the "Mask of Tutankhamen."

The mask, which was on the head of the mummified pharaoh's body, and the inner sarcophagus, which contained the mummy, are made of solid gold. The priceless gold mask is inlaid with semiprecious jewels. The inner coffin itself, which weighs over 200 pounds, is worth millions of dollars by itself. The Mask of Tutankhamen is a baffling piece of art.

The art work is crafted in amazing detail. One wonders how anyone could have created this piece of art with the technology available three thousand years ago. Today you would need modern technology to craft this piece of art.

In the 1990s, I had the chance to see the Amenhotep III exhibit at the Cleveland Museum of Art in Cleveland, Ohio. The exhibit included personal artifacts of Queen Tiye and Amenhotep III, as well as artifacts and information on this very interesting family.

Creation Myths

The different creation myths have so many similarities, it is obvious that they all come from a common source. When we look at the creation myths of Africa/Kemet/Anu, most have common elements: an unknown, hidden, and mysterious creation force; the presence of dark, burning, churning, chaotic (sometimes lifeless) waters; and some type of pyramid-shaped hill arising when the chaotic waters calm down. Other common elements include the presence of sunlight from darkness, bringing light and life; a self-created god or goddess who is a manifestation of a mysterious, hidden, and unknown supreme creator god—who exists outside of the creation, has always existed, and is everlasting; and a self-created supreme god or goddess, who alone, creates the heavens, earth, and all things on earth.

The creation myths of Africa/Kemet/Anu are the same mythical stories with ethnic and geographical variations, depending on where the creation myth was written. There were creation myths from upper Africa/Anu and the Sudan and from lower Africa/Kemet.

When lower and upper Africa was united into a federal state, Kemet/ Anu and almost all of the continent of Africa was considered one country. It should also be noted that the Nile River flows from south to north, so a country like Anu/Ethiopia, in the south, would be considered upper, and a country like Kemet/Egypt, in the north, would be considered lower. As recently as 1650 CE, some maps still showed the South Atlantic as the Ethiopic Ocean, and as mentioned, in ancient times most of the continent of Africa was federalized.

Creation myths varied because people from the upper and lower parts of Africa spoke different dialects and languages; they had different customs, cultures, and beliefs. There were different creation myths from different cities like Memphis, Thebes, Hermopolis (in the present-day city of El Ashmunein), and Heliopolis (all located in present-day Egypt).

We have already reviewed some of the main creation stories: Ptah of Memphis; Khnum and the Potter's Wheel; Atum and the nine Heliopolis Ennead. "Ennead" means the cardinal number that is the sum of eight and one.

Another creation myth (which has at least five variations) is the eight "Ogdoad of Hermopolis" (or "Ogdoad of Khmunu"). "Ogdoad" means the cardinal number that is the sum of seven and one. Khmunu is the native name for this African city, called Hermopolis in Greek. In this creation myth, there were four pairs of gods and goddesses who complemented each other. For every female creator goddess, there was a male counterpart. They were depicted as human beings with the heads of frogs (male) and serpents (female). They also were depicted as four female and four male apes.

The snakes and frogs symbolized animals that inhabited water; the apes were the animals who first inhabited the earth. The Ogdoad were gods and goddesses who inhabited the dark, primordial, chaotic, churning, bubbling waters. Nu and Naunet (male and female) represented the inert primordial waters; Heh and Hauhet represented the boundless eternity of the primordial waters; Kek and Kauket represented the darkness present within the primordial waters; and Amun and Amaunet represented air and the unknown nature of the primordial waters.

At some point, these gods and goddesses interacted in an inappropriate way that caused some type of a great upheaval to occur, causing the waters to recede and a small pyramidal hill (called a Benben) to rise up out of the waters. After the upheaval, the sun rose to light the sky and shine on the small pyramidal hill, and there stood Atum, the first of the gods created.

One of the many variations to this creation myth is about a cosmic egg, which the eight gods and goddesses created while in the primordial waters. The egg was hidden and invisible to all in the dark, primordial, chaotic, churning, bubbling waters of Nu (or Nun). In one version, the egg bursts because of the upheaval of the waters; in another version, the egg is filled with air and bursts. (Note: Amun and Amaunet represent air and the unknown nature of the primordial waters.)

In either case, a bird of light (a falcon or hawk) is released in the form of Ra, who then creates the universe, the earth, and all that inhabit the earth. Ra provides light and the life force that sustains life on earth. In another version, a goose (or ibis) lays the egg in the dark, primordial, chaotic, churning, bubbling waters of Nu (or Nun), and then the goose (or ibis) carries the egg out of the primordial waters to land, where creation takes place.

Other versions of this myth are about a lotus flower rising from Nu (or Nun), the primordial waters, and opening to release either Ra or Khepri (a manifestation of Ra), who then creates the universe and all life on earth.

In this book, I am asserting that the world's religions have many similarities. Some scholars have pointed out that even 4,000 years ago, there were many debates over which of the two major creation stories—the Ogdoad of Hermopolis/Khmunu and the Heliopolis Ennead—came first and which was a reworking of the original. The priests in each city accused the other of repeating their original story, when in fact both of them were just man-made creation myths.

Excerpt from the Papyrus de Turin
Legend of Ra and Isis

The opening paragraph begins by stating the attributes of Ra:

> The chapter of the divine god, who created himself, who made the heavens and earth, and the breath of life, and fire, and the gods, and men, and beast, and cattle, and reptiles, and feathered fowl, and the fish; who is the king of men and gods, the one form, to whom periods of one hundred and twenty years are as single years, whose multitudinous names are unknowable, for even the gods know them not.

Again, these writings and the other texts quoted in this book were found in places like the African/Kemetic/Anu pyramid texts; coffin texts; and the *Book of Coming Forth by Day.* They were also inscribed on funerary stele (a long, tall, narrow slab of stone or wood) and inside temples like the Temple of Hathor at Dendera in Egypt and the Edfu Temple of Horus on the West Bank of the Nile River in Egypt.

Information has been found written on papyri like the Papyrus de Turin; some of the information on the creator god Ptah was taken from stone slabs like the Shabaka Stone, a 25th Dynasty stone slab thirty-six inches in height and fifty-four inches wide, incised with the surviving hieroglyphs from a worm-ridden decaying papyrus.

You can find this material yourself by researching in a library, bookstore, or museum, or by using the Internet, which allows you to access museums around the world.

Let us now look at the Book of Genesis, the first book of the Hebrew/ Tanakh and Christian Bible. These books are said to be the word of God. I will critique the scriptures of the Book of Genesis as reworkings of African/ Kemetic/Anu creation myths, gods, and goddesses. I will also compare the writing style and examine specific words used in Genesis and highlight the references to Africa found in Genesis.

When one is attempting to interpret the Book of Genesis (or any other book in the Bible or Tanakh), it makes sense to look toward Africa/Kemet/ Anu as the true source of these religious books.

The reason why religious scholars don't use Africa/Kemet/Anu to interpret there religious books is because if they do, it will be obvious that the religious myths they claim to be the word of some almighty god are nothing more than the reworkings (if not outright plagiarization) of material taken from African/Kemetic/Anu culture.

No one would waste their cognitive and intellectual energy assigning any religious significance to a Superman, Batman, or Incredible Hulk comic book, let alone base their spiritual self-esteem on them.

It should be noted that the first five books of the Christian Bible— Genesis, Exodus, Leviticus, Numbers, and Deuteronomy—are the same books as Judaism's Torah or "Pentateuch," the five books of Moses. The Torah is also the first five books of the Tanakh, the sacred cannon and holy scriptures of Judaism.

Judaism and Christianity

Genesis 1:1–5

> 1. In the beginning God created the heaven and the earth. 2. And the earth was without form, and void; and darkness was upon the face of the deep. And the Spirit of God moved upon the face of the waters. 3. And God said, Let there be light: and there was light. 4. And God saw the light, that it was good: and God divided the light from the darkness. 5. And God called the light Day, and the darkness he called Night. And the evening and the morning were the first day.

Critique: Again let me summarize the beginning of the African/Kemetic/Anu creation story, the Ogdoad of Hermopolis/Khmunu. In the beginning there were four sets of male and female gods and goddesses who inhabited Nu (or Nun), the dark, primordial, chaotic, churning, bubbling waters. An inappropriate interaction occurred among the gods and goddesses, which caused an upheaval in the primordial waters. The waters receded, and a small pyramid-shaped hill, called a Benben, rose up. The sun was created, then it rose and standing on the Benben was Atum, the first of the gods created.

In the Heliopolis Ennead creation myth, Atum then created Shu, the god of air, and Tefnut, the goddesses of moisture. Shu and Tefnut give birth to the god of the earth, Geb, and the goddesses of the sky, Nut. These goddesses and gods created the physical universe. The creation of days, nights, and the 365-day calendar are also found within the Heliopolis Ennead and the myths of Ra and Tehuti, called the heart, mind, and tongue of the creator, mentioned earlier.

The 354-day lunar calendar, the 384-day revised lunar calendar, the 360-day civic/public calendar, and the 365-day revised civic/public calendar are well documented. African/Kemetic/Anu culture developed the twelve-unit division of day and night, based on equal parts, over 4,000 years ago (more detail in the coming pages).

The writers of religious stories even back then were ascribing cultural and scientific discoveries to gods and goddesses.

One mythical story, "The Legend of Osiris," is found in the historical writings of the Greek historian and biographer Plutarch (46–120 CE).

Plutarch had access to primary, secondary, and tertiary sources regarding this mythical story, which he wrote over 1,900 years ago.

Plutarch lived when Christianity was in its early development. He wrote about African/Kemetic/Anu religious stories that had been around for three thousand years. Assuming he had no ethnic bias and was simply reporting this myth, his account of this story was more accurate than one written by a scholar of today.

Remember, the further back in history one goes, the more accurate the history reported can be—like if your grandmother told you a story about her childhood; and provided detailed (primary) information about her mother, grandmother (your great and great-great-grandmothers), and family events while being raised, it would be more accurate than if your mother told you the same story.

There are several accounts of the "Legend of Osiris." In one version Ra or Re wanted to marry Nut, the goddesses of the sky. Nut, however, married Geb, the god of the earth, who also loved her.

When Ra found out, he became very upset and he ordered Shu, the god of air and the father of Nut and Geb, to separate them. Nut, however, was already pregnant. When Ra found out Nut was pregnant, he said that she could not give birth on any day in the year (a year was 360 days in this myth).

Tehuti, a lunar god and the heart, mind, and tongue of the creator Ra, also liked Nut and decided to help her. So he gambled with the moon for extra light, winning an extra five days to add to the 360-day year. During these five extra days, Nut gave birth to Osiris on the first of these days.

Genesis 1:6–8

> 6. And God said, Let there be a firmament in the midst of the waters, and let it divide the waters from the waters. 7. And God made the firmament, and divided the waters which were under the firmament from the waters which were above the firmament: and so it was so. 8. And God called the firmament Heaven. And the evening and the morning were the second day.

Critique: The concept of heaven was nothing new; it has its origins in African/Kemetic/Anu religious myths. There are many written examples, but here are two excerpts found in the *Book of Coming Forth by Day*.

A Hymn to Ra

Those who are in thy following sing unto thee with joy, and they bow down their foreheads to the earth when they meet thee, the lord of the heaven, the lord of the earth, the King of Truth, the lord of eternity, the prince of everlastingness, thou sovereign of all the gods, thou god of life, thou creator of eternity, thou Maker of Heaven wherein thou art firmly stablished. The company of the gods rejoice at thy rising, the earth is glad when it beholdeth thy rays; the people who have been long dead come forth with cries of joy to behold thy beauties every day. Thou passest over the heights of heaven, thy heart swelleth with joy; and the Lake of Testes [the Great Oasis] is content thereat. The Serpent-fiend hath fallen, his arms are hewn off, and the Knife hath severed his joints.

Opening Up a Way through the Amehet (Gate or Pathway to Heaven)

1. Pe and Tep were capital cities in lower (northern) Kemet/ Egypt.

2. Tem is another name for Atum.

3. The crocodile was the personification of the attributes of the African/Kemetic/Anu god Sobek, depicted in art with a crocodile's head on a man's body. Sobek was worshipped as the source of power of the Nile River. Sobek's attributes were fertility, protection, fear, and rebirth. He was considered at times the ruler of Africa/Kemet/Anu.

I have opened up a way for myself to you. I have become a spirit, in my forms, I have gotten the mastery over my words of magical power, and I am adjudged a spirit; therefore deliver ye me from the Crocodile [which liveth in] this Country of Truth [or law].... When he openeth up his path on the eastern horizon of heaven, when he alighteth towards the western horizon of heaven, may he carry me along with him, and may I be safe and sound.... Let not the Field [Sebau] gain mastery over me, let me not be driven away from the doors of the Other World, let not your doors be shut in my face, for my cakes are in the city of Pe, and my ale is in the city of Tep. And there, in the celestial mansions of heaven which my divine father Tem hath stablished, let my hands lay hold upon the wheat and barley which shall be given unto me therein in abundant measure, and may the son of my own body make ready for me my food therein.

"Firmament" means the vault or arch of the heavens, the sky, the world of space between the stars and planets.

I refer you back to the Heliopolis Ennead creation story of Atum. Atum stood on the Benben and brought forth light and then created Shu and Tefnut. Their creation represented the creation of air and moisture. Shu and Tefnut then gave birth to Geb, the god of the earth, and Nut, the goddess of the sky.

Nut is depicted in artwork as an elongated woman covered in stars, stretched out with her arms and hands touching the ground on one end and her feet touching the ground on the other end, in an arch position. Nut is arching over Geb, the god of the earth.

Shu is depicted in art holding a boat over his head with a sun disk inside of it, symbolizing sailing or floating through the sky. In the Barque of a Million Years, Ra would sail above the horizon through the twelve provinces of daylight; and below the horizon through the twelve provinces of night while he battled the evil serpent Apep.

While sailing through the twelve provinces of night below the horizon, Ra would bring light and comfort to the tortured souls and then reappear above the horizon, reborn in the east.

In the Ogdoad of Hermopolis myth, living within the dark, primordial, chaotic, churning, bubbling waters were four sets of male and female creator gods and goddesses. Nu and Naumet represented the inert primordial waters, Heh and Hauhet the boundless eternity of the primordial waters, Kek and Kauket the darkness of the primordial waters. In relation to firmament, Amun and Amaunet represented air and the unknown nature of the primordial waters as well as space within the primordial waters.

These gods and goddesses interacted in an inappropriate way, and an upheaval occurred, causing the sun to rise in the sky and the Benben to rise out of Nu (or Nun), and there stood Atum, the first god created.

After eight verses of Genesis, one can already see similarities with the African/Kemetic/Anu creation myths. There is the creation of heaven and earth; creation of earth from formlessness; presence of water and darkness; spirit of god, gods, or goddesses moving upon or causing an upheaval in the dark primordial creation waters; creation of light or the sun from darkness; myth of day and night; and the creation of firmament, sky, heaven, space, and stars. The Bible of the Christian religion is a collection of books that were written by men. These men were supposedly inspired by the Holy Spirit (God talked to them) and wrote this book over a 1,500-year period. The Bible is God's revelation of himself and his creation.

These men included Moses, who lived in Egypt and was credited with writing the Hebrew Torah of Judaism, and the first five books of the Christian Bible; Luke, a physician; Matthew, a tax collector; Ezekiel and Jeremiah, priests; Daniel, a minister; Amos, a farmer; Peter and John, fishermen; and Paul, a Pharisee (a member of an ancient Jewish religious group who followed the oral law in addition to the Torah and attempted to live in a state of purity).

Today, if a physician, tax collector, priest, minister, farmer, or fisherman were to say God talked to them through a holy spirit and they have written a book revealing the word of God, would anyone take them seriously? Most people think that people who say God talks personally and literally to them have a serious psychological disorder.

All of the world's religious books like the Christian Bible, Tanakh of Judaism, Islam's Koran, the scriptures of Hinduism and Buddhism are based on hearsay. There is no factual, credible, or direct proof that any of these religious books or scriptures is the word of any supreme god, prophet, or enlightened one. Mythical religious books and scriptures were created by men—then those books and scriptures based on second-hand information were passed down, adopted, and approved by other men at some point in history. All religious books and scriptures are based on nothing but hearsay—in order for mythical religious books and scriptures to be effective they require believers to not question the origin and simply have blind faith, submit, and believe the hearsay.

Before one even begins to read the mythical account of creation in the Book of Genesis, one should understand that the male writers give credit for the authorship of Genesis, Exodus, Leviticus, Numbers, and

Deuteronomy to Moses, who was allegedly born, raised, and educated in Africa/Kemet/Egypt for forty years (Acts 7:17-23 and Exodus 2:1-10), and was married to an Ethiopian woman (Numbers 12:1). Along with Israel, no other countries are mentioned more in the Old Testament of the Christian Bible and Hebrew Torah than the African countries of Egypt and Ethiopia.

Mentioned as either Mitzraim (Hebrew for Egypt), Egypt, Egyptian, Ethiopia, Cush or cognates (words with a common etymological origin), these African countries are mentioned over 650 times in the Christian Bible, so one can understand the extensive political, economic, cultural, and religious influence Africa had on the men who were writing the Bible. The creation stories of the Heliopolis Ennead and the Ogdoad of Hermopolis were around from 3100 BCE to 2465 BCE; the creation characters of the Ennead and Ogdoad are predynastic (before 3100 BCE), thousands of years before the creation story in the Book of Genesis was written.

Genesis 1:9–19

> 9. And God said, Let the waters under the heavens be gathered together unto one place, and let the dry land appear: and it was so. 10. And God called the dry land Earth; and the gathering together of the waters called he Seas: and God saw that it was good. 11. And God said, Let the earth bring forth grass, the herb yielding seed, and the fruit tree yielding fruit after his kind, whose seed is in itself, upon the earth: and it was so. 12. And the earth brought forth grass, and herb yielding seed after his kind, and the tree yielding fruit, whose seed was in itself, after his kind: and God saw that it was good.13. And the evening and the morning were the third day. 14. And God said, Let there be lights in the firmament of the heaven to divide the day from the night; and let them be for signs, and for seasons, and for days, and years: 15. And let them be for lights in the firmament of the heaven to give light upon the earth: and it was so. 16. And God made two great lights; the greater light to rule the day, and the lesser light to rule the night: he made the stars also. 17. And God set them in the firmament of the heaven to give light upon

the earth, 18. And to rule over the day and over the night, and to divide the light from the darkness: and God saw that it was good. 19. And the evening and the morning were the fourth day.

Critique: I will compare this version of the creation of heaven, earth, moon, sun, days and nights, seasons, and years with two excerpts found in African/Kemetic/Anu myths.

Excerpt from Papyrus de Turin, Chapter of the Divine God Legend of Ra and Isis

I am the maker of the heavens and earth. I have knit together the mountains, and I have created everything which existeth upon them. I am the maker of the waters.… I am the maker of heaven. I have made to be hidden the two gods of the horizon. I have placed the soul of the gods in them. I am the Being who openeth his eyes and the light cometh; I am the Being who shutteth his eyes and darkness cometh; I am he who commandeth, and the waters of the Nile flow forth. I am he whose name the gods know not. I am the maker of the hours and the creator of the days. I inaugurate festivals. I make the water to flood. I am the creator of the fire of life through which the products of the workshops come into being. I am Khepera [Khepri] in the morning, Ra at mid-day, and Temu in the evening.… The great god bindeth himself by an oath to give his Eyes.

Critique: The African/Kemetic/Anu men who wrote these stories often refer to the "two lights" as the eyes of Ra (the two lights referred to the sun and moon). The weaker light of the moon is compared to the evening sun. The two lights were also used to refer to the eyes of the god Horus, with the weaker left eye being the moon and the stronger right eye being the sun (called Udjat Eye or the "Eye of Horus," a symbol of protection and royal power).

Excerpts from a Hymn to Amen-Ra
Papyrus of Ani *Book of Coming Forth by Day*

> Lord of Truth, father of the gods, maker of men; creator
> of beasts, lord of things which exist, creator of the staff
> of life, maker of the green herb which nourisheth the
> cattle.... lord of eternity, maker of the everlastingness, lord
> of adorations.... lord of rays, creator of light.... Beloved
> art thou as thou passest through Egypt. When thou risest
> thou sendest forth light from thy beautiful Eyes [i.e., sun
> and moon].

Critique: The importance of agriculture in Africa/Kemet/Anu is illustrated by the 365-day calendar in use more than four thousand years ago—well before Judaism, Christianity, and the Book of Genesis.

The calendar was divided into three seasons, with each season being four months long. There were twelve months, and each month had thirty days; there were three weeks in a month, and one week consisted of ten days. Five festival days were added to the end of the year to celebrate the gods and goddesses Osiris, Horus, Seth, Isis and Nephthys (in this order–not by birth order).

Each twenty-four-hour day was broken up into two twelve-hour periods. The day hours were numbered 1 through 12, and the night 13 through 24. In the summer, the days were longer; in the winter, the nights were longer. They started the day at sunrise, when the sun appeared above the horizon in the east, and they started the night right after the sun sank below the horizon in the west.

During the day, they used the sun to mark the passing of the hours; at night, they marked the passing of the hours by following the rising and falling of the stars, and they determined when the night was ending and a new day was beginning by noting how dark or bright the sky was. Many animals (birds, fish, insects, and others) are on this same celestial clock; they either awakened at sunrise and go to sleep at sunset or awakened at sunset and go to sleep at sunrise.

The seasons were chosen to correspond to the cycles of the Nile River, which was critical to life in Africa/Kemet/Anu. They used the signs from the flow, rising, receding, and flooding of the Nile to divide the seasons of their calendar. They based their agrarian society on farming and agriculture. They viewed subsistence farming and agriculture as a means to achieve a moral spirituality through being one with nature while gaining sustenance and nourishment from nature.

The people also used farming for profit. During the harvest season, once personal needs were met, donkeys were loaded up and taken to market to sell the surplus. Harvest time was also when taxes were due; the tax collectors would come around for the government's share. The revised 365-day civic/public calendar used by Africa/Kemet/Anu society was based on a spiritual link with the Nile River. All of the holidays and festivals honoring gods and goddesses were based on the months, seasons, and days of the 365-day calendar.

When you compare the African/Kemetic/Anu calendar to our Gregorian calendar in use today, you will see that the dates, months, and seasons are different. The African/Kemetic/Anu calendar started in autumn, during the months we call August and September. The African/Kemetic/Anu calendar did not have a spring season; it was incorporated into the end of their winter season and the start of their summer season.

Below, I have listed the months, days, and seasons of the African/Kemetic/Anu 365-day calendar, with the approximate corresponding months and days of the Gregorian calendar (for comparison only).

Akhet (Autumn—Inundation):

> Month: Tekh
> Month: Menhet
> Month: Hwt-Hrw
> Month: Ka-Hr-Ka
> Approximate Gregorian equivalent: August 29 to December 26 (or August to November)

Akhet, the beginning of the year, was when the Nile River flooded the land, depositing rich black silt and dirt, bringing fertility to the land.

Proyet (Winter—Emergence or Growing):

> Month: Sf-Bdt
> Month: Rekh Wer
> Month: Rekh Neds
> Month: Renwett

Approximate Gregorian equivalent: December 27 to April 25 (or December to March)

Proyet was the time of the year when the Nile River receded. The temperatures were cooler. As soon as the fields were accessible, the land was cleared of debris and planting and sowing began. By the end of Proyet, in March or April, new homes were built using bricks made from the silt and dirt. Animals were able to graze on the new herbs and flowers that had sprouted, and birds could find material to make nests to lay eggs and hatch their offspring. The end of Proyet going into the next season was what we call spring.

Shomu (Summer—Low Water or Harvest):

Month: Hnsw
Month: Hnt-Htj
Month: Ipt-Hmt
Month: Wep-Renpet
Approximate Gregorian equivalent: April 26 to August 23 (or April to July)

During Shomu, the sun is hot and the crops are being harvested. Farmers have planted new crops before the season ends to try and make a big profit off the land while it is still possible. Donkeys were loaded up and taken to market to sell off surplus goods.

Tax collectors would come around during this time as taxes were paid to the government. This was a very busy time and happy time, as there was plenty of food, a profit had been made, and people were in a festive mood to give thanks to the gods and goddesses responsible for their good fortune. The ending of this season led into the year-ending festival days.

Again, the 365-day civic/public calendar of Africa/Kemet Anu consisted of three seasons: autumn, winter, and summer. The 365 days were divided into twelve 30-day months. They added five days to the end of the year to give them 365 days. There were between thirty-five and forty-five festivals honoring gods, goddesses, and events during the 365-day calendar year. As mentioned earlier, five festival days were added to the calendar to celebrate Osiris, Horus, Seth, Isis, and Nephthys.

Excerpt from Papyrus de Turin, Chapter of the Divine God Legend of Ra and Isis

I am he whose name the gods know not. I am the maker of the hours and the creator of the days. I inaugurate festivals. I make the water flood. I am the creator of the fire of life through which the products of the workshops come into being. I am Khepera [Khepri] in the morning, Ra at mid-day, and Temu in the evening.

Genesis 1:20–25

20. And God said, Let the waters bring forth abundantly the moving creatures that hath life, and fowl that may fly above the earth in the open firmament of heaven. 21. And God created great whales, and every living creature that moveth, which the waters brought forth abundantly, after their kind, and every winged fowl after his kind: and God saw that it was good. 22. And God blessed them, saying, Be fruitful, and multiply, and fill the waters in the seas, and let fowl multiply in the earth. 23. And the evening and the morning were the fifth day. 24. And God said, Let the earth bring forth the living creature after his kind, cattle, and creeping thing, the beast of the earth after his kind: and it was so. 25. And God made the beast of the earth after his kind, and cattle after their kind, and every thing that creepeth upon the earth after his kind: and God saw that it was good.

Critique: What is interesting to me here is the style of writing and the words used by the men who wrote the myth of creation in Genesis 1:20–25; they sound similar to the African/Kemetic/Anu creation myths.

Excerpt from Grebaut, *Hymne a Ammon-Ra,* Paris 1874; and Wiedemann, *Die Religion*, p. 64ff (Preserved on Papyrus, Giza Egyptian Museum, Cairo)

Father of the gods, thou beautiful bull of the company of gods, thou chief of all gods, lord of Maat, father of the gods, creator of men, maker of beasts and cattle, lord of all that existeth, maker of the staff of life, creator of men, maker of beasts and cattle.... Thou art the creator of things celestial and terrestrial, thou illuminest the universe.... Thou makest the herbs for the use of beasts and cattle, and the staff of life for the need of man. Thou givest life to the fish of the stream and to the fowl of the air, and breath unto the germ in the egg; thou givest life unto the grasshopper, and thou makest to live the wild fowl and things that creep and things that fly and everything that belongeth thereunto. Thou providest food for the rats in the holes and for the birds that sit among the branches.... thou One, thou only One whose arms are many. All men and all creatures adore thee, and praises come unto thee from the height of heaven, from earth's widest space, and from the deepest deepest depths of the sea.... thou One, thou only One who hast no second ... whose names are manifold and innumerable.

Genesis 1:26–31

26. And God said, Let us make man in our image, after our likeness: and let them have dominion over the fish of the sea, and over the fowl of the air, and over the cattle, and over all the earth, and over every creeping thing that creepeth upon the earth. 27. So God created man in his own image, in the image of God created he him; male and female created he them. 28. And God blessed them, and God said unto them, Be fruitful, and multiply, and replenish the earth, and subdue it: and have dominion over the fish of the sea, and over the fowl of the air, and over every living thing that moveth upon the earth. 29. And God said, Behold, I have given you every herb bearing seed, which is upon the face of all the earth, and every tree, in the which is the fruit of a tree yielding seed; to you it shall be for meat. 30. And to every beast of the earth, and to every fowl of the air, and to everything that creepeth upon the earth, wherein there is life, I have given every green herb for meat: and it was so. 31. And

God saw every thing that he had made, and, behold, it was very good. And the evening and the morning were the sixth day.

Critique: This passage (Genesis 1:26–28) is strange. As you know, in the second chapter of Genesis, there is a second creation of man and woman: the more famous Adam and Eve. In this first creation of man in Genesis, man is created not from the dust of the ground but in the image and likeness of God. Second, what and who are the male writers talking about when they use the plural pronouns "us" and "our" and the plural pronoun "them"? ("And God said let us make man in our image, after our likeness and let them have dominion over the fish of the sea…")

Then the writer uses the singular pronouns "he" and "him" ("So God created man in his own image, in the image of God created he him; male and female created he them."), ending with another plural pronoun ("them"). The wording of this part of the creation myth is strange ("in the image of God created he him; male and female created he them").

Genesis 1:26–28 is similar to the Ogdoad of Hermopolis/Khmunu. Atum was created by the four sets of male and female gods and goddesses who inhabited the primordial waters of Nu (or Nun). Their inappropriate interaction caused an upheaval in the dark, primordial, chaotic, churning, bubbling waters of Nu (or Nun), which caused the sun to appear and the Benben to rise out of the primordial waters, and there stood Atum, the first of the gods created.

Atum is a very interesting African/Kemetic/Anu creator god. Atum can create offspring because he is the perfect vehicle for the creation of the gods. He is functionally and physiologically bisexual. His gender is both male and female, and he can impregnate himself; his epithet is "The Great He-She." Because of the epithet associated to him, Atum could easily be referred to as an African/Kemetic/Anu LGBT god.

Atum created himself (in the Heliopolis Ennead version of the creation myth) or was created (in the case of the Ogdoad of Hermopolis). He then depending on the version of his myth, masturbated and ejaculated into his own mouth; had sex with his shadow (Iusaaset); spat (or vomited), and coughed (or sneezed) to produce his children.

Atum gave his shadow a female name (Iusaaset), which comes from the evolution of religious mythology in Africa/Kemet/Anu. Earlier in the culture, individual gods or goddesses, viewed as being separate, are later combined into one god, both male and female. The myth of Atum becomes having a female shadow named Iusaaset that he mates with, then as man and woman they rule the earth together similar to Genesis 1:26–28.

Iusaaset was also spelled Juesaes, Jusas, Iusas, Iusaset, Ausaas, and Saosis; it means "the great one who comes forth." She is described as the grandmother of all the gods and goddesses. The creation myth of man in Genesis 1:26–28 is similar to the creation of a male-female god, with the writer using the common noun "man" instead.

This first created man in Genesis was different from the second man created; he was not created from dust but in the image and likeness of God and was given dominion over all the earth and every living thing that moved on the earth. Dominion means supreme authority or sovereignty; it also refers to the celestial hierarchy: a tradition of angels ranked in the following order: angels (the lowest), archangels, principalities, powers, virtues, dominions, thrones, cherubim, and seraphim (the highest).

This first mythical man created in Genesis was associated with the dominions, made by God in his likeness and image in consultation with the other celestial beings in heaven and given dominion over every living thing that moved on earth. Numerous times in the Bible, celestial beings carry out the will of God; examples include the Archangels Gabriel and Michael. A Cherubim is used by God in the myth of the Garden of Eden. Colossians 1:16 states, "For by him were all things created, that are in heaven, and that are in earth, visible and invisible, whether they be thrones, or dominions, or principalities, or powers: all things were created by him, and for him." There are thousands of African/Kemetic/Anu gods and goddesses. Many were viewed as expressions or extensions of the creator, much like ancestral deities, gods, and angels are viewed by the world's religions today.

Some Biblical scholars try to explain the use of "us" and "our" as an expression of the attributes that God has and man was given. Some say God was talking about himself and nothing more; some say God was talking to angels; and some say God was talking to Jesus and the Holy Spirit, among other explanations.

Remember the influence that African/Kemetic/Anu myths had on the writers of the Book of Genesis; the male writers of Genesis 1:26–28 were writing a myth similar to the creation of a celestial being by a supreme god with the assistance of other celestial beings. This is the same as the African/Kemetic/Anu myths of a supreme creator god and gods who assist with the creation, and are a manifestation and expression of the will of the supreme god.

Here is an example of gods and angels in heaven and on earth who were subservient to the supreme god. Revelation 12:7–10 states that there was a great war in heaven, and the Archangel Michael and his angels (manifestations of God) carry out the will of God and defeat the dragon and his angels. After their defeat, the dragon and his angels were cast out of heaven and sent down to earth because the dragon, also called a serpent, the devil, and Satan, had deceived the whole world.

The second example is found in Genesis 6:2–5, which states that the sons of God saw the daughters of men and found that they were fair, and they took them for their wives as they pleased. Because man is made of flesh, God's spirit will only dwell in him for 120 years. There were giants on the earth in those days, and after that the sons of God came into the daughters of men and they bare them children, the same became mighty men, which were old men of renown. God saw the wickedness of man was great in the earth and saw that every imagination of the thoughts of his heart was evil. (Note: from earlier Papyrus de Turin excerpt: Legend of Ra and Isis: "….king of men and gods, the one form, to whom periods of one hundred and twenty years are as single years….")

We find the mythical god Tehuti described as the heart, mind, and tongue of the creator, voicing the will of the creator. His words brought everything into existence in the heavens and earth. We have Ra, who combined with different gods to accomplish the act of creation. Ra combined with Khepri or with Amen to accomplish the act of creation.

Whether one calls them angels, archangels, dominions, cherubim, seraphim, Jesus, or the Holy Spirit, this is similar to the use of multiple gods that is found in African/Kemetic/Anu myths.

The following excerpts describe lesser gods created in the likeness and image of Ra and Tem (Atum).

The Chapter of Repulsing Slaughter in Hensu
From the Papyrus of Nu

> I am Ra, who stablisheth those who praise him. My hair is the hair of Nu. My face is the face of the Disk. My eyes are the eyes of Hathor. My ears are the ears of Up-uat. My nose is the nose of Khenti-Khabas. My lips are the lips of Anpu. My teeth are the teeth of Serquet. My cheeks are the cheeks of the goddess Isis. My hands are the hands of Baneb-Tet. My forearms are the forearms of Neith, the

Lady of Sais. My backbone is the backbone of Suti. My phallus is the phallus of Beba. My reins are the reins of the Lords of Kher-aha. My chest is the chest of Aa-shefit. My belly and back are the belly and back of Sekhmet. My buttocks are the buttocks of the Eye of Horus. My hips and legs are the hips and legs of Nut. My feet are the feet of Ptah. My fingers and my toes are the fingers and toes of the Living gods. There is no member of my body which is not the member of a god.

The Chapter of Changing into a Divine Hawk
Book of Coming Forth by Day

Let them see that thou hast provided me with food for the festival. I am one of those Spirit-souls who dwell in the Light-god. I have made my form in his form, when he cometh to Tetu [Busiris]. I am a Spirit-body among his Spirit-bodies.... I, even I, am a Spirit-soul, a dweller in the Light-god, whose form hath been created in divine flesh. I am one of those Spirit-souls who dwell in the Light-god, who were created by Tem [Atum] himself, and who exist in the blossoms [i.e., Eyelashes] of his Eye.

Genesis 2:6–7

6. But there went up a mist from the earth, and watered the whole face of the ground. 7. And the LORD God formed man of the dust of the ground, and breathed into his nostrils the breath of life; and man became a living soul.

Critique: Genesis 2:6–7, the creation of the second man in the Book of Genesis, is a reworking of the creation stories of Atum; the Heliopolis Ennead; the creator god Khnum of Philae and Elephantine, Egypt; and passages from Kemetic/Anu religious texts.

Let's review: Atum was self-created in the Heliopolis Ennead version of the creation myth. Atum created his son, the god Shu, and his daughter, the goddess Tefnut. Shu and Tefnut were playing in the dark, primordial, chaotic, churning, bubbling waters of Nu (or Nun). They somehow got into danger and were lost in the waters; Atum sent out his Udjat Eye (symbol of royal power and protection), also called the "Eye of Horus," to find them. The eye finds them, and they all return to Atum, who is so overjoyed at the safe return of his children that he weeps tears of joy.

Excerpt from Hymn to Atum
Papyrus Bremmer-Rhind

> With tears from my eye, I wept and human beings appeared. [Note: some scholars say "as his tears hit the ground."] I created the reptiles and their companions; Shu and Tefnut gave birth to Geb of the earth and Nut of the sky; Geb and Nut gave birth to Osiris and Isis, Seth and Nephthys; Osiris and Isis gave birth to Horus; one was born right after another; these nine [the Heliopolis Ennead] gave birth to all the multitude of the land.

Khnum of Philae and Elephantine was worshipped as a water god and is associated with being the source of the Nile River. The Nile would deposit black silt onto the river banks and make the banks fertile. The silt could also be used to make clay, which in turn was used to make pottery. Khnum was associated with pottery and art. He was self-created and was the creator of all things and all things that will be. Epithets associated with his name were "Father of Fathers," "Mother of Mothers," "to create," "to join," "to unite," and "to build."

Khnum is depicted in art as a man with the head of a ram (remember, animals are the personification of personal attributes; the ram symbolized fertility), sitting at his potter's wheel, creating all of mankind out of clay. He created children on his potter's wheel and breathed life into them, giving them "ka" (spirit).

Let's see the similarities between Genesis's second creation of man and the Kemetic/Anu creation myths just mentioned. We have a self-created god; a god who created a man; tears; water; mist; forming man from dust; creating mankind with his hands; dust; dirt; ground; silt; clay; art; pottery; children created on a potter's wheel; breathing; life; breathing life into; soul; ka; tears from a gods eyes (which are part of his face), hitting the ground/earth and humans are created; and a mist went up from the earth, watering the whole face of the ground, and the LORD God formed man of the dust of the ground.

Here are some excerpts from various African/Kemetic/Anu religious texts that deal with some type of a scenario associated with wind, breath, soul, nostrils, life, spirit, and creation by a god or goddess. The following excerpts are from the Papyrus de Turin and the *Book of Coming Forth by Day*: Papyrus of Ani.

Magical Texts in the Mummy Chamber and the Funeral Chamber Speech of Isis

> Isis saith: I have come to be a protector unto thee. I waft unto thee air for thy nostrils, and the north wind which cometh forth from the god Tem [Atum] unto thy nose. I have made whole for thee thy windpipe. I make thee to live like a god.

Papyrus de Turin, Chapter of the Divine God
Legend of Ra and Isis

> Then his children came unto him, and every god was there uttering cries of lamentation. And Isis came with her words of power, and in her mouth was the breath of life.

A Hymn to Osiris

> Thou art the beneficent one, and art praised in Nart. Thou makest thy soul to be raised up. Thou art the Lord of the Great House in Khemenu/Khnum [Heliopolis].… thou art the beneficent Spirit among spirits. The god of the Celestial Ocean [Nu] draweth from thee his waters. Thou sendest forth the north wind at eventide, and breaths from thy nostrils to the satisfaction of thy heart.… The stars in the celestial heights are obedient unto thee.… Thou art he to whom praises are ascribed in the southern heaven, and thanks are given for thee in the northern heaven.

The Doctrine of Eternal Life

> I am whole, even as my father Khepera [Khepri] was whole, who is to me the type of that which passeth not

41

away, Come then, O Form, and give breath unto me, O lord of breath.

A Hymn of Praise to Ra when He Riseth on the Horizon and when He Setteth in the Land of Life

Let me breathe the air which cometh forth from thy nostrils and the north wind which cometh forth from thy mother Nut. Make thou my Spirit-soul to be glorious, O Osiris, make thou my Heart-soul to be divine.

Chapter of Snuffing the Air with Water in Khert-Neter (Underworld)
Spell against Heart Robbers

Hail Tem [Atum]. Grant thou unto me the sweet breath which dwelleth in thy nostrils, I am he who embraceth that great throne.... I keep watch over the Egg of Kenken-ur [i.e., the Great Cackler, a goose]. I grow and flourish [as] it groweth and flourisheth. I live [as] it liveth. I snuff the air [as] it snuffeth the air [or, my breath is its breath].

The Prayer of Ani
The Weighing of the Heart

May there be no parting of thee from me in the presence of him that keepeth the Balance! Thou art my Ka [spirit], which dwelleth in my body; the god Khnemu [Khnum] who knitteth together and strengtheneth my limbs.

Genesis 2:9

9. And out of the ground made the LORD God to grow every tree that is pleasant to the sight, and good for food; the tree of life also in the midst of the garden, and the tree of knowledge of good and evil.

Genesis 3:21–22

> 21. Unto Adam also and to his wife did the LORD God make coats of skins, and clothed them. 22. And the LORD God said, Behold the man is become as one of us, to know good and evil: and now, lest he put forth his hand, and take also of the tree of life, and eat, and live for ever:

Critique: Let's compare these verses with excerpts from the *Book of Coming Forth by Day*.

The Doctrine of Eternal Life
Papyrus of Ani

> He is clothed in the finest raiment, like unto the raiment of those who sit on the throne of living right and truth. He thirsts not, nor hungers, nor is sad; he eats the bread of Ra and drinks what he drinks daily, and his bread also is that which is the word of Keb [Geb], and that which comes forth from the mouths of the gods. He eats what the gods eat, he drinks what they drink.... Not only does he eat and drink of their food, but he wears the apparel which they wear.... He goeth to the Great Lake in the midst of the Field of Offerings whereon the great gods sit; and these great and never failing gods give unto him [to eat] of the "Tree of Life" of which they themselves do eat that he likewise may live.... The bread which he eats never decays, and his beer never grows stale. He eats of the "bread of eternity" and drinks of the "beer of everlastingness."

As mentioned earlier, Iusaaset was considered the grandmother of all the gods and goddesses. She was worshipped as the shadow/wife of Atum of the Heliopolis Ennead. Iusaaset was also associated with the acacia tree, considered in Africa/Kemet/Anu as the "Tree of Life." The many uses of the acacia tree made it an important symbol in African/Kemetic/Anu culture.

Using education again to understand history, the acacia tree is known for and used for its medicinal properties; as a food source in soups, sauces, and honey; tree gum and sap; tannin (complex phenolic resins used in tanning and in medicine); perfumes; wood; paints; and ornamentals in gardens, of which there are at least six types used to decorate and dress gardens: "And the Lord God took the man, and put him into the Garden of Eden to dress it and to keep it" (Genesis 2:15).

African/Kemetic/Anu culture often used trees and plants in symbolic writings and art. Several types of trees and plants were sacred: acacia, sycamore, tamarisk (two were said to stand by the eastern gate to heaven), myrrh, willow, palm, lotus, persea (associated with rebirth, standing on the horizon of the eastern rising sun), and evergreens (associated with everlasting life and renewal because they have green leaves in all seasons; they are also associated with Osiris, whose symbolic color was green). Several gods (Horus and Osiris) and goddesses (Nut, Hathor, and Isis) were associated with trees.

The following excerpt is a myth about the Great Cat in the form of Ra, who fought the battle of good versus evil against the giant serpent Apophis (Apep) by the sacred persea or ished tree.

The *Book of Coming Forth by Day*, Chapter 17

> I am the cat [Mau], which fought hard by the Persea or Ished tree, in Annu [Heliopolis] on the night when the foes [Apep and his cohorts] of Neb-er-tcher [Osiris] were destroyed.

There are several paintings and vignettes depicting this battle of good versus evil between the Great Ra and Apophis by the sacred persea or ished tree. One painting is in the tomb of Inherkha (Inherka) in Thebes, Africa.

The concept of good versus evil is found in several African/Kemetic/Anu mythical conflicts between gods: Ra versus Apep, Seth versus Apep, and Horus versus Seth. Horus, the divine child of Isis and Osiris, represented good. He waged war against Seth, who represented evil and was the murderer of Osiris. The two of them waged several brutal wars against each other, with their supporters, for the control of earth. Seth took control of earth when he murdered Osiris, but Horus (also called Heru) won the final battle, and a truce was reached when Tehuti intervened. Even with the truce, there was still the threat of hostilities and the never-ending battle of good versus evil on earth.

Here are some of the similarities between the creation myth in Genesis 2:9, 2:15, 3:21–22 and the African/Kemetic/Anu religious excerpts: a creator god; a man created by God in a garden versus a man in the presence of gods in eternity; clothed in coats of skin versus being clothed in the finest raiment and wearing the apparel of the gods; the presence of food to eat from a tree provided by God versus eating the food of the gods; the Trees of Life and Knowledge of good and evil in the midst of the garden versus a Tree of Life and a Great Lake in the midst of the field of offerings where the great gods sit.

Eating from the Tree of Life to live like the gods versus being prohibited and being ordered not to eat from the Trees of Life and Knowledge of good and evil respectively, to prevent humans from acquiring the knowledge of good and evil and living forever like God; the battle of good versus evil; a created man being told by God to dress and keep a garden versus the acacia tree, a symbolic African/Kemetic/Anu tree. Some species of the acacia tree have their flowers and leaves used as ornamentals to decorate and dress gardens.

Genesis 3:3–5, 11, 13–14, and 24

> 3. But of the fruit of the tree which is in the midst of the garden, God hath said, Ye shall not eat of it, neither shall ye touch it, lest ye die. 4. And the serpent said unto the woman, Ye shall not surely die: 5. For God doth know that in the day ye eat thereof, then your eyes shall be opened, and ye shall be as gods, knowing good and evil.… 11. And he said, Who told thee that thou wast naked? Hast thou eaten of the tree, whereof I commanded thee that thou shouldest not eat? 13. And the Lord God said unto the woman, What is this that thou hast done? And the woman said, The serpent beguiled me, and I did eat. 14. And the Lord God said unto the serpent, Because thou hast done this, thou art cursed above all cattle, and above every beast of the field; upon thy belly shalt thou go, and dust shalt thou eat all the days of thy life:… 24. So he drove out the man; and he placed at the east of the garden of Eden Cherubims, and a flaming sword which turned every way, to keep the way of the tree of life.

Critique: The religious myths of African/Kemetic/Anu culture also use the serpent to create deception, chaos, and destruction, and to take the side of evil against good. Apep is usually depicted in art as a giant snake (and sometimes as a crocodile). He commanded an army of evil cohorts who battled Ra for the souls of mankind.

We have Horus, the son of Osiris and Isis, who battled Seth, the murderer of Osiris, for control of earth. Seth is represented as various animals in art; in one form, he is a snake. In African/Kemetic/Anu myths, before Seth became evil, he battled Apep, the giant snake (or sometimes a crocodile), in a constant battle of good versus evil.

The following African/Kemetic/Anu myth is about the battle between Horus and Seth. In this battle, Horus (good) fights with Heru-behutet (a dualistic form of Horus combined with Ra).

In this myth, Horus becomes two different gods with the same form and appearance, working together to defeat Seth. They club, spear, cut off limbs, shoot arrows, and drag Seth and his cohorts all over the battlefield of Aat-shatet (middle/Africa/Kemet/Anu).

Seth decides to turn himself into a serpent (which he can do because he is a god) and starts to hiss loudly and looks for a hole in the ground to hide and live in.

Excerpt from the Wall of the Temple of Edfu
Located on the West Bank of the Nile River in Edfu, Egypt

The Legend of Heru-Behutet and the Winged Disk

> The monster Ba [soul], hath turned himself into a hissing serpent, let Horus, the son of Isis, set himself above his hole in the form of a pole on the top of which is the head of Horus, so that he may never again come forth therefrom.

Critique: Again let's take a look at the similarities between the verses in Genesis mentioned previously and the myths of Africa/Kemet/Anu: a supreme creator god; an evil, deceitful serpent; a supreme god placing an upright serpent on his belly, eating dust for the rest of his life; an upright, walking god (Seth) turning himself into a serpent to hide and live in a hole in the ground; a level of Christian celestial beings called Cherubim's, placed by a Supreme God at the east of the Garden of Eden to guard the Tree of Life; a flaming sword that also protects the Tree of Life east of the

46

Garden of Eden; Horus and Heru-behutet, acting on orders from Ra, sit like a pole on the hole so the serpent Seth can never come forth again.

Other similarities include Heru-behutet (a combination of Horus and Ra), who symbolized the sun, which can be said to be flaming; Horus and Heru-behutet fought the evil Seth with clubs, spears, and arrows; a flaming sword protected the Garden of Eden; a "Tree of Life" and a "Tree of Knowledge" in the Garden of Eden and the sacred acacia tree in African/Kemetic/Anu culture called the "Tree of Life"; Cherubim's and a flaming sword placed east of the Garden of Eden to protect the "Tree of Life" and the tamarisk tree, a sacred tree in African/Kemetic/Anu mythology, associated with guarding the eastern gates of heaven.

Genesis 2:11–18 and 21–24

> 11. The name of the first is Pison: that is it which compasseth the whole land of Havilah, where there is gold; 12. And the gold of that land is good: there is bdellium and the onyx stone. 13. And the name of the second river is Gihon: the same is it that compasseth the whole land of Ethiopia. 14. And the name of the third river is Hiddekel: that is it which goeth toward the east of Assyria. And the fourth river is the Euphrates. 15. And the LORD God took the man, and put him into the garden of Eden to dress it and to keep it. 16. And the LORD God commanded the man, saying, Of every tree of the garden thou mayest freely eat: 17. But of the tree of the knowledge of good and evil, thou shalt not eat of it: for in the day that thou eatest thereof thou shalt surely die. 18. And the LORD God said, It is not good that the man should be alone; I will make him an help meet for him.… 21. And the LORD God caused a deep sleep to fall upon Adam, and he slept: and he took one of his ribs, and closed up the flesh instead thereof; 22. And the rib, which the LORD God had taken from man, made he a woman, and brought her unto the man. 23. And Adam said, This is now bone of my bones, and flesh of my flesh: she shall be called Woman, because she was taken out of Man. 24. Therefore shall a man leave his father and his mother, and shall cleave unto his wife: and they shall be one flesh.

Critique: First of all, this is sexist; the woman was created as a help meet, taken out of the rib of the man, and then named by the man with part of his name: woman. The woman is responsible for the so-called apple incident in the Garden of Eden, and "cleaving" to a woman (or anyone) can be dangerous. The woman in Genesis was almost created as an afterthought (or the need for more hired help).

I mentioned earlier that the creation myth of the first man in Genesis is different from the creation myth of the second man. The first man was made in the image and likeness of God and his hierarchy of celestial beings. He was associated with the word "dominion," one of the levels of the celestial hierarchy of beings. He was given authority over every living thing that moved on earth. He was told to be fruitful, multiply, and replenish the earth and subdue it. "Subdue" means repress, put down by force or intimidation.

Adam was created because God had no man to till the ground or do the work in the garden, so he made a man from dust (dirt); God breathed into the man's nostrils the breath of life, and man became a living soul (Genesis 2:5–7). God placed this man in a garden, naked like an animal; the man was given food to eat like a dog or cat; given instructions to stay away from the Tree of Knowledge of good and evil (despite the fact that there was a deceitful and evil serpent in the garden); and told to dress and work the garden without help.

The borders of this garden are two rivers we can be sure of: one river, encompassing the whole land of Ethiopia, had to be the Nile River. The second river we can be sure of is the Euphrates River, which runs from Turkey to the Persian Gulf. So we can say that Adam had to till the ground, dress, and keep a garden that was approximately 5,800 miles in length (the Nile River is approximately 4,100 miles long and the Euphrates River is approximately 1,700 miles long), not including the other two rivers mentioned in Genesis.

How many people would like this job? No pay; given herbs and fruit to eat; walking around naked like an animal; placed in a garden with boundaries; not allowed to gain knowledge or have a concept of good versus evil (which would allow you to know if you were being taken advantage of); and have to work in a garden almost twice the horizontal length of the United States of America with no help.

On top of that, you have a person over you whose job description is to subdue and have dominion over you. Then your god feels sorry that you are alone and decides "I will make him a help meet for him" (Genesis 2:18), a woman whose function is to help meet the labor demands of tilling the ground and keeping a garden approximately 5,800 miles in length. So he puts you to sleep, takes one of your ribs, and makes a being that you are allowed to give the name "woman" to.

When this mythical woman breaks the law and simply learns the knowledge of good versus evil, she is punished for it with pain, sorrow, and behavioral domination: "Unto the woman he said, I will greatly multiply thy sorrow and thy conception; in sorrow thou shalt bring forth children; and thy desire [shall be] to thy husband, and he shall rule over thee" (Genesis 3:16). "Rule" means to govern or exercise authority over.

This creation myth about the Garden of Eden provides an excuse for the male subjugation of women. It uses the word of God to justify sexism, discrimination, and abusive behavior against women. When I read about the Garden of Eden, for some reason the words "slave" and "plantation" come to mind. I will cover the numerous and indefensible slavery passages in the scriptures of religions like Christianity, Judaism, and Islam in the next chapter.

Another example of sexism and disrespect towards women can be found in I Peter 3:1-7 of the Christian Bible. Excerpts from I Peter 3:1-7 state: "Likewise, ye wives, be in subjection to your own husbands"—"While they behold your chaste conversation coupled with fear"—"In the old time the holy women also, who trusted in God, adorned themselves, being in subjection unto their own husbands"—"Even as Sara obeyed Abraham, calling him lord"—"Likewise, ye husbands, dwell with them according to knowledge, giving honour unto the wife, as unto the weaker vessel."

Sara "obeying" Abraham (her husband) and referring to women as "the weaker vessel" is bad enough, but the use of the word "subjection" to describe a women's relationship to her husband is something only a man could have written. I Peter 3:1-7 is an example of a male writer using a man-made mythological god in an attempt to control women.

Note: Subjection means: Domination; the bringing of a person or people under the control of another; owing allegiance to another; to submit to the authority of another; the act of conquering.

Buddhism

The complex religion of Buddhism is generally vague regarding a creation myth. It is a forward-looking religion; Buddhism regards speculating about creation to be a waste of time because the origin of creation is beyond human comprehension. Intelligence and spiritual/mental energy should not be spent trying to comprehend creation, because self-empowerment is more important.

Buddhism says nothing can exist or start to exist because time and space have always existed. You only have transformations: recycling of universal cosmic energy, one episode after the next. On earth, we are doomed to a continuing cycle of death and rebirth, unless we use our intellect and energy to pursue a lifestyle of mental and spiritual awareness that allows us to rise above the superficial material vices, desires, and temptations of this life and reach a state of Nirvana.

Nirvana is the extinction of desire, suffering, and individual consciences; becoming one with nature; a place of complete bliss, delight, and peace (or as some jokingly say, when you are dead). Buddhism is often described as complex, vague, and evasive, because there are many sects and schools that have varying beliefs when it comes to creation myths, like a recycling universe; existence is made up of three parts; time and space have always existed; creation started with a contraction and expansion of space (similar to the Big Bang theory of science).

The oldest surviving school of Buddhism, Theravada (with over 100 million followers), presented a creation myth called the Agganna Sutta, found in the Digha Nikaya, the first of five books that are part of the Sutta Pitaka, a division of the standard collection of texts called the Pali Canon or Tipitaka. The Tipitaka is recognized as canonical by the Theravada Buddhists. (Note: Buddhism partially arose out of the brutal oppression of the discriminatory caste system of Hinduism. "Caste" means social status or position based on class.) In this mythical story, Buddha presents an alternative creation myth to Hinduism's creation myth, which justified a caste system that engaged in interethnic discrimination.

Excerpts from the Agganna Sutta
On Knowledge of the Beginnings of Humankind (the Buddhist Cosmology)

"Abhassara" means the radiant ones, divine beings of the fine material world; a class of higher devas. "Brahma" is a Hindu god of creation, one of the three major deities in Hinduism. (Note: There is a difference between Brahman, Brahma, and Brahmin. Brahman is the supreme god of Hinduism. Brahma is the god of creation who is part of a trilogy and a manifestation of the supreme god Brahman. Brahmin is the highest level of the Hindu caste system, which was created from the mouth of the god Purusha, a manifestation of Brahman.)

The Beginning of Earth and Humankind

> There comes a time, Vasettha [a person Buddha is talking to who is in training to become a monk], when, sooner or later after a long period, this world contracts. At a time of contraction, beings are mostly born in the Abhassara Brahma world. And there they dwell, mind-made, feeding on delight, self-luminous, moving through the air, glorious—and they stay like that for a very long time. But sooner or later, after a very long period, this world begins to expand again. At a time of expansion, the beings from the Abhassara Brahma world, having passed away from there, are mostly reborn in this world. Here they dwell, mind-made, feeding on delight, self-luminous, moving through the air, glorious—and they stay like that for a very long time.
>
> At that period, Vasettha, there was just one mass of water, and all was darkness, blinding darkness. Neither moon nor sun appeared, no constellations or stars appeared, night and day were not yet distinguished, nor months and fortnights, nor years and seasons, there were no male and female, beings being reckoned just as beings. And sooner or later, after a very long period of time, savory earth spread itself over the waters where those beings were. It looked just like the skin that forms itself over hot milk as it cools. It was endowed with color, smell, and taste. It was the color of fine ghee or butter and it was very sweet, like pure wild honey.
>
> And then the creepers had disappeared, rice appeared in the open spaces free from powder and husks, fragrant and clean grained. And what they had taken in the evening for supper had grown again and was ripe in the morning, and what they had taken in the morning for breakfast was ripe again by evening, with no sign of reaping. And these beings set to and fed on this rice, and this lasted for a very long time. And as they did so, their bodies became coarser

still, and the difference in their looks became even greater. And the females developed female sex organs and the males developed male sex organs. And the females became excessively preoccupied with the men, and the men with the women. Owing to this excessive preoccupation with each other, passion was aroused, and their bodies burnt with lust. And later because of this burning, they indulged in sexual activity. But those who saw them indulging threw dust, and ashes, or cow dung at them, crying, "Die, you filthy beast! How can one being do such things to another?".... Then some being of a greedy nature said: "I say, what can this be?" And tasted the savory earth on its finger. In doing so, it became taken with the flavor, and crave arose in it. Then other beings, taking their cue from that one, also tasted the stuff with their fingers. They too were taken with the flavor, and craving arose in them. So they set to with their hands breaking off pieces of the stuff in order to eat it. And the result was that their self-luminance disappeared. And as a result of the disappearance of their self-luminance the moon and the sun appeared, night and day were distinguished, months and fortnights appeared, and the year and its seasons. To that extent the world re-evolved.

Critique: There are several similarities with this Buddhist account of creation and the creation myths of Africa/Kemet/Anu mentioned earlier. We have contraction and expansion; upheaval of the dark primordial waters; mass of blinding dark water; Atum, a mythical creator sun god; self-luminous celestial beings; creation of light, sun, moon, and stars; four sets of male and female creator gods and goddesses; asexual beings born from the Abhassara Brahma, over time becoming males and females; savory earth spreads itself over the water; earth rises out of the primordial waters of Nu (or Nun); creation of days, nights, months, years, seasons, and celestial signs; asexual beings evolving into males and females; male-female god Atum creating male and female gods and goddesses; mythical celestial beings from the Abhassara Brahma world pass away and are reborn in a new world; Ra going beneath the horizon to die on the western horizon and rising on the eastern horizon to be reborn every morning; eating and drinking what the gods consume so one can become a god and live forever in eternity versus the opposite: eating the food which makes a self-luminous asexual celestial being from the Abhassara Brahma degenerate and turn into a lustful male or female human, thus losing their self-luminance.

Hinduism

There is no one single Hindu myth of creation; there are many texts and myths concerning creation. The oldest collection of sacred canonical texts comes from the Vedic Sanskrit: Rig Veda Hymns. Two of these hymns are presented below.

Nasadeeya (Nasadiya): The Creation Hymn of Rig Veda 129th hymn of the 10th Mandala

> At first neither being nor nonbeing. There was not air nor yet sky beyond. What was its wrapping? Where? In whose protection?
>
> Was water there, unfathomable and deep? There was no death then, nor yet deathlessness; of night or day there was not any sign. The one breathed without breath, by its own impulse. Other than that was nothing at all. Darkness was there; all wrapped around by darkness, and all was water indiscriminate. Then that which was hidden by the void, that one emerging, stirring, through power of Ardor [Tapas], came to be. ["Ardor" means heat, fire, warmth, fervour, fervidness, and intensity.] In the beginning love arose, which was the primal germ cell of the mind, the Seers, searching in their hearts with wisdom, discovered the connection of being and nonbeing.
>
> A crosswise line cut being from nonbeing. What was described above it, what below? Bearers of seed there were mighty forces, thrust from below and forward move above. Who really knows? Who can presume to tell it? Whence was it born? Whence issued this creation? Even the gods came after its emergence. Then who can tell from whence it came to be? That out of which creation has arisen, whether it held it firm or it did not; He who surveys it in the highest heaven, He surely knows or maybe He does not!

Critique: Some historians say this hymn was written to astound and confuse rather than explain the Hindu account of creation. However, there is nothing confusing about this creation myth. It is similar to African/Kemetic/Anu creation myths, with the writer attempting to dress this Hindu myth up as some sort of riddle of creation.

If one is familiar with the Heliopolis Ennead and Ogdoad of Hermopolis/Khmunu creation myths, one can see the similarities with this creation myth riddle.

Hindu creation myth: At first there was no beings or nonbeings, no air, no sky, no sky beyond. The Heliopolis Ennead creation myth: nothing exists except the dark, primordial, chaotic, churning, bubbling waters of Nu (or Nun). Hindu creation myth: There was no death or deathlessness; no sign of day or night; the One breathed without breath by its own impulse, other than that there was nothing else at all. Heliopolis Ennead creation myth: Atum created himself rising up out of Nu (or Nun), standing on a Benben, the first of the living breathing gods, bringing life, light, and the first day.

Hindu creation myth: Darkness was there wrapped around by darkness, and water was indiscriminate. Ogdoad of Hermopolis/Khmunu creation myth: We have the dark, primordial, chaotic, churning, bubbling waters of Nu (or Nun) inhabited by four sets of male and female creator gods and goddesses. Nu and Naumet represented the inert primordial waters; Heh and Hauhet represented the boundless eternity of the primordial waters; Kek and Kauket represented the darkness of the primordial waters; and Amun and Amaunet represented air within and the unknown nature of the primordial waters.

Hindu creation myth: Then that which was hidden by the void/emptiness, that one emerging through the power of Ardor (fire, heat, warmth, fervour, fervidness, and intensity), came to be. Ogdoad of Hermopolis/Khmunu creation myth: The four sets of gods and goddesses who inhabit the dark, primordial, chaotic, churning, bubbling waters of Nu (or Nun) interacted in an inappropriate way, causing an upheaval in the primordial waters, which caused the sun to rise in the sky and creating Atum, the first of the gods. Heliopolis Ennead creation myth: Atum creates himself and then rises up out of the dark, primordial, chaotic, churning, bubbling waters, standing on the pyramidal-shaped mound, bringing light and the sun.

Hindu creation myth: In the beginning "love arose," which was the primal germ cell of the mind (the One in the beginning). The Seers (visionary, foresight) discovered the connection of being and nonbeing. Bearers of seed there were the mighty forces thrust from below and forward move above. In the Ogdoad of Hermopolis/Khmunu creation myth: the four sets of gods and goddesses below in the primordial waters created an upheaval (mighty force) that created the sun, light, and Atum.

In the Heliopolis Ennead creation myth: once Atum was created, he went on a self-pleasuring "love fest." Atum, who is physiologically bisexual (male and female), cried tears of joy, and as they hit the ground, human beings were created; mates with his own shadow; masturbates and ejaculates into his own mouth, impregnating himself; coughs (or sneezes) and spits (or vomits) to produce his offspring.

Excerpt from Hymn to Purusha

"Purusha" means "eastern dawn"; manifestation of the infinite and supreme being Brahman; cosmic man; the self which pervades the universe; the supreme male principle in the universe.

"Viraj" means the brightest of all stars; intelligent and classy woman/person; splendor; true beauty; forgiving.

"Yajus" means sacrificial prayer or formula.

Brahmins, Rajanya, Vaisya, and Sudra are four of the five levels of the caste system of Hinduism.

"Indra" means mythical king of the gods; god of thunder and rain; god of battle; defeated the serpent thus creating land, ocean and life.

"Agni" means mythical god of fire; the messenger of the gods; acceptor of sacrifice.

"Vaya" means mythical god of the wind.

> A Thousand heads hath Purusha, a thousand eyes, a thousand feet. On every side pervading earth he fills a space ten fingers wide. This Purusha is all that yet hath been an all that is to be: The Lord of immortality which waxes greater still by food. So mighty is his greatness; yea greater than this is Purusha. All creatures are one-fourth of him, three-fourths eternal life in heaven. With three-fourths Purusha went up: one-fourth of him again was here.

Thence he strode out to every side what eats not and what eats. From him Viraj was born; again Purusha from Viraj was born.... From the great general sacrifice the dripping fat was gathered up. He formed the creatures of the air, and animals both wild and tame.... There from were spells and charms produced; the Yajus had its birth from it. From it horses were born, from it all cattle with two rows of teeth. From it were generated kind [buffalo, bison, and ox], from its goats and sheep were born.

When they divided Purusha how many portions did they make? What do they call his mouth, his arms? What do they call his thighs and feet? The Brahmin was his mouth, of both his arms was the Rajanya made [some refer to this caste system level as Kshatriya]. His thighs became the Vaisya; from his feet the Sudra was produced. The Moon was gendered from his mind, and from his eye the Sun had birth. Indra and Agni from his mouth were born, and Vaya from his breath.

Forth from his navel came mid-air, the sky was fashioned from his head. Earth from his feet and from his car [language] the regions. Thus they formed the worlds.... When the gods, offering sacrifice, bound, as their victim, Purusha. Gods sacrificing sacrificed the victim, these were the holy ordinances. The mighty ones attained the height of heaven, there where the Sadhyas, gods of old, are dwelling.

Critique: In the myth of Purusha, we find the same attributes and epithets associated with the African/Kemetic/Anu mythical gods Osiris, Ra, Amen-Ra, Atum, and Khepri. Purusha is a manifestation of the eternal supreme being Brahman; Khepri and Atum are manifestations of the supreme god Ra. Mighty is Purusha's greatness, inconceivably extended in time and space; his growth is incomprehensible; his evolutions are manifold; he is the self that pervades the universe (Amen-ra and Ra). Purusha is associated with immortality and everlastingness; he is called "Lord" (Osiris and Amen-ra) and is the creator of animals, gods, and humans (Amen-ra, Atum, and Ra).

The myth of Purusha is associated with offerings and sacrificial ceremonies. The same offerings and sacrificial ceremonies are found earlier in the African/Kemetic/Anu religious myths. Offerings and sacrificial ceremonies are made to placate the gods; for the dead; and to bring good fortune to the spirit (ka). Offerings and sacrificial ceremonies are found in spiritual texts of African/Kemetic/Anu religions and are easy to investigate.

One African/Kemetic/Anu myth, the Book of Gates: the second section of the Tuat (Underworld) concerns propitiatory offerings and sacrifices. "Propitiatory" means offered in order to atone for a wrong or the act of placating.

Ra combines with Osiris (ruler of the Underworld) and is called Afu-Ra on his journey through the Tuat (Underworld). There are twelve sections, hours or gates of the Tuat, which symbolizes Ra's journey through the twelve hours of night in the Barque of a Million Years. Each section is guarded by a god or goddess. In the second section, Afu-Ra weighs each person's words and deeds. The good people stand on the right side of Afu-Ra and give offerings and praise, which are rewarded with a good outcome, and the wicked stand to the left of Afu-Ra and are tortured, sacrificed, and destroyed.

Lastly, the most sacred sound of the Hindu dharma (spiritual and religious term that means one's righteous duty or virtuous path) is Aum (OM). This primordial sound, the essence of the Hindu spiritual scriptures, is the sound of the sun and the sound of light; it is used in chants as an affirmation; it is used as a mantra capable of creating transformation; it permeates all the elements of the universe: earth, air, fire, and water. Aum resides in intelligence and consciousness. It is the sound of ascent as it uplifts the soul; it is the sound of the sacred eagle or falcon.

One can see the obvious similarity to the African/Kemetic/Anu self-created sun god Atum. The name "Atum" and the word "Aum" look and sound similar; both have a connection to the sun; one rises out of the primordial waters, while the other is the primordial sound; one is self-created and creates; the other produces the sound that creates; one represents the sun and creates the gods and goddesses that rule the air, moisture, sky, and earth; the other permeates the elements of earth, air, water, and fire; one is the sound of the ascent of the soul represented in the divine eagle or falcon; the supreme self-created sun god Ra is often represented as a man with the head of a divine hawk or falcon, symbolizing rising to the sky or heavens.

The African/Kemetic/Anu mythical gods Sia (Sa) and Hu were created from the blood of the self-mutilated penis of Ra. These two gods represented the creative powers of Ra. They are the bodyguards of Ra, standing at the front of the boat during Ra's daily journey through the gates of the twelve hours of day and twelve hours of night.

Hu represented the creative powers of Ra and was the personification of the sense—meaning general consciousness and awareness; taste; physiological method of perception; and method by which a word, situation, or expression can be interpreted. Hu was considered the divine food upon which the gods in heaven lived. Hu is referred to as "The Divine Utterance," "The Voice of Authority," "The God of Relish," "The God of Pronunciation," and "The Creative Word." Hu is the god of the first sound and word spoken during creation; depending on the time and place, he was associated with the creator gods Atum of the Heliopolis Ennead, and at times he was confused with Tehuti, known as the heart, mind, and tongue of the creator, and the creator god Ptah, who created the universe by word.

Hu and two other gods—Sia, who represented divine infinite knowledge (omniscience), and Heke, who represented magic, spells, and incantations—represented the manifestation of the supreme god's creation as a trilogy. Hu and Sia are also two of the twelve gods who sit as jurists in the judgment day weighing of the deeds/heart of Ani in the Judgment Scene found in the Papyrus of Ani.

In Hinduism, the divine vibration is Aum, the primordial sound, the sound of the sun, light, and transformation. Aum permeates the universe: earth, air, water, fire; it resides in intelligence and consciousness. Aum is the essence of the Hindu spiritual scriptures.

Some scholars have made the claim that the ancient African/Kemetic/Anu people would chant to recreate the sound of the creator god's first exhale of breath during the creation. When some people exhale, they make an "Hhhaaaaa" or "Hhhuuuuu" sound. This is the sound of Hu manifested through Atum exhaling after breathing in the first breath of life in yet another creation myth.

The sound "Hhhuuuuu" or "Hhhaaaaa" is woven into the universe, and when chanted it sounds like the harmonics of a cosmic breeze. This cosmic, universal sound, associated with primordial creation, the essence of consciousness, relaxation, and peace, has been chanted as "Hhhaaaaa," "Hhhuuuuu," or "Aum."

These chants/sounds are still used today in Hinduism as well as the followers of the Minnesota-based religion of Eckankar. The Eckankar spiritual religion is actually one of the few religions that have knowingly or unknowingly incorporated an African/Kemetic/Anu myth (like the god Hu) into their spiritual and religious practice.

Islamic Creation Myth

The creation myth of Islam can be found in the Koran, the religious book of Islam. The Islamic creation story is spread out over several suras (chapters). The Islamic creation myth is the youngest of the dominant world religions. This creation myth was written after the creation myths of Africa/Kemet/Anu, Hinduism, Buddhism, Judaism, and Christianity.

It is a reworking of African/Kemetic/Anu creation myths and some parts of the creation myths of Judaism, Christianity, Hinduism, and Buddhism; it adds unique Islamic perspectives regarding creation. Islam's creation myths are written in the Koran to make the reader think about Allah's gift of creation, the heavens, earth, and all living things on it. The writers want the reader to examine the order of the creation and the believer's place in it. The writers make the case for the positive attributes of Allah: his greatness, wonder, and majesty, and the believer's path to salvation.

Islam Creation Myth
The Koran

Sura 15:26–30

> 26. And certainly we created man of clay that gives forth sound, of black mud fashioned in shape. 27. And the jinn we created before, of intensely hot fire. 28. And when your Lord said to the angels: surely I am going to create a mortal of the essence of black mud fashioned in shape. 29. So when I made him complete and breathed into him of my spirit, fall down making obeisance [obedience] to him. 30. So the angels made obeisance to him, all of them together.

Critique: This is almost the same mythical story as the African/Kemetic/Anu creator god Khnum. Khnum created all of mankind out of clay with his hands. It should be noted that the silt from the Nile River gives us the word "Kemet" (Egypt), which means black land. He created children on his potter's wheel and breathed life into them, giving them "ka" (spirit).

This chapter presented various African/Kemetic/Anu sources that describe breath, soul, spirit, and breathing of life into nostrils.

"Jinn" means a supernatural creature that occupies a parallel world to that of mankind, and together with humans and angels makes up the three sentient (endowed with feeling and unstructured consciousness) creations of Allah. Jinns are able to assume human or animal form; they are created out of fire and can be either good or bad. They can be controlled by humans with the use of a talisman (an object marked with magic signs and believed to confer on its bearer supernatural powers of protection).

In African/Kemetic/Anu myths, the god Seth, the evil jealous brother who murdered Osiris, was good before he became evil. In myths he was depicted as a good god who fought the evil giant serpent Apep. When Seth became an evil god, he fought battles against Horus, the good son of Osiris, for the control of earth and the souls on it.

Both Seth and his cohorts had the ability to take on any form: animal, human, or god. The Eye of Horus is a symbol of royal power and protection from disease and evil gods like Seth and Apep. The Eye of Horus was one of the most popular and common amulets or trinkets worn in ancient Africa/Kemet/Anu; it was believed to ward off evil and disease.

The Islamic Jinn is very similar to the creation myths of the Ogdoad of Hermopolis/Khmunu. The four sets of male and female creator gods and goddesses of Hermopolis/Khmunu were depicted as humans with the heads of frogs (male) or serpents (female) or depicted as animals (apes). The city Hermopolis (Khmunu) in Egypt was known as "Isle of Flame"; the primordial waters of Nu (or Nun) were bubbling and churning, and in myth, the Ogdoad of Hermopolis/Khmunu create the universe and all life on earth, both good and bad.

Sura 15:31–40

> 31. But Iblis … refused to be with those who made obeisance. 32. He said: O Iblis what excuse have you that you are not with those who make obeisance? 33. He said: I am not such that I should make obeisance to a mortal whom thou hast created of the essence of black mud fashioned in shape. 34. He said: Then get out of it; for surely you are driven away. 35. And surely on you is curse until the Day of Judgment. 36. He said: My Lord! Respite me till the time when they are raised. 37. He said: So

surely you are among the respited ones. 38. Till the period of the time made known. 39. He said: My Lord because thou hast made life evil to me, I will certainly make [evil] fair-seeming to them on earth, and I will certainly cause them all to deviate. 40. Except Thy servants from among them, the devoted ones.

Critique: The myth of the battles between the god Horus, the good son of Osiris, and the god Seth, the evil brother of Osiris, over control of earth and the souls on earth are well documented. Seth, who is jealous of his brother Osiris, murders him to gain control of earth and wages a brutal war against Horus, who eventually avenges his father's murder to take back control of earth. Seth turns into a snake and is driven underground, where he hides in a hole.

There is a reworking of this story in Revelation 12:7–10, where the dragon and his cohorts wage war against Michael and his angels in heaven. When defeated, the dragon and his cohorts are cast out of heaven to earth. The serpent is called devil and Satan, because he had deceived the whole world.

The myth of Iblis is similar, as Iblis disobeyed Allah and refused to make obeisance (show deference) to Allah's created man and was driven away from heaven by Allah. This is also similar to Eve in the Garden of Eden disobeying God and eating from the Tree of Knowledge. Iblis was cast out of heaven, like Adam and Eve were cast out of the Garden of Eden, and like the devil was cast out of heaven. The myth of Iblis is also similar to the myth of Cain and Abel (Genesis 4:13–16), where Cain was cursed and marked after he slew his brother Abel and cast out into the land of Nod on the east of Eden.

Sura 15:41–46

> 41. He said: This is a right way with me. 42. Surely, as regards my servants, you have no authority over them except those who follow you of the deviators. 43. And surely Hell is the promised place of them all. 44. It has seven gates; for every gate there shall be a separate party of them. 45. Surely those who guard [against evil] shall be in the midst of the gardens and fountains. 46. Enter them in peace, secure.

Critique: "Surely those who guard [against evil] shall be in the midst of the gardens and fountains." These words in the Koran are similar to the words used in the African/Kemetic/Anu myth written in the Papyrus of Ani and found in the Doctrine of Eternal Life mentioned earlier. There is a Great Lake in the midst of the field of offerings where the great gods sit and give of the Tree of Life for other gods to live.

This myth in the Koran is also similar to the myth of the Garden of Eden. Both Christianity and Judaism are older than Islam, the world's youngest and last major religion. The Book of Genesis account of the Garden of Eden is a reworking of African/Kemetic/Anu myths evolving into a Tree of Knowledge and a Tree of Life in the midst of a garden. The men who wrote the Koran used someone guarding against evil in the midst of gardens and fountains; this is just a reworking of African/Kemetic/Anu, Judaism, and Christianity myths.

The Islamic depiction of Hell having seven gates (and for every gate there is a separate party and those who guard against evil shall be in the midst of the gardens and fountains – Enter them in peace secure) is another reworking of African/Kemetic/Anu myths. One myth mentioned earlier is where Ra travels in a boat through the twelve hours (provinces) of daylight and below the horizon in the west thru the twelve hours (provinces) of night.

Each hour is called a gate and is guarded by different gods and goddesses along the journey. These gods announce, welcome, allow entrance, assist in transport, and help protect Ra from the evil giant serpent Apep. As long as one can see the sun in the morning, then Ra wins the battle with Apep and returns from his journey safe to the eastern horizon, symbolizing resurrection or rebirth each morning. In the morning if it was overcast with clouds in the sky, blocking the sun from visibility, then Apep had won the night, and the battle starts again the next night.

From the Theban Recension of the *Book of Coming Forth by Day*, one can find two other myths dealing with the Underworld kingdom of the god Osiris in Sekhet Aaru (heaven; heavenly Underworld; abode of blessed gods). In one there are seven halls, mansions, and doors that must be passed through by the deceased before they could see Osiris. Each door had three gods: a lookout, a doorman, and a watchman. If the deceased could not answer the watchman's questions, they were not allowed to proceed.

In the other versions of this myth from the same papyrus, there are four, six, ten, or eleven secret gates of the House of Osiris in Sekhet Aaru.

The common number of secret gates is ten, with each gate actually having an address with spells and requirements of the deceased to express respect and honor to Osiris and the gods once entering.

The concepts of a heaven; heavenly Underworld; hell; Duat or Tuat (land of the dead), or Underworld, divided by gates; regions; sections; halls; doors; houses; and mansions are found in African/Kemetic/Anu myths. Through research, one can easily find sources of these African/Kemetic/Anu concepts. There are the Gates of Akert (the Underworld); Gates of Tchesert (northern gate of the Underworld); the Gates of Shu (the god of air); Gates of the Gods; Gates of the North; and so on.

Sura 32:7–9

> 7. Who made good everything that he has created, and he began the creation of man from dust. 8. Then he made his progeny of extract, of water held in light estimation. 9. Then he made him complete and breathed into him of his spirit, and made for you ears and eyes and the hearts; little is it that you give thanks.

Critique: As mentioned earlier, Islam is younger than Judaism and Christianity. These three verses in the Koran are a reworking of the creation myths of Africa/Kemet/Anu, Judaism, and Christianity. Islam, Judaism, and Christianity used the mythical story of the African/Kemetic/Anu creator god Khnum as the source of their creation of man. As mentioned earlier, Khnum, of Philae and Elephantine, Egypt, was worshipped as a water god and is associated with being the source of the Nile River.

After flooding each year, the Nile River deposits fertile black silt, which brings life to the farming communities along the river. The silt is also used to make clay, which in turn is used to make pottery. Khnum was associated with art and pottery. Khnum created all of mankind out of clay with his hands. He created children on his potter's wheel and breathed life into them, giving them "ka" (spirit). He was self-created and was the creator of all things and all things that will be.

In this sura, man is created from dust instead of black mud found in Sura 15:26; either way, we still have similarities of a man being created out of dirt, black mud, clay, or dust by a self-created supreme god. As cited earlier in this chapter, we have multiple excerpts of mythical writings like Khnum about African/Kemetic/Anu gods breathing life into a man or god giving them life, ka, soul, or spirit.

This creation of a second man in Sura 32:7–9 and the first creation of man in Sura 15:26 are different, with the second man having his progeny (offspring) created from the "extract of water held in light estimation." "Extract" means to remove, usually with some force or effort.

In Genesis 2:21–22, Eve was created by God, who put Adam into a deep sleep and removed (extracted) one of his ribs to create Eve.

Some think this "extract of water held in light estimation" refers to a light-skinned man or offspring. The African/Kemetic/Anu myth of Atum, who was depicted in myth as having the gender of both male and female and being anatomically/physiologically bisexual—masturbates in one version of his myth and ejaculates into his own mouth to impregnate himself and produce his offspring.

In the Islamic creation myth, a supreme god uses the first man's "extract of water held in light estimation" to create his offspring. "Extract of water held in light estimation" is similar to semen and sperm. It should be noted that there is no woman present during the creation of the offspring of man in Sura 32:7–9, like there was no independent or separate woman present during the creation of the offspring of the anatomically/physiologically bisexual Atum.

Sura 7:189

> 189. He it is who created you from a single being, and of the same [kind] did he make his mate, that he might incline to her; so when he covers her she bears a light burden, then moves about with it; but when it grows heavy, they both call upon Allah, their Lord: If thou givest us a good one, we shall certainly be of the grateful ones.

Critique: This sura refers to a woman giving birth as "of the same [kind] did he make his mate, that he might incline to her; … she bears a light burden, then moves about with it; but when it grows heavy…" Women, according to this sura, are created so a man can incline (sleep) with them. Religious texts are written by men who have no respect for women as equals.

What you have is a bunch of men sitting down saying to themselves, how can I control, discriminate against, and subjugate women? I know! I will incorporate control of women into some narrow-minded dogma characterized by stolen myths, false assertions, fables unproved, and unprovable myths, and call it Hinduism, Judaism, Christianity, Islam, or religion.

Then we can say, "It's the word of God," "It's the way God planned it," or in the case of Buddhism, "The situation you find yourself in is only because of misdeeds in a previous life."

Then men can use religion to sanction, practice, and require obedience to this dogmatic discrimination and disrespect toward women. Religion sanctions discrimination against women and the LGBT community; the Bibles of Christianity and Judaism, and the Koran of Islam, were used as the blueprint and instructional manual for the institution of slavery, not only in America but Europe and all over the world.

Some of the fiercest opponents of the LGBT community and the most anti-gay marriage advocates, writers, and speakers are religious leaders representing some narrow, simple-minded belief. In the next chapter, I will cover religion's role in world slavery, which is exactly the same as religion's role in opposition to gay marriage across America.

Sura 71:13–17

> 13. What is the matter with you that you fear not the greatness of Allah? 14. And indeed he has created you through various grades. 15. Do you not see how Allah has created the seven heavens one above the other? 16. And made the moon therein a light, and made the sun a lamp. 17. And Allah has made you grow out of the earth as a growth.

Critique: We have already covered the many passages found in the texts of the African/Kemetic/Anu *Book of Coming Forth by Day*. One finds the same myths of a god creating the heavens, moon, and sun, with humans created when Atum's tears hit the ground, or Khnum creating humans out of clay made from the silt of the Nile River at his potter's wheel. The "various grades" in this sura one could believe refer to the biological evolution of humans on earth.

Sura 21:30–33

> 30. Do not those who disbelieve see that the heavens and the earth were closed up, we have opened them; and we

have made of water everything living, will they not then believe? 31. And we have made great mountains in the earth lest it might be convulsed with them, and we have made in it wide ways that they may follow a right direction. 32. And we have made the heaven a guarded canopy and [yet] they turn aside from its signs. 33. And he it is who created the night and the day and the sun and the moon; all [orbs] travel along swiftly in their celestial spheres.

Critique: Here again we see familiar characterizations of a creator god's act of creation, almost identical to African/Kemetic/Anu creation myths. One can also see similarities to the creation myths of Hinduism, Buddhism, Judaism, and Christianity, which reworked the African/Kemetic/Anu creation myths. The myth of water being at the center of creation; the creation of night and day; the creation of the celestial order; and the creation of the sun, moon, and universe were covered earlier in the chapter.

The part of this sura that says "And we have made the heaven a guarded canopy and [yet] they turn aside from its signs" is almost identical to the myth of Nut, the African/Kemetic/Anu goddess of the sky in the Heliopolis Ennead myth. As mentioned earlier, Nut is depicted in artwork on papyri as an elongated woman covered with stars. She is stretched out with her arms and hands touching the ground on one end and her feet touching the ground on the other end in an arch position.

Nut provides a guarded celestial canopy for the creator sun god Ra. In a similar depiction of artwork Nut is arching over the mythical god of the earth Geb, again providing a guarded celestial canopy.

Sura 24:40–45

40. Or like utter darkness in the deep sea: there covers it a wave above which is another wave, about is a cloud, [layers of] utter darkness one above another; when he holds out his hand, he is almost unable to see it; and to whomsoever Allah does not give light, he has no light. 41. Do you not see Allah is he whom does glorify all those who are in the heavens and the earth, and the [very] birds with expanded wings? He knows the prayer of each one and its glorification, and Allah is cognizant of what they do. 42. And Allah's is the kingdom of the heavens and the

earth, and to Allah is the eventual coming. 43. Do you not see that Allah drives along the clouds, then gathers them together, then piles them up, so that you see the rain coming forth from the midst? And he sends down of the clouds that are [like] mountains where in is hail, afflicting there with whom he pleases and turning it away from whom he pleases; the flash of his lightning almost takes away the sight. 44. Allah turns over the night and the day; most surely there is a lesson in this for those who have sight. 45. And Allah has created from water every living creature: so of them is that which walks upon its belly and of them is that which walks upon two feet and of them is that which walks upon four; Allah creates what he pleases; surely Allah has power over all things.

Critique: African/Kemetic/Anu creation myths and culture have been reworked into the creation myth of Islam, just like the other major world religions. One can find the same words, epithets, and stories used. This signals that we are not talking about the word of some god but instead are reading a book written by men using a common mythical source. Because Islam is the youngest of the world's major religions, the men who wrote the Koran not only used African/Kemetic/Anu myths and culture in their creation myth, they also used some of the unique ethnic creation myths of Hinduism, Buddhism, Judaism, and Christianity.

As with the other major world religions, we find the same common similarities: a supreme, all-encompassing creator god; the use of a plural pronoun "we" when man, the universe, and earth are created (Sura 15:26-27 and 21:30–33); the presence of angels during creation; a god who creates days and nights; a supreme god who creates the sun, moon, stars, heaven, earth, and animals; during the creation there is the presence of darkness, deep sea, water, waves, and light.

There are common similarities found in all man-made creation myths, whether the myth is African/Kemetic/Anu, one of the dominant world religions, or the many world aboriginal religions. The world's diverse aboriginal creation myths have many of the same similarities found in African/Kemetic/Anu creation myths.

Whether one is reading about the creation myths of the Zulu of South Africa; Boshongo (Bantu) of Central Africa; Ekoi and Efik of Southeastern Nigeria; and Fans (Bantu) of Central Africa, Southern Africa, and West

Africa, the myths are similar and some scholars make the case that these oral myths were reworked by the men of Kemet/Anu into their creation myths.

We find the same similarities in the creation myths of the aboriginal people of Australia and New Zealand; Ainu (the aboriginal people of Southern Russia and North Central Japan); Apache of the Southwestern United States; Seminole of Florida and Oklahoma; Choctaw of the Southeast United States; Comanche of Eastern New Mexico and Southern Colorado; Navajo of the Southwest United States; Chelan in Eastern Washington State; or the Iroquois of Southern Canada and North Central United States.

In South America and the Caribbean, we have the same creation myth similarities found among the Inca of Peru; Aztec of Central Mexico; Maya of Southern Mexico and Central America; and the Rastafarians of Jamaica and the Caribbean.

Because the world's aboriginal creation myths and religious practices are passed down from generation to generation by oral tradition, their accuracy can be questioned. Many myths have been lost or negatively influenced when their cultures were invaded, colonized, and exploited by people with an ethnic and monetary agenda, starting in the 1400s until the present day. Most of the interpretations and writings have been done by anthropologists and scholars who were a part of the colonization of aboriginal lands and had unfettered access to; and control over what information the aboriginal people were telling them. Despite this handicap, one can still be certain of similarities among all aboriginal creation myths, which are similar to African/Kemetic/Anu creation myths.

Most aboriginal creation myths begin with the presence of darkness, chaos, shapelessness, or void. We find the presence of some type of flowing water, floods, moisture, lake, ocean, sea, or primordial water. Rising out of the water, we find some type of land, pyramid-shaped mound, great mound, or dirt. Sitting on the new earth, we find a bird placing (or laying) a creation egg or the egg appearing to rise out of the primordial water to sit on land.

The egg either bursts from the wind or is dropped (or cracked) by the bird; this action releases the sun or light and brings life. A god or goddess either rises out of the primordial water or is self-created from nothing and appears standing on land, the first created bringing forth light or the sun. We find the presence of fire, wind, and air, with some type of reference to breath of life, blowing of air, or breathing life into a human or animal.

Almost all aboriginal creation myths have some type of supreme creator god or goddess who is either self-created or created by hidden creator gods. The gods or goddesses are female, male, combination male-female, androgynous, asexual, a creator sun god or sun goddess, a creator moon god or moon goddess. These goddesses or gods create man, woman, the universe, heaven, the stars, the planets, the moon, and the earth. The newly created man or woman names the animals and is given dominion over them. Some type of disobedience or conflict occurs, and the supreme creator god administers some form of discipline to the offending human, god, or goddess. We can find aboriginal myths of a god hiding in a cave or underground to avoid discipline by the supreme creator god.

We can find the presence of sacred trees, gardens, flowers, mountains, lakes, and fountains. Sacred creation animals include frogs, birds (falcons, eagles, hawks, ibises); alligators, crocodiles, hippopotamus, lizards, other reptiles, and lots and lots of snakes. We can find the aboriginal belief in animism (all nature objects and the universe have souls) or ancestral/folk creation spirits who inhabit caves, volcanoes, mountains, lakes, streams, the wind, and animals.

Some aboriginal creation myths refer to repeated cycles of creation or various levels of celestial/universal and human creation. The constant ongoing battle of good versus evil over the control of life on earth and the heavens after creation is found in some aboriginal creation myths. Required sacred offerings and sacrifices to the creation gods are found within certain aboriginal creation myths. The concept of cosmic sound and vibrations playing a role in creation is also found within certain aboriginal creation myths.

Despite being one of the dominant world cultures, China has no one dominant creation myth. There are many versions of Chinese aboriginal creation myths, depending on which Chinese ethnic group, school, or sect you are talking about. Two of the better known creation myths from China are the creation myths of Pan-Ku and Pan-Ku/Yin and Yang.

Pan-Ku

In the beginning there was no heaven or earth, all was one, in a state of chaos. The universe was like a big black egg inside of which Pan-Ku slept. When Pan-Ku awoke he felt suffocated and used an ax to break open the egg. The light clear part of the egg floated up to form the heavens; the yolk sunk down to form the earth. Pan-Ku stood in between the heaven and earth with his head touching and holding up the heavens and his feet touching and holding down the earth. With the heavens and earth starting to separate, Pan-Ku used tools like a hammer and chisel to help facilitate the further separation of the heavens from the earth.

As the heavens and earth began to grow and separate at the rate of ten feet per day, Pan-Ku grew as well, becoming a giant man nine million li in height (li is the traditional Chinese unit of length). After 18,000 years the heavens and earth were far enough apart that they would never converge again and the giant Pan-Ku could rest. With Pan-Ku finally able to rest, he falls asleep and dies. With his last breath he created the wind and clouds.

His eyes become the sun and moon; his hair and beard become the stars in the sky; his voice becomes thunder and lightning; his limbs and torso become the five major mountains; his sweat becomes the rain; his flesh becomes the soil; his blood and sperm become the lakes, rivers, seas, and oceans; his bones become rocks; his muscles become fertile land; his marrow turns into jade and pearls; and the parasites from his decaying body become humans.

Pan-Ku/Yin and Yang

The universe was contained inside a giant egg of chaos all commingled together. Pan-Ku inside the egg grew too large and cracked the egg. He emerged from the giant egg and began to separate yin from yang [opposites]. He separated light from darkness, male from female, hot from cold, fire from water, heaven from earth, etc.

Tired from the exhaustion of creation, Pan-Ku dies and from his eyes the moon and sun are created; from his limbs and torso the five mountains are created; from his sweat the rain and dew are created; from his voice thunder and lighting are created; from his body all the features of the earth are created; and humans are created from pure vapor. This Chinese creation myth of Yin and Yang is a creation philosophy that sees the earth as a continual evolving living creation with dependent opposites that must always be in balance.

If one creation force is out of balance, then yin and yang are out of balance. The earth must be respected, cared for, and kept in order for the creative forces of yin and yang to stay in balance.

Chapter 3

Religion, Slavery, and Same-Sex Marriage

Many religious leaders and members today are opposed to same-sex marriage, in the same way religious institutions and individuals were in favor of the immoral institution of slavery. Religion was used to not only justify and sanction slavery, but one can find instructions within the Bible of Christianity, the Torah of Judaism, and the Koran of Islam, which provide an operational manual, a do's and do not's blueprint on how to enslave humans. Some of the most ardent supporters of slavery in America were Christian religious institutions and their members. There were a few exceptions like the Mennonites, Amish, Quakers, and dissenting members of the various religious denominations who supported slavery. Many dissenting members of the various religious denominations that supported slavery faced persecution because of their dissent.

Many of the founders of America left England for religious freedom and the right to live as they pleased (as long as one is not breaking the law or hurting anyone). Some of the founding fathers were opposed to slavery, but unfortunately not enough to prevent slavery from becoming an institutionalized part of early American history.

Today in America, we see religious institutions projecting their beliefs of what is right or wrong when it comes to same-sex marriage. Many political, civic, and social leaders are against same-sex marriage. With few exceptions, their views are based on discriminatory and judgmental anti-LGBT religious scriptures that are nothing more than man-made myths and fables. Many religious denominations did not change their official positions supporting slavery until after the Civil War was fought, congressional legislation was passed, or public opinion became so overwhelmingly against their position that they had to change. However, religious scriptures that sanction and support slavery are still extant today.

Anti-LGBT religious scriptures like Leviticus 18:22 and 20:13 will not be revised and religious institutions will always officially be opposed to same-sex marraige, even if the Supreme Court makes the correct judicial decision and supports same-sex marriage, congressional legislation is passed legalizing same-sex marriage, or public opinion becomes overwhelming in favor of same-sex marriage. The religious community will have to be forced to accept the fact that despite its man-made scriptures, two consenting adults have the civil and human right to marry.

The practice of slavery had its origins in African/Kemetic/Anu culture, and this too has been reworked and incorporated into several of the worlds dominant religions. Scholars debate how slavery was defined in Africa/Kemet/Anu, but there is no question that it existed.

A person could become a slave in African/Kemetic/Anu culture under several circumstances: owing a debt, punishment of a crime, becoming a prisoner of war, negotiated servitude, and becoming an indentured servant to escape poverty.

We can be sure that the many circumstances under which a person could become a slave could easily be manipulated, and some people were probably enslaved against their will. Slaves were restricted to the rich, either the pharaoh and royal family or nobles. Slaves worked in households, fields, temples, and the dreaded mines, digging for gold and copper.

There is no evidence that slaves in African/Kemetic/Anu culture were ever sold at slave auctions; however, I tend to think that, at some point in time, there had to be some type of financial transactions involving slaves. Prisoners of war and criminals were enslaved for life—exceptions were made for indentured servants, negotiated servitude, and someone working off a debt; these individuals maintained some civil rights and could eventually become free again after fulfilling their work or negotiated agreement.

Slaves who worked in households and temples had a much easier existence than slaves who worked in the mines or fields. However, slaves who worked for nobles and the pharaoh were often executed and placed in their masters' graves to accompany the body into the afterlife. Women were often taken as concubines (mistresses) and wives, and sometimes their children grew up to become nobles or pharaohs.

Thutmose III, son of a concubine, became one of the greatest military geniuses in history, expanding the borders of his kingdom from Syria to the southern part of the Sudan. Many scholars believe that the mother of Pharaoh Siptah, who ascended to the throne as a child, was a Canaanite (present-day Israel, Lebanon, West Bank, and Gaza Strip) who was a concubine of the pharaoh.

What do the Christian Bible, the Tanakh of Judaism (which includes the Hebrew Torah), the Koran of Islam, Hinduism, and Buddhism say about slavery?

The Bible and Hebrew Torah

Leviticus 25:44–46

> 44. Both thy bondmen, and thy bondmaids, which thou shalt have, shall be of the heathen that are round about you; of them shall ye buy bondmen and bondmaids. 45. Moreover of the children of the strangers that do sojourn among you, of them shall ye buy, and of their families that are with you, which they begat in your land: and they shall be your possession. 46. And ye shall take them as an inheritance for your children after you, to inherit them for a possession; they shall be your bondmen for ever: but over your brethren the children of Israel, ye shall not rule one over another with rigour.

Exodus 21:2–11

> 2. If thou buy a Hebrew servant, six years he shall serve: and in the seventh he shall go out free for nothing. 3. If he came in by himself, he shall go out by himself: if he were married, then his wife shall go out with him. 4. If his master have given him a wife, and she have born him sons or daughters; the wife and her children shall be her master's, and he shall go out by himself. 5. And if the servant shall plainly say, I love my master, my wife, and my children; I will not go out free: 6. Then his master shall bring him unto the judges; he shall also bring him to the door, or unto the door post; and his master shall bore his ear through with an aul; and he shall serve him for ever. 7. And if a man sell his daughter to be a maidservant, she shall not go out as the menservants do. 8. If she please not her master, who hath betrothed her to himself, then shall

he let her be redeemed: to sell her unto a strange nation he shall have no power, seeing he hath dealt deceitfully with her. 9. And if he had betrothed her unto his son, he shall deal with her after the manner of daughters. 10. If he take him another wife; her food, her raiment, and her duty of marriage, shall he not diminish. 11. And if he do not these three unto her, then shall she go out free without money.

Exodus 21:20–21

20. And if a man smite his servant, or his maid, with a rod, and he die under his hand; he shall be surely punished. 21. Notwithstanding, if he continue a day or two, he shall not be punished: for he is his money.

What Does the New Testament in the Christian Bible Say about Slavery?

Ephesians 6:5–9

5. Servants, be obedient to them that are your masters according to the flesh, with fear and trembling, in singleness of your heart, as unto Christ; 6. Not with eyeservice, as menpleasers; but as the servants of Christ, doing the will of God from the heart; 7. With good will doing service, as to the Lord, and not to men: 8. Knowing that whatsoever good thing any man doeth, the same shall he receive of the Lord, whether he be bond or free. 9. And, ye masters, do the same things unto them, forbearing threatening: knowing that your Master also is in heaven; neither is there respect of persons with him. (Note: "forbearing" means showing patience, self-control, restraint under adversity.)

1 Timothy 6:1–2

1. Let as many servants as are under the yoke count their own masters worthy of all honour, that the name of God and his doctrine be not blasphemed. 2. And they that have

believing masters, let them not despise them, because they are brethren; but rather do them service, because they are faithful and beloved, partakers of the benefit. These things teach and exhort.

This next passage from the Book of Luke is Jesus the Son of God himself delivering a parable to his disciples. ("Parable" means a short moral story; any of the stories told by Jesus to relay his religious message.) Jesus is talking about the expectations, requirements, and consequences of a man that the lord has blessed and made ruler over his household. The parable is found in Luke 12:41–48. Let's see how Jesus of Christianity speaks out against slavery and in defense of slaves, called menservants and maidens.

Luke 12:41–48

> 41. Then Peter said unto him, Lord, speakest thou this parable unto us, or even to all? 42. And the Lord said, Who then is that faithful and wise steward, whom his lord shall make ruler over his household, to give them their portion of meat in due season? 43. Blessed is that servant, whom his lord when he cometh shall find so doing. 44. Of truth I say unto you, that he will make him ruler over all that he hath. 45. But and if that servant say in his heart, My lord delayeth his coming; and shall begin to beat the menservants and maidens, and to eat and drink, and to be drunken; 46. The lord of that servant will come in a day when he looketh not for him, and at an hour when he is not aware, and will cut him in sunder, and will appoint him his portion with the unbelievers. 47. And that servant, which knew his lord's will, and prepared not himself, neither did according to his will, shall be beaten with many stripes. 48. But he that knew not, and did commit things worthy of stripes, shall be beaten with few stripes. For unto whomsoever much is given, of him shall be much required: and to whom men have committed much, of him they will ask the more.

Critique: So, according to Jesus of Christianity, the "Son of God," the lord will reward a faithful and patient servant of the Lord, one who is a slave owner, with blessings and make him ruler over his household. According to Jesus, the reward for this type of person is "unto whomsoever much is given." If the ruler of his household loses patience, however, gets drunk and beats his slaves called menservants and maidens, but "knew not," they will only get beaten with a few stripes.

If you knew the Lord's will and "prepared not," then got drunk and beat your slaves, you will get beaten with many stripes. This is because so much is given unto you (like slaves) and much is required of you. If you are a slave getting beaten to within an inch of your life or, even worse, a maiden getting beaten to within an inch of your life by a drunken slave master, I guess you could think to yourself that Jesus has great compassion for you and really thinks slavery is wrong and you shouldn't be a slave.

The men who wrote and attributed this parable to the mythical Jesus show disregard for the immoral social condition of slaves. Slavery is treated in this parable with a dismissive, marked lack of interest. Nowhere in the Christian Bible does Jesus the "Son of God" say that slavery is aberrant, deviant, and immoral. Nowhere in the Christian Bible does Jesus say that there is no place in Heaven for a slave owner or someone who engages in slavery. I wonder if there are slaves (or, as Jesus calls them, menservants and maidens) in heaven with God. Heaven must be a much better place to go than Hell if you're a slave.

Remember this parable. To those who demonize the LGBT community, how aberrant, deviant, and immoral is this "Slave Parable of Jesus"?

> Colossians 3:22: Servants, obey in all things your masters according to the flesh; not with eyeservice, as menpleasers; but in singleness of heart, fearing God;
>
> Colossians 4:1: Masters, give unto your servants that which is just and equal; knowing that ye also have a Master in heaven.
>
> 1 Peter 2:18: Servants, be subject to your masters with all fear; not only to the good and gentle, but also to the froward.
>
> Titus 2:9–10: 9. Exhort servants to be obedient unto their own masters, and to please them well in all things; not answering again; 10. Not purloining, but schewing all good fidelity; that they may adorn the doctrine of God our Saviour in all things.

What Does the Koran of Islam Say about Slavery?

Sura 33:50

O prophet surely we have made lawful to you your wives whom you have given their dowries, and those whom your right hand possesses out of those Allah has given to you as prisoners of war....

Sura 23:6

Except before their mates or those whom their right hand possess, for they surely are not blameable.

Sura 24:32

And marry those among you who are single and those who are fit among your male slaves and your female slaves; if they are needy, Allah will make them free from want out of his grace; and Allah is ample-giving, knowing.

Sura 4:24–25

24. And all married women except those whom your right hand possess this is Allah's ordinance to you; and lawful for you are all women besides those, provided that you seek them with your property taking them in marriage not committing fornication.... 25. And whoever among you has not within his power ampleness of means to marry free believing women, then he may marry of those whom your right hands possess from among your believing maidens and Allah knows best your faith; you are [sprung] the one from the other; so marry them with the permission of their masters and give them their dowries justly....

Sura 4:92

And it does not behove a believer to kill a believer except by mistake, and whoever kills a believer by mistake, he should free a believing slave….

Sura 24:58

O you who believe let those whom your right hand possess and those of you who have not attained to puberty ask permission of you three times; before the morning prayer….

Sura 24:31

And say to the believing woman that they cast down their looks and guard their private parts and do not display their ornaments except what appears thereof, and let them wear head-coverings over their bosoms, and not display their ornaments except to their husbands or their fathers.… or their brothers, or their brother's sons or their sister's sons, or their women, or those whom their right hand possess, or the male servants not having need [of women]….

Sura 33:55

There is no blame on them in respect of their fathers nor their brothers, nor their brother's sons, nor their sister's sons, nor their own women, nor of what their right hand possess; and be careful of your duty to Allah; surely Allah is a witness of all things.

Note: In the above excerpts from the Koran, Islam's use of the phrases "your right hand" and "their right hand" can be found in varying forms within the older Bible of Christianity and Torah/Tanakh of Judaism. The phrases: "He is at my right hand"; "thou that savest by thy right hand"; "thy right hand hath holden me up"; "the saving strength of his right hand"; "thy right hand upholdeth me"; "Sit thou at my right hand, until I make thine enemies thy footstool"; and "thy right hand, O Lord, hath dashed in pieces the enemy" can be found in the books of: Psalms 16:8, 17:7, 18:35-36, 20:6-7, 63:8-9, 110:1, and Exodus 15:6 respectively.

The Caste System of Hinduism

The caste system of Hinduism can be described as a rigid form of interethnic discrimination, stratification, and social boundaries. The caste system, still practiced in some parts of India today, was created and sanctioned by Hinduism. The Hindu caste system uses religious myths and dogma to divide humans into fixed interethnic strata; it divides humans based on their name, skin color, and where they were born. People have died, been born, and married within the rigid social boundaries of the Hindu caste system.

Depending on what part of India one is talking about, the origin, number of levels, and names of the caste system levels varies. One well-known Hindu creation myth, "Hymn to Purusha" (see chapter 2), tells the story of Purusha, a manifestation of the supreme Hindu god Brahman, who creates the four castes of Hinduism (the fifth, the lowest caste level, was added later by Hindu culture).

The Brahmins were created from his mouth, symbolizing teachers and priests; Rajanya (some refer to this caste system level as Kshatriyas) from his arms, symbolizing warriors and rulers; Vaisyas from his lap, symbolizing agriculturists, skilled traders, merchants, and minor officials; and Sudras from his feet, symbolizing unskilled workers. A fifth class, called Pariah (Harijans), was added later, symbolizing outcasts; they were called "Untouchables." Gandhi called this caste "Children of God" because of the discrimination and persecution they endured.

The Pariah were (and are) the lowest of the lowest in the Hindu caste system. Forced to carry out polluting and menial work relating to dirt and decay, they were associated with sanitation workers, latrine cleaners, handlers of the dead bodies of humans and animals, the ones to clean up the feces of animals, leather workers, butchers, launderers, and so on.

They lived in extreme poverty and despair, working for very little (or no) pay and living in minimal housing, with poor food, clothing, and shelter. Their lives were very similar to slaves working on a plantation. If a person from one of the other higher castes happened to come into contact with one of the Untouchables, it was considered an abomination and the person had to scrub and clean himself thoroughly so as to not be contaminated by the lowest of the lowest. To even walk in the footsteps of an Untouchable was undesirable, and the lowest of the lowest was not even allowed to spit upon the ground because this would pollute the earth.

"Bride Burning" is the by-product of the brutal interethnic caste system of Hinduism, coupled with a sexist cultural dowry system that places a materialistic value on the lives of women. This results in some men having no respect for women as equals. The psychotic, brutal, and violent practice of bride burning is so unbelievable that a whole book could be written on this human rights violation. The fact that a husband would set his bride on fire or burn her to death if he thought he did not receive the proper dowry from her family is beyond the bounds of reality. This is what happens when you have a caste system that has degenerated into male supremacy grounded in rigid religious myths.

Two other unbelievable human rights violations "Acid Throwing" and "Dowry Death" are also the by-product of a Hindu caste system that has degenerated into male supremacy, grounded in rigid religious beliefs. Dowry Death and Acid Throwing occur when a husband or in-laws, harass torture, disfigure, and blind a married woman in an attempt to extort a greater dowry from her family. If no dowry is forthcoming, the husband or in-laws harass the young wife into committing suicide, kill her themselves, or the husband throws acid in her face in retaliation for not receiving the appropriate materialistic dowry compensation.

The Hindu caste system uses myths to arrange people into divisions and justify elevating one human over another, thereby forcing people to accept an inferior position in life. The myth of the Hindu scriptures asserts that the caste system was formed and created by the supreme god Brahman, manifested through the god Purusha, and is the natural order of things needed for society to function orderly.

Buddhism and Slavery

Buddhism partially arose in India as an alternative to Hinduism's discriminatory caste system. Some scholars say Buddha, the spiritual leader of Buddhism, did not try to do away with the caste system and the slave-like conditions of the Untouchables. They say Buddha was more concerned with finding the meaning of life and reaching Nirvana.

Buddhism teaches that we are doomed to repeat the endless cycle of birth, death, and rebirth until we attain spiritual enlightenment and reach Nirvana; the suffering we find on earth, like slavery, is the result of not reaching Nirvana in a previous life. The focus of our life must be on reaching spiritual enlightenment, which will end our suffering; this enlightenment enables us to become one with nature and reach Nirvana.

There are many sects and schools of Buddhism. This diversity means that one can probably find slaves described as servants within some sects. However, unlike Judaism, Christianity, Hinduism, and Islam, there are no official writings where Buddha advocates the practice of slavery or sanctions the caste system.

The religious texts of Buddhism clearly reject slavery in several cases, stating one should not deal in the business of trading human beings and one should abstain from accepting male and female slaves. Buddhism teaches compassion and equality. It does not advocate for human rights; instead, it focuses on the individual need for self-spiritual enlightenment.

The LGBT community should remember that religions used man-made myths in defense of slavery, just like they use those myths against the LGBT community and the same-sex marriage initiative today. Religion has no moral authority or credibility when it comes to social issues. Any religion whose current scriptures support and promote slavery including children has lost all credibility. Religion is based on fables and myths; it is only the word of men; and within its ranks are some of the most violent, sexist, anti-family sexual predators that the world has ever known.

Religion would be better served to learn the African/Kemetic/Anu phrase (usually attributed to the Greeks): "know thyself," meaning that you cannot begin to address any cultural problem until you have, morally, mentally and physically, healed yourself first. For religion, that should be an everlasting, eternal, boundless, and infinite task.

Some Quotes on Slavery and Religion

"In all the ages the Roman Church has owned slaves, bought and sold slaves, authorized and encouraged her children to trade in them. There were the texts; there was no mistaking their meaning; she was doing in all this thing what the Bible had mapped out for her to do. So unassailable was her position that in all the centuries she had no word to say against human slavery."—Mark Twain

"Let the gentleman go to Revelation to learn the decree of God, let him go to the Bible. I said that slavery was sanctioned in the Bible, authorized, regulated, and recognized from Genesis to Revelation. Slavery existed then in the earliest ages and among the chosen people of God; and in Revelation we are told that it shall exist till the end of time shall come. You find it in the Old and New Testaments, in the prophecies, psalms, and the epistles of Paul; you find it recognized and sanctioned everywhere."—Jefferson Davis, president of the Confederate States of America

"The delegates of the annual conference are decidedly opposed to modern abolitionism and wholly disclaim any right, wish, or intention to interfere in the civil and political relation between master and slave as it exists in the slave-holding states of the union."—Methodist Episcopal Church, 1836 General Conference, Cincinnati, Ohio

"It [slavery] has exercised absolute mastery over the American Church. With the Bible in their hands, her priesthood have attempted to prove that slavery came down from God out of heaven. They have become slaveholders and dealers in human flesh."—William Lloyd Garrison, Abolitionist leader

"There was no place in the land where the seeker could not find some small budding sign of pity for the slave. No place in all the land except one, the pulpit. It yielded at last; it always does. It fought a strong and stubborn fight and then did what it always does, joined the procession at the tail end. Slavery fell. The slavery text in the Bible remained; the practice changed; that was all."—Mark Twain

"I assert, most unhesitatingly, that the religion of the South is mere covering for the most horrid crimes, a justifier of the most appalling barbarity, a sanctifier of the most hateful frauds, and a dark shelter under which the darkest, foulest, grossest, and most infernal deeds of slaveholders find the strongest protection. Were I to be again reduced to the chains of slavery, next to that enslavement, I should regard being the slave of a religious master the greatest calamity that could befall me. I hate the corrupt slaveholding, woman-whipping, crude-plundering, partial, and hypocritical Christianity of this land."—Frederick Douglass

In summary, slavery is sanctioned in the scriptures of Christian, Judaism, and Islamic religions. A brutal caste system similar to slavery is found in the myths of the scriptures of Hinduism. Slavery was being practiced in African/Kemetic/Anu culture thousands of years ago and had an influence on the different man-made religious texts when they were written by men.

There is no excuse for slavery in any form, no matter what terms you use: bondmen; bondmaid; serfdom; serf; manservant; maidservant; debt slavery; forced labor; servitude; menials; servant; workman; slave; indentured servant; concubine; mistress; maiden; Untouchables; right hand possess; caste system; negotiated servitude; foreign war captive; lowest of the lows; inferior person; or Pariah.

Religion has been used to justify slavery, sexism, and the denial of same-sex marriage rights. It has been used to discriminate against the LGBT community. Only a self-righteous person with a need to control the lives of others could use religious myths to induce individuals to discriminate and pass judgment against others, such as the LGBT community. These cognitively and intellectually challenged individuals carry out, without thinking, rigid religious dogma that are based on man-made myths.

Some of the most outspoken opponents of the LGBT community claim that they are upholding "family values"; these individuals are engaged in fake moral superiority and are often afflicted with guilt about their own transgressions. They are hypocrites in conflict with their own sexual lifestyle. A number of ardent critics of the LGBT community turn out to be LGBT or engage in heterosexual affairs.

Chapter 4

*Birth-Myth of Divine Saviors, Sons of God,
Prophets, or Enlightened Ones*

African/Kemetic/Anu culture and religious myths, which include Heru (Horus), Isis, and Osiris have been reworked and retold by men from many religious groups of the world. Almost all religions have some type of divine savior or son of god who is born into the world to bring a message (peace, love, compassion, enlightenment, and salvation) or to combat some evil force or resistance on earth in a battle of good versus evil. Scholars have listed over thirty religious figures with similar myths from different parts of the world.

The similarities to African/Kemetic/Anu myths that are referenced in this chapter are found in the savior myth concepts of Christianity (Son of God); Hinduism (divine savior); Judaism (attributes of a prophesized savior); Islam (prophet/messenger of Allah/God); and Buddhism (enlightened one).

The African/Kemetic/Anu sources are taken from the pyramid texts, coffin texts, *Book of Coming Forth by Day*, funerary texts, temples, papyri, and stele inscriptions.

The Annunciation, Conception, Birth, and Adoration of the Child

The nativity scene of Amenhotep III in the temple of Amun (Amen) at Luxor, Egypt, is referred to as the Annunciation, Conception, Birth, and Adoration of the Child; it is a four-part vignette depicting the mythical birth of a divine son. In the first scene of the nativity vignette, the mythical god Tehuti (Thoth), the heart, mind, and tongue of the creator, announces to the royal mother the impending birth of her son, descended from the creator god Amun.

In the second scene, the creator god Khnum (or the god Kneph) are standing to one side of the royal mother; both personify breath as spirit and are depicted as a man with the head of a ram (symbolizing fertility). Khnum (or Kneph) holds with one hand the royal mother's hand, and with the other hand he holds an ankh, the symbol of life, up to the royal mother's mouth, indicating that she is conceiving. On the other side of the royal mother is Isis, the original "Madonna" (or Hathor, who personifies love, motherhood, and joy), also holding the ankh of life, up to the mouth of the royal mother while holding her hand.

In the third scene, the divine child is born with two gods (or goddesses) holding her hands, one on each side, while other gods and goddesses observe and assist with the birth.

In the fourth scene, the gods and goddesses gather around the newborn infant to praise and adore him while holding the ankh of life up, symbolizing giving the newborn breath, life, spirit, and soul.

The Birth-Myth and Concealment of the Infant Child Heru (Horus)

Heru along with his mother Isis formed the original "Madonna and Divine Son" described earlier. Heru was born during chaotic and turbulent times. The earth was being ruled by the evil Seth. Heru was born to Isis after she and her sister Nephthys retrieved the scattered body parts of Isis's husband Osiris.

Osiris had been murdered by his jealous brother Seth, who took over as ruler of earth. The two goddesses found all of Osiris's body parts except his phallus (penis). According to several interpretations, Isis used magic to draw the essence of Osiris; fashioned a phallus of gold to replace Osiris's phallus; or used divine fire to become impregnated.

Once Isis knew she was pregnant, she fled to the Nile Delta marshlands to hide from Seth, who wanted to kill her son. In the marshlands, Isis gave birth to Heru.

Heru (Horus) was hailed as the coming avenger of his father's murder, who would retake the throne and restore peace, love, and tranquility to earth. Heru waged a long, brutal, and bloody war against his evil uncle Seth in a good-versus-evil battle for control of earth and the souls of the gods and humans who inhabited earth.

Eventually, Heru won and negotiated a settlement through Tehuti establishing himself as ruler of earth and avenging the murder of his father, thus restoring peace, love, and tranquility to earth with the ever-present danger of evil trying to overcome good and righteousness.

The Papyrus of Ani
Hymn to Osiris

Note: remember Isis and Osiris from the Heliopolis Ennead creation myth are brother and sister as well as husband and wife.

> She sought him untiringly, she wandered round and round about this earth in sorrow, and she alighted not without finding him. She made light [or air] with her feathers, she created air with her wings, and she uttered the death wail for her brother. She raised up the inactive members of him whose heart was still, she drew from him his essence, she made an heir, she reared the child in loneliness, and the place where he was not known, and he grew in strength and stature, and his hand was mighty in the House of Keb [Geb]. The Company of Gods rejoiced, rejoiced at the coming of Horus [Heru], the son of Osiris, whose heart was firm, the triumphant, the son of Isis, the heir of Osiris.

The following myth can be found in the Papyrus de Turin's Legend of Ra and Isis and the Papyrus of Ani's Chapter of the Divine God.

(Note: In this myth, Ra refers to himself as a prince and son of a god. The bulk of the myth is unrelated to divine saviors, sons of god, prophets, or enlightened ones but tells a myth of one of the dominant females in African/Kemetic/Anu culture and religion, the mother of Heru and the wife of Osiris, whose birth-myth will be examined next.)

In the following summary of an African/Kemetic/Anu myth, we find a female goddess on an equal level with her male counterpart and not in a submissive or subservient role. There is sexism in the religious and cultural myths of Africa/Kemet/Anu, but one can find more equality of men and women than one finds in the world's dominant religions. This myth could have very well have been written by a female and shows the cunning, intellect, and desire for power found in some myths concerning females in African/Kemetic/Anu culture.

This myth is about the "Legend of Ra and Isis." In this myth the name of the Holy God is hidden to all and only known by the Holy God himself. The Holy God has grown old, and his health is declining to the point where he can no longer control his bodily functions. The Holy God dribbles at the mouth and cannot control his emissions, which fall to the ground.

The goddess Isis in this myth has taken the form of a woman who had acquired the knowledge of words of power. She is living with the Holy God in heaven because she has become disgusted with the men of earth and decided to live among the gods and goddesses again. Even still she wonders what it would be like to live in heaven and earth as a mighty goddess; and mistress of the earth by means of the knowledge of the name of the Holy God.

The only way Isis can become a supreme or mighty goddess is to find out the hidden name of the Holy God, and the only one who knows it is the Holy God himself. So Isis decides to create a deadly scenario that would force the Holy God to reveal to her his name. She makes a deadly serpent out of dirt and the Holy God's spit and emesis and creates a sacred serpent with sharp, deadly fangs.

Isis, then, knowing where the Holy God walks every day, places the deadly snake in the pathway so there is no way it can be avoided. The Holy God goes on his daily walk, is bitten by the serpent, and becomes sick; he does not know what has happened to him.

He calls out to the other gods for help because he does not know what has stung or bitten him. "Can it be water?" he asks; "Can it be fire?" He is in intense pain, both cold and shivering as well as hot and burning from the snake bite; he is also losing his eyesight. The other gods and goddesses who are the children of the Holy God, like Isis, have the knowledge of words of power and the breath of life, which can heal the Holy God.

Excerpt from the Legend of Ra and Isis

> I have been stung by some deadly thing, of which my heart hath no knowledge, and which I have neither seen with my eyes nor made with my hands. I have no knowledge whatsoever of that which hath done this thing to me. Never before have I felt pain like unto this, and

no pain can be worse than this. I am a Prince and son of a Prince, I am a divine emanation, I was produced by a god, I am a Great One, and the son of a Great One, and my father determined for me my name. My names are multitudinous, my forms are manifold, and my being existeth in every god.... My father and my mother uttered my name and they hid it in my body when I was born, so that none of those who would use against me words of power might succeed in making their enchantments to have dominion over me.

All the gods and goddesses, including Isis, come to see what is wrong with the Holy God. The three questions in this part of the myth are funny to me. Isis, who created the deadly snake in the first place and knows what is wrong with the Holy God, plays some serious mind games by asking him, "What is the matter? Hath anything which thou hast fashioned [dared] to lift up his head against thee? Hath a serpent shot his venom into thee?"

The Holy God tells Isis what happened and how he feels. Isis then asks the Holy God to tell her his name because whoever pronounces it will live forever as a mighty god or goddess. The Holy God goes on to describe his personal attributes: "I am the maker of the waters, the mountains; I am he whose name the gods know not; I am the maker of the heavens," and so on.

Isis then tells the Holy God he still has not told her his name, and if he does, she will make the poison leave his body. Finally the Holy God allows Isis to search his body and allows his name to come forth from his body into hers. Isis, upon learning the name of the Holy God, says, "Flow poison, come out of Ra," and Ra is healed. Isis becomes the queen of the gods and goddesses in heaven and on earth through the knowledge of Ra's name.

The Myth of Osiris

There are two birth-myths associated with Osiris that I have already covered earlier in the book. The first is the Heliopolis Ennead version, where Osiris is born to Geb and Nut (see chapter 1).

In the second version of his birth-myth, the goddess Nut gives birth to Osiris on the first of five extra days that have been added to the end of the year by the god Tehuti, who gambled with the moon for the extra days (see chapter 2).

Myths about Osiris are the most prevalent in African/Kemetic/Anu religions. The myth of Osiris is a fragmented compilation of writings from various sources over an extended period of time, beginning with the pyramid texts and constantly revised by writers over thousands of years, leading up to first-and second-century CE historians.

Osiris myths are found in all the dynasties of Africa/Kemet/Anu; he is a predynastic god with roots that go back into Anu/Ethiopia. The myth of Osiris's birth, death, and resurrection have had the greatest influence on the world's dominant religions: Hinduism, Judaism, Buddhism, Christianity, and Islam.

Personal attributes ascribed to Osiris were reworked, crystallized, and incorporated into two very long hymns: Hymn to Osiris and Hymn to Osiris Un-nefer (Un-nefer, another name for Osiris, means to open, to appear, or to make manifest good things). The hymns are found in the Papyrus of Ani: the *Book of Coming Forth by Day*.

Osiris is depicted in art as a man whose body is wrapped like a mummy; his face and hands, which are colored green, are exposed. The exposed green face and hands and the mummy wrappings symbolized everlastingness (evergreen trees found in Africa maintain their green color all year) and resurrection (the mummification process involved wrapping and preserving the body in cloth to ensure the person's eternal existence in the afterlife).

In his hands he is holding a shepherd's crook and flail, symbolizing he is a shepherd king, and a scepter—the symbol of power, dominion, and royal authority. On top of his head is the ancient feathered Atef crown associated with Osiris and Ra.

The Atef crown is a combination of the predynastic white crown of upper Anu/Ethiopia situated between two ostrich feathers, which symbolized truth, justice, morality, and balance; Osiris was the ruler of the Underworld, where departed souls went to have their lifelong deeds and hearts judged in the Hall of Judgment.

Osiris is the son of a god (Geb) and the first born of the goddess (Nut). The following personal attributes are ascribed to Osiris: the King of Kings; Lord of Lords; Prince of Princes; Lord of Everlastingness; Everlasting Lord; King of Eternity; Governor of the Gods; Beneficent Spirit among Spirits; Beneficent One; Lord; Shining Spirit Body; Governor of Spirit-Bodies; Great Chief; Prince of the Gods; Son who was set on the Throne of his

Father; Beloved of thy Mother; Lord of Eternity; King of the Gods; King of Men; Soul of Ra; Prince of Divine Food; and God of the Celestial Ocean.

In several African/Kemetic/Anu myths, Osiris ascends to heaven by way of the "Ladder to Heaven." The following excerpt is taken from the Papyrus of Nu and describes the Ladder to Heaven. (Note: "Osiris Nu" means Osiris, god of the Celestial Ocean, and Suti is Seth, who was a good god before he became an evil god.)

> Osiris Nu, whose word is truth, appeareth upon the Ladder that Ra hath made for him, and Horus and Suti hold him tightly by the arms as he ascendeth it.

The following excerpt is taken from the text inscriptions on the walls of the Pyramid of Pepi I:

> Hail to thee, O ladder of God, hail to thee, O Ladder of Set. Stand up, O Ladder of God, stand up, O Ladder of Set, stand up, O Ladder of Horus, whereon Osiris went forth into heaven.

The following excerpt is taken from the text inscriptions on the walls of the Pyramid of Unas:

> Ra setteth upright the ladder for Osiris, and Horus raiseth up the ladder for his father Osiris, when Osiris goeth to find his soul.

The myth of Osiris is that of the son of a god (Geb) who is beloved by his mother (Nut); he rules over the earth, bringing peace, love, and kindness through persuasion. Osiris is part of the trinity of Osiris, Isis, and Horus: the Father, Mother, and Divine Son.

Osiris is associated with resurrection (like Jesus); he was tortured (like Jesus), mutilated (like Jesus), and murdered (like Jesus) by his jealous brother Seth. His dismembered body is reassembled and resurrected by Isis using magic and incantations, with the help of Nephthys, the sister of Isis and Osiris.

Once alive again, Osiris cannot rule over earth again because Seth is now the ruler of earth, so he becomes ruler of the Underworld, replacing the god Anubis (son of Nephthys and Seth; in some myths, Osiris or Ra is the father of Anubis).

The Underworld (also called Amenta, Duat, Tuat, or Otherworld) is a place where departed souls of gods and humans must go to have their deeds or heart weighed in the balance. Once their deeds or heart are weighed, using the "Scale of Truth or Justice," a decision is made to either send the deceased to heaven or keep them in the Underworld to be devoured.

The judgment is rendered after the deceased enters the Hall of Judgment and is brought before the twelve members of the Company of Gods: Sa (Sia), Hu, Hathor, Heru, Isis, Nephthys, Nut, Geb, Tefnut, Shu, Atum, and Ra-Harmachis (Ra, the supreme solar creator god, manifested as "Horus of the Horizon"), with Osiris on the throne as ruler and judge.

The "Scale of Truth or Justice" and the "Company of Gods" is depicted in art in the Judgment Scene from the Papyrus of Ani (see chapter 5). The Judgment Scene of Ani is similar to many judgment day scenarios in the world's dominant religions; it is also striking in similarity to the criminal and civil courtrooms in America and around the world.

Osiris was murdered and resurrected; he is also associated with ceremonial and sacrificial offerings; the souls of the deceased had to consume bread, cakes, sweet meats, wine, and ale as a requirement for acceptance into heaven.

The myth of the Underworld is complicated; it is associated with fire; hell; evil demons and darkness; Osiris; resurrection; gates the deceased must pass through; complex pathways and transformations for souls on the way to immortality; the Hall of Judgment; weighing of deeds or the heart; and rebirth and ascension to heaven.

The following excerpt can be found in the Papyrus of Nu, *Book of Coming Forth by Day.*

(Note: "Utchat" is another spelling for Udjat, the "Eye of Horus.")

Address to the Gods of the Taut: from the Papyrus of Nu

> Therefore shall thy name be announced to the god Thoth, who saith: Tell me, who is he, whose heaven is of fire, whose walls are living serpents, and whose ground is a stream of water? Who is he? He is Osiris. Thoth saith: Advance now, thy name shall be announced to him. Thy cakes shall come from the Utchat, thy ale shall come

from the Utchat, and the offerings which shall appear to thee at the word upon earth [shall proceed] from the Utchat. This is what Osiris hath decreed for the steward of the overseer of the seal, Nu [i.e. Osiris Nu, god of the Celestial Ocean; not Nu or Nun, the primordial waters], whose word is truth.

Birth-Myth of Krishna of Hinduism

The myth of Krishna can easily be researched. His myth has been passed down in the form of oral legends, and accounts of his myth have been written about by historians and scholars. His myth can be found in the varied sacred texts and scriptures of Hinduism.

Some of the sources of the birth, life, and teachings of Krishna can be found in the sacred texts and scriptures of the Bhagavad-Gita, Vishnu Purana, Devi-Bhagavata Purana, Bhagavata Purana, Upanishads, and Mahabharata. Unlike Christianity, which has only one Bible, Hinduism has many scriptures, and not all of the sects recognize the same texts as sacred.

The name "Krishna" has been interpreted as meaning dark one, attractive one, black one, and dark complexion; some scholars use the words "bluish-black" to describe Krishna. Krishna was born during chaotic and turbulent times. King Kamsa (or Kansa), an evil, demonic, powerful, and cruel tyrant, ruled the land of Mathura in India. King Kamsa had overthrown and jailed his very own father King Ugrasena, who had been a good, fair, and loving king, to ascend to the thrown.

Before Krishna was born, a voice called out from the sky during the wedding of his parents, Devaki (the sister of King Kamsa) and Vasudeva, announcing to all that their eighth child would kill King Kamsa and restore peace, love, and harmony to India. King Kamsa, upset and afraid for his life and throne, proceeded to kill the first six babies born to Devaki and Vasudeva.

Vasudeva took the seventh newborn to safety in the faraway Indian city of Gokula and left the male newborn named Balarama with his second wife Rohini (some myths have the birth of Balarama being miraculously transferred to Rohini). King Kamsa was told Devaki had had a miscarriage; he believed this but still was suspicious. With the prophesized birth of the eighth child next, Kamsa put Devaki and Vasudeva in chains and locked them up in prison to await the birth of their eighth child so he could kill it.

There is a debate among some Christian scholars as to whether Krishna was born to a virgin mother like Jesus. Devaki had already given birth to seven other children; this part of the myth is without question. The similarity can be found in several Hindu texts where Vishnu (or Visnu), in order to accomplish the goal of the gods, grows inside Devaki's womb and is born as a god in human form, manifested as Krishna.

Vishnu is part of the Hindu divine trinity, which consists of Brahma, the god of creation; Shiva, the destroyer or transformer; and Vishnu, the preserver and protector of creation.

Vishnu is depicted with four hands resting on a coiled giant snake. In each of his four hands he holds: a sea shell (conch, or Sankha), which can be blown into to sound the beginning of battle; a club (mace); a serrated disk (Vaijra) with over a hundred sharp edges; and the lotus flower, which symbolizes eternity, purity, divinity, primordial birth, cosmic waters, beauty, prosperity, and fertility; he also carries a bow (Sarnga) and sword (Nandaka).

This is one god who is loaded down for battle; why? Most times the battle of good versus evil on earth is equally matched, but sometimes evil gets the upper hand, like during the rule of King Kamsa. The myth of Vishnu is that he, at the request of the gods, takes on human or animal form and defeats evil, returning love, peace, and harmony to the earth, thus restoring the balance of good versus evil.

Once Devaki and Vasudeva are in prison, Krishna is born; the gods all rejoice and thunder and lightning are present in the skies. The birth of Krishna is similar to the Christian myth of an earthly mother, giving birth to a celestial god (Vishnu as Krishna), descended from heaven than it is to a virgin birth.

After the birth, a voice from heaven tells Vasudeva to take the newborn Krishna to Gokula, where Yashoda, the wife of his friend Nanda, had just given birth to a newborn girl; Vasudeva is instructed to switch the newborns and bring the baby girl back to prison.

The voice from heaven released Vasudeva's chains, opened the prison doors, and allowed him to slip past the guards (who had been put into a deep sleep). Outside, it began to rain torrents of water, and the rivers swelled. A giant serpent came along and provided shelter for the baby Krishna, and the rivers calmed down. Vasudeva made it safely to the house of Nanda and switched the male baby with the newborn girl; then he returned to the prison undetected.

When King Kamsa heard of the birth of the eighth child, he came to the prison to kill the child. When he saw that it was a girl child, he was confused because he was expecting the eighth child to be a male.

After reflecting on what to do with the newborn female, King Kamsa held the newborn baby up in the air to smash her against a stone; as he did, she slipped out of his hands and flew over to a window. The baby girl then turned and said to King Kamsa, "What will you get by killing me? Your powerful enemy is already born on earth. O vilest of men! Disgrace to your family! He, the excellent human being who is very difficult to be worshipped, will certainly kill you." The female newborn then disappeared.

King Kamsa ordered his soldiers to kill all the newborn babies they found and to search for and kill the newborn child of Vasudeva and Devaki. Krishna, however, was safe in Gokula and went on to be raised by his foster parents, Nanda and Yashoda.

Krishna grew up and became a great military leader, fighting in many battles of good versus evil. One such battle is depicted in the Hindu scriptures of the Bhagavad-Gita—the long, violent, and bloody Kurukshetra War was a battle over justice, righteousness, universal harmony, duty, and good versus evil. Krishna eventually fulfilled the prophesy by leading an army to overthrow and kill King Kamsa, restoring King Ugrasena to the throne and once again restoring peace, love, harmony, and tranquility to the land of Mathura and all of India.

Critique: The first obvious similarity between Krishna and African/ Kemetic/Anu religious myths is that the name Krishna is interpreted as meaning dark one, black one, of a dark complexion, or being bluish-black. African people have varied skin hues, from pale to very dark. With Africa/ Kemet/Anu as the geographical location of the myths of Osiris and Heru, the people who developed those myths could be described as dark one, black one, of a dark complexion.

Krishna, like Heru, was born during chaotic and turbulent times; Krishna was born during the rule of the evil, powerful, demonic, and oppressive King Kamsa, and Heru was born during the rule of the evil, powerful, demonic, and oppressive Seth. King Kamsa had overthrown and jailed his own father King Ugrasena, who had been a good, compassionate, fair, and loving king, and ascended to the throne. Seth murdered his brother Osiris, who was a good, compassionate, fair, and loving ruler of earth in order to become ruler of earth.

Before Krishna was born, a voice from the sky announced during the wedding of his parents, Devaki and Vasudeva, that their eighth child would kill King Kamsa and restore peace, love, and harmony to India. The Annunciation, Conception, Birth, and Adoration of the Child, the four-part vignette from the Nativity Scene of Amenhotep III in the temple of Amun at Luxor, Egypt, shows Tehuti, the heart, mind, and tongue of the creator, announcing to the royal mother the impending birth of her son, who was descended from the creator god Amun.

After the birth of Heru, he was hailed as the coming avenger of the murderer of his father Osiris, and the god who would retake the throne and restore peace, love, and tranquility to earth.

The Hindu god Vishnu impregnated Devaki in order to be born as a god in human form, manifested as Krishna. In the Annunciation, Conception, Birth, and Adoration of the Child, the goddesses and gods, Isis or Hathor and Khnum or Kneph impregnated the royal mother by holding her hand and holding the ankh of life up to her mouth, indicating that she is conceiving a child descended from the creator god Amun (Amen). Osiris was the son of a god, Geb, and his mother, the goddess Nut, was impregnated by Geb.

The holy trinity of Hinduism is Brahma, the god of creation; Shiva, the destroyer or transformer; and Vishnu, the protector and preserver of creation. One of the holy trinities of African/Kemetic/Anu religions is Osiris, the father; Isis, the mother; and Heru, the divine child. In one of the four hands of Vishnu, he is holding a lotus flower, a Hindu religious symbol that represents eternity, purity, divinity, primordial birth, cosmic waters, beauty, prosperity, and fertility.

One can easily research two types of lotus flowers, used as sacred symbols; numerals for counting; varying mythical stories; funeral garlands or wreaths; temple offerings; cosmetics; nourishment; medical uses; as well as art depictions in African/Kemetic/Anu culture.

The blue lotus and white lotus are day blooming and night blooming water flowers, respectively, that open and close daily or over a period of days. The blue lotus, which opens in the midmorning and closes in midafternoon, is yet another variation of a creation myth.

Symbolized as the creation of the sun, the blue lotus rises out of the primordial waters and opens in the morning; the solar creation god Atum rises out of its center. The white lotus opens at dusk and closes at midday.

The blue and white lotus flowers also symbolize the twenty-four-hour cycle of day and night, which is symbolic of birth, death, and rebirth.

Lotus flowers are depicted in the Judgment Scene from the Papyrus of Ani as coverings for the offerings Ani makes to Osiris at his judgment. Also, a long-stemmed lotus flower is in front of the throne of the seated Osiris, with the four children of Horus standing on its petals. The lotus flower in African/Kemetic/Anu culture symbolizes birth, death, and rebirth; resurrection; eternity; primordial birth; primordial waters; divinity; prosperity; nourishment; and fertility.

Krishna was born in an unusual place, a prison, while Heru was born in an unusual place, the Nile Delta marshlands. King Kamsa planned to kill the newborn Krishna to save his throne, and Krishna's father had to flee with the newborn and hide him in the city of Gokula.

Isis, in the African/Kemetic/Anu myth of Heru, gave birth to and hid Heru in the Nile Delta marshlands to protect him from the evil Seth, who wanted to kill the newborn to prevent him from avenging his father and taking back control of earth.

Krishna was raised by foster parents, Nanda and Yashoda. Krishna grew older and became a great military leader, fighting in many great battles and eventually killing King Kamsa and returning the throne to King Kamsa's father, King Ugrasena, fulfilling the prophecy of the gods and restoring peace, love, harmony, and tranquility to the land of Mathura and all of India.

Heru fought many bloody battles with Seth, winning most of them and eventually forcing a truce negotiated by Tehuti, thus avenging the murder of his father (Osiris) and regaining control of earth and restoring peace, love, and tranquility with the ever-present danger of evil trying to overcome good and righteousness.

It should be noted that another similarity between Heru (Horus) and Krishna, is that both wage war in defense of family members who were overthrown or killed. Krishna is the grandson of King Ugrasena, the father of King Kamsa; Krishna is the son Devaki, the sister of King Kamsa. Heru is the son of Osiris and Isis, the brother and sister of Seth. Heru (Horus) attempts to kill and eventually overthrows his evil uncle Seth, the murderer of Osiris. Krishna overthrows and kills his evil uncle King Kamsa who had overthrown and jailed his own father, King Ugrasena.

It is easy to see the similarities between the personal attributes associated with Krishna and the African/Kemetic/Anu gods: Osiris; Heru; creator gods: Atum; Ra; and Ra manifested as Khepri and Amen-Ra.

These similar personal attributes can be found in the Papyrus of Ani *(Book of Coming Forth by Day)*: Chapter of Praises and Glorifyings of Coming out from and of Going into the Glorious Khert-Neter. Similar attributes can also be found in the Hymn to Ra; Hymn to Osiris; and Hymn to Amen-Ra.

Krishna's personal attributes can be found in various Hindu scriptures and texts. For this comparison I will use Mahabharata, book 13, and Anusasana Parva, part 2, section CLVIII.

When reading the similar personal attributes listed below, the reader should also take note of the personal attributes of Krishna and the African/ Kemetic/Anu gods— in comparison to the personal attributes ascribed to the supreme gods of Christianity, Judaism, and Islam.

The man-made belief in a supreme god was already being worshipped long before the man-made religions of Christianity, Judaism, and Islam were created. The following five excerpts are long—but provide numerous examples of similar personal attributes ascribed to a supreme god. The following five excerpts were compiled from the sources mentioned above.

Krishna

> This Krishna takes birth in the race of either the gods or among men. Staying on righteousness, this Krishna of cleansed soul [on such occasion] protects both the higher and lower worlds. Sparing those that deserve to be spared, Krishna sets himself to the slaughter.... It is he who is all acts proper and improper.... He is the destroyer and he is the creator of the universe.... He is of human form; and he is of terrible form. All creatures sing his praises.... He is the enhancer of wealth: He is the one victorious being in the universe. In sacrifices, eloquent men hymn his praises.... It is unto him that the sacrificial priests pour their libations.... This Krishna of foremost feats rescued the earth. It is unto him that the people dedicate diverse kinds of food.... It is Krishna who is god of the wind.... it is he who is that first of gods, viz., the sun possessed of a thousand rays. He is the soul of the deities and human beings.... It is he who is the sacrifice performed by those persons that are conversant with the rituals of sacrifices. It is he who rises every day in the firmament [in the form

of the sun] and divides time into day night.... He is the sun, the dispeller of all darkness. He is the creator of all.... It is he who created the earth.... It is this Krishna of immeasurable and blazing energy who has created the forests and mountains.... He is the creator of the universe. He creates everything from his own nature.... He is the seasons; He is fortnights; he is day and night.... He at first created the waters.... He is the soul of the universe.... He is these diverse wonderful vegetations of nature which we see.... He it is that then creates the Earth and Wind, the Sky, Light, and also Water.... He who causes all things to exist through his puissance.... Know that good and evil, mobile and immobile, have all flowed from this One who is Vishwaksena [another name for Vishnu]. Whatever exists, and whatever will spring into existence, all is Keshava [Krishna]. This Krishna is also the death that overtakes all creatures when their end comes. He is eternal and it is he who upholds the cause of righteousness.

Hymn to Osiris

Lord of eternity, King of the gods, whose names are manifold, whose forms are holy ... whose Ka [spirit] is holy ... thou being of hidden form in the temples ... thou art the prince of divine food in Anu ... the hidden Soul ... The ruler supreme in the White Hall [Memphis, Egypt]. Thou art the soul of Ra.... Thou art the beneficent one.... Thou makest the soul to be raised up.... Thou art the mighty one of victories.... Lord of eternity ... Thy name is established in the mouths of men. Thou are the substance of the two lands of Egypt.... The stars in the celestial heights are obedient unto thee.... Thou art he to whom praises are ascribed in the southern heaven, and thanks are given for thee in the northern heaven.... Offerings appear before thee at the decree of Geb. The Companies of the Gods praise thee, and the gods of the Taut [Underworld] smell the earth in paying homage to thee. The uttermost parts of the earth bow before thee, and the limits of the skies entreat thee with supplications when they see thee.

The holy ones are overcome before thee, and all Egypt offereth thanksgiving unto thee when it meeteth.… Thou art a shining Spirit-body, the Governor of Spirit-bodies; permanent is thy rank, established is thy rule … Gracious is thy face, and beloved by him that seeth it. Thy fear is set in all the lands by reason of thy perfect love, and they cry out to thy name, making it the first of names, and all people make offering to thee. Thou art the lord who are commemorated in heaven and upon earth.… Thou art the Great Chief, the first among thy brethren, the Prince of the Company of the Gods, the stablisher of Right and Truth throughout the world, the son who was set on the throne of his father Geb.… Thou didst stand up and smite the enemy and set thy fear in thine adversary. Thou dost bring the boundaries of the mountains.… Thou hast made this earth with thy hand, and the waters, and the winds, and the vegetation, and all the cattle, and all the feathered fowl, and all the fish, and all the creeping things, and all the wild animals thereof.… Thou rollest up into the horizon, thou hast set light over the darkness. Thou sendest forth air [or light].… Thou art the companion of the stars and the guide of every god.

Hymn to Ra

Homage to thee, O thou who hast come as Khepera [Khepri], the creator of the gods. Thou art seated on thy throne [or, thou art crowned], thou risest up in the sky, illumining thy mother [Nut]; thou art seated on thy throne as the King of the gods.… The goddess Maat embraceth thee at the two seasons of the day [morning and evening]. May Ra give glory, and power of truth-speaking and the appearance as a living soul.… O all ye gods of the House of the Soul, who weigh heaven and earth in a balance, and who give celestial food [to the dead].… Thou creator of mortals and of the Companies of the Gods of the South and of the North, of the West and of the East, ascribe ye praise to Ra, the Lord of heaven.… The earth becometh light at his birth each day; he proceedeth until he reacheth the place where he was yesterday.... Let Ra grant me a view of the Disk [the sun], and a sight of Ah [the moon] unfailingly each day. Let my Ba [soul] come forth to walk about hither and thither and whithersoever it pleaseth.... Let meals from the sepulchral offerings be given to me in the presence of Osiris as to those who are in the following of Horus.

Hymn to Amen-Ra

Amen-Ra, the Bull of Heliopolis, president of the gods ... Prince of Punt [Anu/Ethiopia, Somalia, Horn of Africa], lord of the heavens, eldest son of the earth, lord of things which exist, stablisher of things, stablisher of all things ... Lord of Truth [or Law], father of the gods, maker of men, creator of beasts, lord of things which exist, creator of the staff of life [wheat], maker of the green herb which nourisheth the cattle ... His Majesty, their Lord, the lord of fear, the mighty one of victory, the mighty of Will, the lord of crowns, who maketh offerings to flourish, and createth the divine food ... lord of eternity, maker of the everlastingness, lord of adorations ... lord of rays, creator of light ... His name is hidden from his children, in his name Amen.

Papyrus of Ani
Chapter of Praises and Glorifyings of Coming out from and of Going into the Glorious Khert-Neter

I am the god Tem [Atum] in rising. I am the Only One, I came into existence in Nu [primordial waters], I am Ra who rose in the beginning, the ruler of this creation.... I am the Great God who created himself, even Nu.... It is Ra, the creator of the names of his limbs, which came into being.... It is Temu [Atum], the dweller in the disk, but others say that it is Ra when he riseth in the eastern horizon of the sky. I am Yesterday, I know Today.... Yesterday is Osiris and Today is Ra, when he shall destroy the enemies of Neb-er-tcher [lord to the uttermost limit;

Osiris], and when he shall establish as prince and ruler his son Horus.... The things which have been made, and the things which shall be made [refer to] the dead body of Osiris.... Others again say that the things which have been made are Eternity, and the things which shall be made are Everlastingness, and that Eternity is the Day and Everlastingness the Night.

Birth-Myth of Buddha

Varied, ethnically diverse, confusing, and inconsistent best describe the multiple birth-myths, multiple earthly forms at birth, final birth, and life of Buddha that are found in Buddhist schools: conservative early sects, Theravada, Mahayana, Vajrayana, Tibetan, Chan, Tendai, Nichiren, Zen, Shin Buddhist, and so on.

Most of the birth-myths of Buddha were written between 600 BCE and 900 CE. One could write a dozen books to critique all the birth-myths attributed to Buddha. "The Golden Age of Buddhism" in Asia was 600 CE to 900 CE. This was a time when Buddhist kingdoms flourished and magnificent monuments to the heavens were constructed, similar to the Golden Age of Africa/Kemet/Anu, when society flourished, and the great Egyptian/Kemetic pyramids and other monuments were built.

I will attempt to summarize the birth-myths of Buddha; sources on his various birth-myths are easy to research. One source is *The Jataka Tales* from the Pali Canon of Theravada Buddhism, a series of 545-plus birth-myths of previous Buddha lives, passed down from folklore accounts. Other sources include *The Lalitavistara Text: Vaipulya Sutras,* summaries of the Mahayana school of Buddhism, taken from 120 bas-relief panels.

The last source is from *The Golden Age of Buddhism,* over 2,600 individual bas-reliefs which include the following: over 1,400 narrative panels (which include the 120 of the Lalitavistara); and over 1,200 decorative panels, located in the world's largest Buddhist monument, the impressive and awe-inspiring Temple of Borobudur in Indonesia. The temple was constructed between 700 and 850 CE and is considered to be one of the Seven Wonders of the Modern World.

The birth-myth of Buddha begins in the heavens. He is surrounded by divine radiance and encircled by twelve thousand monks and thirty-two thousand Bodhisattvas (anyone striving to attain perfect enlightenment). The sound of eighty-four thousand drums fills the heavens, and the gods implore Buddha to go down to earth and reveal the teachings of the Vaipulya Sutras for the salvation and blessing of the world.

After long consultations and deliberation with the gods, Bodhisattvas, and monks trying to decide what physical form he would assume on earth (animal or human) and who would be his mother, Buddha decided to be born into the royal family of King Shuddhodana and enter the womb of Queen Maya in the form of a white elephant (the white elephant symbolizes fertility and wisdom).

Queen Maya was the only woman in all of India capable of bearing Buddha because she possessed the strength of ten thousand elephants. She was also perfect in her beauty, chastity, and virtue. She then has a dream of a white elephant as a sign that she would give birth to a great leader.

The conception of Queen Maya is accomplished with the assistance of the gods. Buddha did not reside inside the womb of his mother like other babies; instead, to avoid contamination, the gods provided a jeweled box for him to stay in while inside his mother's womb. A shining, glorious light is emitted from the divine child inside of Queen Maya, and while she is pregnant, she is able to perform miracles like healing the sick just by touching them.

Nine months after her dream of a white elephant, Queen Maya traveled to Koliya, the city where her father lived—it was customary for a woman to have her baby in the house of her father.

On the way to Koliya, the queen's great procession passed a garden in Nepal called Lumbini Park. This park was located near the foot of the Himalayan Mountains. The queen was attracted to the park because of its sala trees, scented flowers, birds, and bees; she ordered the procession to stop so she could rest.

As she rested, Queen Maya reached up to touch one of the leaves hanging down from a branch of the sala tree; she then gave birth to Buddha. The newborn Buddha stood up and began to walk, taking seven steps; as he did, lotus flowers appeared after each step. On the seventh step, he stopped and said, "I am chief of the world, eldest am I in the world. Foremost am I in the world. This is the last birth. There is now no more coming to be."

Born as an exalted being and a great spirit, Queen Maya and the newborn Buddha returned home, where there was a celebration in the entire kingdom. Seven days after giving birth, Queen Maya died, and Buddha was raised by his aunt, Queen Pajapati.

Critique: The Buddhist birth-myth is similar to both African/Kemetic/Anu and Hindu birth-myths. (Note: Buddhism arose out of philosophical differences with Hinduism over its caste system, rigid social structure, and lack of individual spiritual and cultural empowerment. Some scholars describe Buddhism as a more humane and philosophically divergent sect of Hinduism.)

The first similarity is the reason for the birth of the divine child. Something is happening on earth that requires intervention by the gods, and it is necessary for a savior to come to earth to bring salvation and restore peace, love, and tranquility.

The birth-myth of Buddha begins in heaven. The gods implore Buddha to go down to earth to bring blessings and salvation to the world.

In the Hindu birth-myth of Krishna, India is ruled by the evil, demonic, oppressive, and cruel King Kamsa. In the African/Kemetic/Anu birth-myth of Heru, the evil and oppressive Seth rules the earth.

Buddha decides to enter the womb of Queen Maya as an elephant in order to be born and save earth. Queen Maya has a dream of a white elephant as a sign that she would give birth to a great leader. The conception of Queen Maya is accomplished with the assistance of the gods.

In the myth of the Hindu god Vishnu, the protector and preserver of creation, the battle of good versus evil is out of balance, with evil dominating; Vishnu manifests himself through a divine birth on earth (Krishna) and defeats evil, thus restoring the balance of good versus evil on earth.

In order to accomplish the goal of the gods, Vishnu grows inside the womb of Devaki and is born as a god in human form, manifested as Krishna. In the Hindu birth-myth, at the wedding of Devaki and Vasudeva a voice from heaven announces that their eighth child would kill King Kamsa and restore peace, love, and harmony to all of India.

In the African/Kemetic/Anu birth-myth of Heru, he is born to the goddess Isis and is hailed as the coming avenger of the murderer of his father Osiris, who would retake the throne and restore peace, love, and tranquility to earth.

Buddha, Krishna, and Heru were all born in unusual places. Buddha was born in a garden beneath a sala tree, Krishna was born in a prison, and Heru was born in the Nile Delta marshlands.

Buddha's mother, Queen Maya, died seven days after his birth, and he was raised by his aunt and foster mother, Queen Pajapati. Krishna's father took him to the city of Gokula to hide him because King Kamsa wanted to kill him. He was raised by his foster parents Nanda and Yashoda.

Buddha brings peace, love, compassion, harmony, and tranquility to earth. Krishna and Heru restore peace, love, compassion, harmony, and tranquility to earth.

Islam: Birth-Myths of Yahya, Isa, and Muhammad
Birth-Myth of Yahya: Sura 19:5–15

> 5. And surely I fear my cousins after me, and my wife is barren, therefore grant me thyself an heir. 6. Who should inherit me and inherit from the children of Yaqoub, and make him, my Lord, one in whom thou art well pleased. 7. O Zakariya! Surely we give you good news of a boy whose name shall be Yahya: We have not made before anyone his equal. 8. He said: O my Lord! When shall I have a son, and my wife is barren, and I myself have reached indeed the extreme degree of old age? 9. He said: So shall it be; your Lord says: It is easy to me, and indeed I created you before, when you were nothing. 10. He said: my Lord! Give me a sign. He said: Your sign is that you will not be able to speak to the people three nights while in sound health. 11. So he went forth to his people from his place of worship, then he made known to them that they should glorify Allah morning and evening. 12. O Yahya! Take hold of the book with strength, and we granted him wisdom while yet a child. 13. And tenderness from us and purity, and he was one who guarded against evil. 14. And dutiful to his parents, and he was not insolent, disobedient. 15. And peace on him on the day he was born, and on the day he dies, and on the day he is raised to life.

Critique: The birth-myth of Yahya is similar to the Christian birth-myth of John the Baptist. Let us see just how similar the two birth-myths are.

Luke 1:6–7

6. And they were both righteous before God, walking in all the commandments and ordinances of the Lord blameless. 7. And they had no child, because that Elisabeth was barren, and they both were now well stricken in years.

Luke 1:13–16

13. But the angel said unto him, Fear not, Zacharias: for thy prayer is heard; and thy wife Elisabeth shall bear thee a son, and thou shalt call his name John. 14. And thou shalt have joy and gladness; and many shall rejoice at his birth. 15. For he shall be great in the sight of the Lord, and shall drink neither wine nor strong drink; and he shall be filled with the Holy Ghost, even from his mother's womb. 16. And many of the children of Israel shall he turn to the Lord their God.

Luke 1:18–20

18. And Zacharias said unto the angel, Whereby shall I know this? for I am an old man, and my wife well stricken in years. 19. And the angel answering said unto him, I am Gabriel, that stand in the presence of God; and am sent to speak unto thee, and to shew thee these glad tidings. 20. And, behold, thou shalt be dumb, and not able to speak, until the day that these things shall be performed, because thou believest not my words, which shall be fulfilled in their season.

Luke 1:57 and 60

57. Now Elisabeth's full time came that she should be delivered; and she brought forth a son…. 60. And his mother answered and said, Not so; but he shall be called John.

Luke 1:67–69

> 67. And his father Zacharias was filled with the Holy
> Ghost, and prophesied, saying, 68. Blessed be the Lord
> God of Israel; for he hath visited and redeemed his people,
> 69. And hath raised up an horn of salvation for us in the
> house of his servant David;

When I first read the second of these two myths, I had to double check
to see if I was reading the same myth over and had forgotten that I had
read it. The birth-myth of Yahya of Islam is supposed to be the word of
Allah; however, the myth of John the Baptist of Christianity is older and
almost identical.

Birth-Myth of Isa (Marium)

Sura 19:16–25

> 16. And mention Marium in the book when she drew
> aside from her family to an eastern place. 17. So she took
> a veil to screen herself from them; then we sent to her our
> spirit, and there appeared to her a well-made man. 18. She
> said: Surely I fly for refuge from you to the beneficent god,
> if you are one guarding against evil. 19. He said: I am only
> a messenger of your Lord: That I will give you a pure boy.
> 20. She said: When shall I have a boy and no mortal has
> yet touched me, nor have I been unchaste? 21. He said:
> Even so; your Lord says: It is easy to me: and that we may
> make him a sign to men and a mercy from us; and it is a
> matter which has been decreed. 22. So she conceived him;
> then withdrew herself with him to a remote place. 23. And
> the throes of childbirth compelled her to betake herself to
> the trunk of a palm tree. She said: Oh, would that I had
> died before this, and had been a thing quite forgotten! 24.
> Then the child called out to her from beneath her: Grieve
> not; surely your Lord has made a stream to flow beneath
> you. 25. And shake towards you the trunk of the palm
> tree; it will drop on you fresh ripe dates.

Sura 19:29–36

> 29. But she pointed to him. They said: How should we speak to one who was a child in the cradle? 30. He said: Surely I am a servant of Allah; He has given me the book and made me a prophet. 31. And he has made me blessed wherever I may be, and he has enjoined on me prayer and poor-rate so long as I live. 32. And dutiful to my mother, and he has not made me insolent, unblessed. 33. And peace on me on the day I was born and on the day I die, and on the day I am raised to life. 34. Such is Isa, son of Marium, this is the saying of truth about which they dispute. 35. It beseems not Allah that he should take to himself a son, glory be to him; when he has decreed a matter he only says to it "Be" and it is. 36. And surely Allah is my Lord and your Lord, therefore serve him; this is the right path.

Critique: Like the birth-myths of Yahya and John the Baptist are similar, this birth-myth of Isa is similar to the birth-myth of Jesus of Christianity. Islam views Adam, Noah, Abraham, Moses, David, John the Baptist, and Jesus as part of Islam; they were all great messengers and prophets of Allah, with Muhammad being the last of the great prophets.

The birth-myths of Yahya and Isa and their mothers are about women who are, respectively, barren (incapable of having children) or chaste (virgin: never having sexual intercourse) and being impregnated by Allah. There is an announcement from an angel or messenger from Allah of the impending birth; a sign that the birth is going to occur; the birth is a sign to earth of Allah's mercy; and the birth occurring itself.

The birth-myths of Yahya and Isa are similar to the four-part African/Kemetic/Anu birth-myth vignette the Annunciation, Conception, Birth, and Adoration of the Child.

In the birth-myths of Yahya and Isa, their mothers are impregnated by Allah; a messenger or angel of Allah informs the father of Yahya (Zakariya) and mother of Isa (Marium) that a son will be born unto them. A sign is given that the birth of Yahya will occur, and the births of Yahya and Isa occur, with the birth of Isa being a sign to the earth of the mercy of Allah.

In the Annunciation, Conception, Birth, and Adoration of the Child, the first vignette depicts the god Tehuti announcing to the royal mother the impending birth of her son, descended from the creator god Amun. In the second part of the vignette, the creator god Khnum (or Kneph) stands on one side of the royal mother and the goddess Isis (or Hathor) stands on the other side of the royal mother. They hold the hand of the royal mother while holding the ankh, the symbol of life, up to the mouth of the royal mother, indicating that she is conceiving. In the third part of the vignette, the royal mother gives birth to a newborn child.

The birth-myth of Buddha states that he is in heaven, where the gods are imploring him to go down to earth and reveal the teachings of the Varipulya Sutras for the blessing and salvation of earth. Buddha has a long deliberation and consultation with the gods, monks, and Bodhisattvas (anyone who is striving to attain perfect enlightenment).

Buddha decides to enter the womb of Queen Maya in the form of a white elephant. Queen Maya is chosen because of her beauty, chastity, and virtue. She then has a dream of a white elephant (symbol of fertility and wisdom), the sign that she will give birth to a great leader.

In the Islamic birth-myth of Isa, Isa is born at the trunk of a palm tree and spoke at birth, saying, "Grieve not … And shake towards you the trunk of the palm tree, it will drop on you fresh ripe dates…. Surely I am a servant of Allah; he has given me the book and made me a prophet. And he has made me blessed wherever I may be…. And peace on me on the day I was born and on the day I die, and on the day I am raised to life."

Buddha in his birth-myth was born in the Garden of Lumbini Park under a sala tree. As his mother, Queen Maya, began to rest, she reached up to touch one of the leaves hanging down from a branch of the sala tree and gave birth to Buddha. At birth, Buddha spoke, saying, "I am chief of the world, eldest am I in the world. Foremost am I in the world. This is the last birth. There is now no more coming to be."

The birth-myth of Krishna states that a voice from the sky announced during the wedding of Devaki and Vasudeva that their eighth child would kill the evil King Kamsa and restore peace, love, and harmony to India.

The Hindu god Vishnu decides to grow inside the womb of Devaki and be born as a god in human form, manifested as Krishna. Vishnu is a part of the Hindu trinity of Brahma, the supreme god of creation; Shiva, the destroyer or transformer; and Vishnu, the protector and preserver of creation.

Yahya and Isa are similar to the older African/Kemetic/Anu birth-myth of Heru (Horus), who is the son of a god (Osiris) and goddess (Isis). Yahya is also similar to the birth myths of Buddha and Krishna because he is raised by someone who is not his biological parent. Buddha is raised by his foster mother, Queen Pajapati, and Krishna is raised by his foster parents, Nanda and Yashoda. Yahya is raised by his step-father Zakariya, and John the Baptist is raised by his step-father, Zacharias.

Birth-Myth of Muhammad

There is no mention in the Koran of a birth-myth of Muhammad. The accounts of his birth-myth are handed down by scholars in the hundred years following the date attributed to his death on June 8, 632 CE. The following is a brief summary of the details of his birth-myth.

Muhammad was born in 570 CE in Mecca, Saudi Arabia. Mecca is located in a remote valley surrounded by the Sirat mountains, which include Mount Ajyad, Mount Abu Qubays, and Mount Hira. He was born during the Year of the Elephant; Muhammad's father died before he was born, and his mother died when he was six years old. Muhammad was adopted by his grandfather, Abdul Muttalib, who raised him for two years. Then at the age of eight until maturity, he was adopted and raised by his uncle Abu Talib.

Around the age of forty, Muhammad received a revelation in Mecca from Allah during the month of Ramadan. The myth states that over the next twenty-two years, until his death, Allah, through the angel Jabril (Gabriel), would reveal the Koran to Muhammad. Jabril verbally recited these revelations to Muhammad, whose followers wrote them down to become the Koran.

During the early years of Muhammad, Islam had become more of a polytheistic religion with an emphasis on what will happen if one does not follow the teachings of Islam. This was a divergence from the monotheistic teachings of Adam, Noah, Abraham, Moses, David, John the Baptist, and Jesus.

Muhammad's revelations and teachings were more about regulations of behavior and rules for society. Muhammad taught that he was a messenger of Allah, the last of the great prophets. He began to teach a monotheistic version of Islam with Allah as the only supreme god; believers must submit and surrender to the will of Allah.

Muhammad's teachings were met with fierce resistance from the Islamic religious establishment in Mecca, who felt he was disrespectful to the current version of Islam. Muhammad and his followers were persecuted and attacked, and they had to flee Mecca in different directions. Muhammad fled to Medina, Saudi Arabia, to continue to spread his teachings.

Muhammad gained more followers in Medina and led many military battles against Mecca over the direction of Islam. Muhammad and his followers finally conquered Mecca and united the Arabian Peninsula into a government of social organization and civil order; they restored the original monotheistic version of Islam as the religion of the land.

Critique: Muhammad's successful campaign to reform Islam from a polytheistic religion to a monotheistic religion is similar to the unsuccessful attempt by Pharaoh Akhenaten (see chapter 2) to transform the religion of Africa/Kemet/Anu from a polytheistic religion with multiple gods and goddesses and one supreme god to a monotheistic religion with the god Aten as the one and only supreme god.

One can find within Islam, the youngest of the world's dominant religions, similarities with African/Kemetic/Anu religious myths and culture and the religions of Hinduism, Buddhism, Judaism, and Christianity.

Muhammad was born in a house located in a valley situated between several mountains in Mecca, Saudi Arabia. He was born in 570 CE during the Year of the Elephant. Being born in a house was not unusual, but being born in a remote valley surrounded by mountains which has become the most sacred site in Islam is symbolic and unusual.

Other divine saviors, sons of god, or prophets happened to be born in unusual places. Heru was born in the Nile Delta marshlands in his African/Kemetic/Anu birth-myth; Krishna of Hinduism was born in a prison cell. Mountains are a part of the birth myth of Buddha, who was born in an unusual place, under a sala tree in the gardens of Lumbini Park, near the foot of the Himalayan Mountains; and Jesus of Christianity was born in a manger inside a barn.

Moses, a prophet, law-giver, and religious leader, is viewed as an important and central figure in the religions of Islam, Judaism, and Christianity. The birth-myth of Moses is also unusual. He was born to a mother who immediately hid him for three months because there was a decree from the evil pharaoh to kill all newborn Hebrew children.

Neither the Christian Bible nor the Hebrew Torah mention exactly where Moses was born (a house, barn, garden, prison), just that he was looked upon by his mother, who saw that he was goodly (good, pleasing in appearance).

He was then immediately hidden for three months. Then when he could no longer be hidden, in an attempt to save him from death, his mother placed him in an ark of bulrushes, daubed with slime and pitch, then placed the ark with the baby inside in the flags by the river's brink. According to Muhammad's birth-myth, he was born in 570 CE during the Year of the Elephant. In the birth-myth of Buddha, he decided to enter the womb of Queen Maya in the form of an elephant. Queen Maya was chosen because she is perfect in her beauty, chastity, and virtue.

Queen Maya also possessed the strength of ten thousand elephants. She then had a dream of a white elephant (symbol of fertility and wisdom), the sign that she would give birth to a great leader.

Muhammad's father died before he was born, and his mother died when he was six years old. He was adopted and raised by his grandfather and foster parent, Abdul Muttalib. Then at the age of eight until maturity, he was adopted and raised by his uncle and foster parent, Abu Talib.

Krishna of Hinduism was taken by his father and hidden in the city of Gokula because King Kamsa was trying to kill him. He was left there to be raised by his foster parents, Nanda and Yashoda.

Buddha was born to Queen Maya, who died seven days after his birth; Buddha was raised by his aunt and foster mother, Queen Pajapati. Moses was placed in a small ark, which was then placed by the river's edge, where he was found and raised by his foster mother, the pharaoh's daughter.

Muhammad considered himself a prophet and messenger of Allah, and he had to wage war against the polytheistic religious establishment in Mecca in order to bring about the return of Islam as a monotheistic religion based on the teachings of Adam, Noah, Abraham, Moses, David, John the Baptist, and Jesus. Muhammad's religious war resulted in Islam returning to a philosophy of regulations of behavior, rules for society, and submitting and surrendering to the will of Allah. After many years of war, Muhammad reestablished the original form of Islam to all the land of Arabia.

Heru of the African/Kemetic/Anu religious myths had to wage war against his evil uncle Seth for control of earth. Heru fought to retake the throne and avenge the death of his father, Osiris, who was murdered by Seth.

Eventually Heru wins the war and a negotiated settlement through Tehuti reestablishes Heru as the ruler of earth, restoring peace, love, and tranquility to earth with the ever-present danger of evil trying to overcome good and righteousness.

Krishna of Hinduism became a great military leader, fighting many battles like the bloody Kurukshetra War. He eventually fulfilled his prophesy and led an army to overthrow and kill the evil King Kamsa. Krishna then restored to the throne the good and loving father of King Kamsa, who had been overthrown by his evil son, thus restoring peace, love, harmony, and tranquility to the land of Mathura and all of India.

Hebrew Mashiach

Judaism does not believe that any of the following events have occurred to date: a divine Son of God sacrifices himself on earth for the sins of humans (Jesus); a divine celestial being or god manifests himself in a physical form on earth to save the earth (Krishna) or bring enlightenment (Buddha); or the last great prophet of Allah is born on earth and reveals Allah's will (Muhammad). According to Judaism, the savior or messiah has not yet come to earth.

The word "Mashiach" is not found within the scriptures of the Tanakh, the religious book of Judaism. Mashiach is the Hebrew word for messiah. Principle number twelve of Maimonides's Thirteen Fundamental Principles of the Jewish faith is a belief in the arrival of the messiah (or Mashiach) and the messianic era.

Jewish religious scholars use "Mashiach" to describe a Jewish leader descended from a king. The Mashiach will be anointed king in the end days and reunite the scattered people of Israel and bring about global peace, harmony, love, tranquility, justice, and fairness.

"Mashiach" means "the anointed one" or "anointed king"; he is not a god, son of god, or celestial being. The Mashiach will be a charismatic political, religious, civic, or military leader descended from the mythical character King David. The following quotes from Hebrew Scriptures (the Tanakh of Judaism) describe the Mashiach:

> **Jeremiah 23:5–6:** 5. He will be descended from the line of King David. He will reign, prosper and execute judgment and justice in the earth. 6. Judah shall be saved

and Israel shall dwell in safety. He shall be called "HaShem [lord] our righteousness."

Isaiah 11:2–5: 2. And the spirit of HaShem shall rest upon him, the spirit of wisdom and understanding, the spirit of counsel and might, the spirit of knowledge and of the fear of HaShem. 3. He shall not judge after the sight of his eyes, neither decide after the hearing of his ears. 4. He shall judge the poor with righteousness and decide with equity for the meek of the land. He shall smite the land with the rod of his mouth and with the breath of his lips shall he slay the wicked. 5. Righteousness shall be the girdle of his loins, and faithfulness the girdle of his reins.

Isaiah 11:10–12: 10. And it shall come to pass in that day, that the root of Jesse, that standeth for an ensign of the people, unto him shall the nations seek; and his resting place shall be glorious. 11. It will come to pass for the second time the lord will set out to recover the remnant of his people, that remain from Assyria [present-day Iraq]; Egypt in Africa; Cush [present-day southwest Ethiopia and central-southeast Sudan in Africa]; Pathros [present-day southern Egypt]; Elam [present-day southeast Iran]; Shinar [along the borders of Iran, Syria, Iraq, Turkey]; Hamath [central Syria]; and from the Islands of the sea [Red Sea and Mediterranean Sea]. 12. He will set up an ensign for the nations and will assemble the dispersed of Israel and gather together the scattered of Judah from the four corners of the earth.

Isaiah 2:4: And he shall judge between the nations, and decide for many peoples. They will destroy their weapons and nations shall not lift up sword against nation; neither shall they learn war any more.

Critique: When the mythical Mashiach or messiah does finally come, one can apply retroactive similarities, attributes, and characteristics already found in the African/Kemetic/Anu myths of Heru and Osiris; Krishna of Hinduism, which existed before Judaism; Buddha of Buddhism, which is younger than Judaism by about four hundred years (however, the dates of some myths have the two religions parallel to each other); Jesus, the mythical Son of God, who is referred to as the messiah of Christianity; and Muhammad of Islam, which is the youngest of the dominant world religions.

Whether you call the mythical savior a human, god, or celestial being, who is descended from a king on earth (Mashiach), human on earth (Muhammad), god and goddess on earth (Heru), god in heaven (Jesus and Krishna), or celestial being in heaven (Buddha), it is still the myth of a earthly savior being descended from some type of celestial, heavenly, or earthly source.

The below compilation of attributes and characteristics of the Mashiach are from the verses just cited in the books of Jeremiah and Isaiah. The attributes and characteristics are similar to those of Osiris, Heru, Krishna, and Muhammad.

> The Mashiach will reign, prosper, and execute judgment and justice in the earth, he shall be called HaShem [lord] our righteousness. He shall judge the poor with righteousness and decide with equity for the meek. Faithfulness shall be the girdle of his reins. He shall judge between the nations and decide for many people. The lord will rest upon him the spirit of wisdom, understanding, counsel, knowledge, and might. He will bring about global peace, harmony, love, tranquility, justice, and fairness.

The man-made myth of Osiris states that he is the ruler of the Underworld, where departed souls go to have their lifelong deeds and hearts judged in the Hall of Judgment. He is called the Beneficent One, the Great Chief, and King of Men. Osiris wears the Atef crown, whose feathers symbolize truth, justice, morality, and balance. Osiris, before his murder at the hands of Seth, brought to earth as its ruler peace, love, and kindness through persuasion.

The Mashiach will "smite the land with the rod of his mouth and with the breath of his lips shall he slay the wicked." Heru, in the African/Kemetic/Anu myth, fights a good-versus-evil battle against his evil uncle Seth for control of earth and the souls of the gods and humans who inhabit the earth, eventually winning and negotiating a settlement through Tehuti, establishing himself as ruler of earth and avenging the murder of his father, Osiris, thus restoring peace, love, and tranquility to earth.

Krishna of Hinduism becomes a great military leader, fighting many battles of good versus evil. One such battle over justice, righteousness, universal harmony, duty, and good versus evil was the long, violent, and bloody Kurukshetra War found within the Bhagavad-Gita. Krishna then fulfills his prophecy and kills the evil King Kamsa, then restoring King Kamsa's father (King Ugrasena) to the throne and once again bringing peace, love, harmony, and tranquility to the land of Mathura and all of India.

Islam, the youngest of the dominant world's religions, states that the mythical Prophet Muhammad and his followers fought and finally conquered Mecca and united the Arabian Peninsula into a government of social organization and civil order, restoring the original monotheistic version of Islam as the religion of the land.

The Hebrew Mashiach Being Anointed King in the End Days

Anointing of kings, queens, pharaohs, the deceased, guests, soldiers, and so on, by pouring or smearing some type of perfumed oil, milk, melted butter, or other substances on the subject, can be found depicted in reliefs inside of several African/Kemetic/Anu temples. Mariette, Dendirah IV 70, depicts the myth of the god Anubis anointing the mummy of Osiris with the goddess Isis giving instructions.

The following is an excerpt from the *Book of Coming Forth by Day: The Papyrus of Ani.*

Description of the Ceremonies of Opening of the Mouth Anointing of the Mummy

> I have anointed thy face with ointment, I have anointed thine eyes. I have painted thine eye with uatch [green ointment] and with mestchem [eye paint]. May no ill-luck happen through the dethronement of his two eyes in his body, even as no evil fortune came to Horus through the overthrow of his eye in his body. Thy two eyes are decked there—within its name Uatch, which maketh thee to give forth fragrance, in its name of Sweet-smelling.

King Tut Anoints His Wife with Perfumed Oil or Water

"The Golden Shrine," a part of the Tutankhamen exhibit at the Egyptian Museum in Cairo, is a small shrine made in the form of the sanctuary within the Temple of Nekhbet mounted on a sledge. (Nekhbet is a mythical predynastic goddess and protector of the kings from infancy till death and the mother of female divine nature.) Every exposed surface of the shrine is covered with scenes, inscriptions, and decorations.

The panels show King (Pharaoh) Tutankhamen and his queen at different moments of relaxation and intimacy. One of the panels shows King Tutankhamen seated while holding lotus flowers in his left hand and anointing the queen by pouring perfumed oil or water from a small vessel with his right hand. The queen is sitting in front of the king in a relaxed position, with her left elbow on his knee, looking up at him while the perfumed oil or water is poured into her right hand, which she holds up to her chin as the two young lovers gaze into each other's eyes.

Judaism has deep roots in African/Kemetic/Anu culture, and the men who wrote the Judaic myths were influenced by African/Kemetic/Anu religious myths.

Exodus 1:1–8

> 1. Now these are the names of the children of Israel, which came into Egypt; every man with his household came with Jacob. 2. Reuben, Simeon, Levi, and Judah, 3. Issachar, Zebulun, and Benjamin, 4. Dan, and Naphtali, Gad, and Asher. 5. And all the souls that came out of the loins of Jacob were seventy souls: for Joseph was in Egypt already. 6. And Joseph died, and all his brethren, and all that generation. 7. And the children of Israel were fruitful, and increased abundantly, and multiplied, and waxed exceeding mighty; and the land was filled with them. 8. Now there arose up a new king over Egypt, which knew not Joseph.

Judaism's Tanakh (Isaiah 11:11–12) cites several geographical locations where, the Lord will set out to recover the remnant of his people that remain on earth. Three of these locations are (northern) Egypt, Pathros (southern Egypt), and Cush (central-southeast Sudan and southwest Ethiopia).

Two of the most sacred religious symbols in Judaism are the Star of David (African/Kemetic/Anu "Star of Creation") and the "Tablets of Stone," "Stone Tablets," or "Tablets of Testimony" (which look exactly like the royal double-plumed crown worn by the religious gods of Africa/Kemet/Anu).

The Thirteen Fundamental Principals of Faith, the widely accepted list of Jewish beliefs, was developed by Maimonides (Rambam, Rabbi Moshe ben Maimon, 1135–1204 CE). Maimonides, a physician, philosopher, and Torah scholar, was born in African/Moorish-ruled Cordoba, Spain; he also lived in the Middle East and North Africa. He was a leader in the Jewish community in Cairo, Egypt.

The name for the Bible of Judaism, the Tanakh, is also spelled Tenakh or Tenak; it is considered the authoritative, valid, and fundamental scriptures of Judaism. The sacred African/Kemetic/Anu symbol for life is called the Ankh. The names of some of the pharaohs include Akhenaton, Sankhkare Mentuhotup III, Akheprure Amenhotep II, Senakhtenre Tao I, and Tefnakhte.

Menkheperre was the first prophet of Amun and a high priest at Thebes, Egypt. Located at Thebes is the Grande Lodge of Wa-Set (or Wo-Se), "The Scepter," called Luxor by the Arabs. The giant complex, the ruins of which still stand today, was an educational, spiritual, and religious site.

Some of the structures located inside of Wa-Set are the Temple of Ipet (called Temple of Luxor by the Arabs); the Great Hypostyle Hall of Karnak; the Temple of Ipet-Isut, the Holiest of Places (called Temple of Karnak by the Arabs); a rectangular-shaped cleansing and baptismal pool; and several Tejens (called obelisks by the Greeks).

Picture the rectangular-shaped reflecting pool near the Washington Monument (and if you are old enough, maybe you can remember Johnny Carson and Ed McMahon on "The Tonight Show" doing the skit "Karnak the Magnificent"). The designer of the Washington Monument and the writers of the Karnak skit had to be aware of the history of the Grande Lodge of Wa-set.

The African/Kemetic/Anu symbol of life, the Ankh, along with the names of the pharaohs, are similar to the words Tanakh, Tenakh, or Tenak. Many scholars say the word Tanakh is an acronym made up from parts of the words Torah (Pentateuch), Nevi'im (Prophets), and K'tuvim (Writing), which are the three main sections of the Tanakh.

That may be so, but Judaism, like all the world's dominant religions, was written by men who were influenced by African/Kemetic/Anu culture.

The words Tanakh, Tenakh, or Tenak could easily be an acronym taken from Tefnakhte, Ankh, Akhen, Sankh, Akhe, Senakh, Menkh, and Karnak. If you remove the "f" and "te" from King Tefnakhte, the two alternate spellings of the Hebrew Bible (Tenakh and Tenak) are identical in sequence to Te_nakh_ _.

Judaism claims that the Mashiach will not be a god, goddess, or celestial being but will be a human descended from King David. This concept is the same as Buddha coming into the world as the newborn baby of Queen Maya and into the royal family of King Shuddhodana, or Heru coming into the earth as a newborn baby of a queen (Isis) and a king (Osiris).

King David might as well have been a mythical god of Judaism. He is the ancestor of Joseph, the stepfather of Jesus; he slayed the giant Goliath; he was a great military leader like Heru (Horus), Krishna, and Muhammad; he became king of Israel; both royalty and lineage are established by tracing ancestry to him, referred to as the "House of David."

King David's name is associated with the spiritual symbol of Judaism, the Star of David, which looks like a star but has much more symbolic meaning. It is referred to in African/Kemetic/Anu myth as the "Star of Creation," two interlaced triangles or pyramids, one pointing to earth, the other pointing to heaven, symbolizing "as above so as below," meaning that our spiritual existence is everlasting.

We come from a heavenly spiritual form to earth manifested in a physical form, and when we die, our eternal spirit leaves our physical form and returns back to a spiritual form (more about this symbol in chapter 6).

Birth-Myth of Moses

Exodus 1:11–14

> 11. Therefore they did set over them taskmasters to afflict them with their burdens. And they built for Pharaoh treasure cities, Pithom and Raamses. 12. But the more they afflicted them, the more they multiplied and grew. And they were grieved because of the children of Israel. 13. And the Egyptians made the children of Israel to serve

with rigour: 14. And they made their lives bitter with hard bondage, in morter, and in brick, and in all manner of service in the field: all their service, wherein they made them serve was with rigour.

Critique: In the birth-myth of Moses, he is born during a difficult and turbulent time for Hebrews. Joseph, a great respected leader in the Hebrew community who was a social, economic, and political force within Egypt, has died. The Hebrew people are being targeted and persecuted for religious, economic, political, and social reasons. They are being beaten, tormented, enslaved, and killed by the evil and wicked pharaoh of Egypt.

Note: The mythical birth of Moses is distinguished from the social, economic, and political persecution of Jewish people, which is a historical fact. Despite debates over the action, it is a fact that between 1984 and 2010, over 100,000 African Jews emigrated out of East Africa into Israel, escaping drought, famine, and religious and social persecution. The persecution and expulsion of Jewish people at the very beginning of the Spanish Inquisition in the late 1400's and early 1500's is a historical fact, and the genocide inflicted on Jewish people at the hands of the Nazis of Germany is another well-known fact.

As mentioned earlier, Moses was born during difficult and turbulent times. In the African/Kemetic/Anu birth-myth of Heru, he was born during chaotic and turbulent times when the earth was being ruled by the evil incarnate Seth.

Krishna of Hinduism was also born during chaotic and turbulent times, when King Kamsa, the evil, demonic, powerful, and cruel tyrant, ruled the land of Mathura in India.

This birth-myth of Moses applies to the religions of Judaism and Christianity, since the first five books of the Hebrew Tanakh, called the Torah, are the same as the first five books of the Christian Bible.

Exodus 1:15–22

15. And the king of Egypt spake to the Hebrew midwives, of which the name of the one was Shiphrah, and the name of the other Puah: 16. And he said, When ye do the office of a midwife to the Hebrew women, and see them upon the stools; if it be a son, then ye shall kill him: but if it be a daughter, then she shall live. 17. But the midwives feared

God, and did not as the king of Egypt commanded them, but saved the men children alive. 18. And the king of Egypt called for the midwives, and said unto them, Why have ye done this thing, and have saved the men children alive? 19. And the midwives said to Pharaoh, Because the Hebrew women are not as the Egyptian women; for they are lively, and are delivered ere the midwives come in unto them. 20. Therefore God dealt well with the midwives: and the people multiplied, and waxed very mighty. 21. And it came to pass, because the midwives feared God, that he made them houses. 22. And Pharaoh charged all his people, saying, Every son that is born ye shall cast into the river, and every daughter ye shall save alive.

Critique: In this birth-myth, we find a king trying to kill all the male-born children. He is concerned that his kingdom is in jeopardy because the persecuted Hebrew men might join and fight with the enemy against Egypt. (Exodus 1:10: "Come, let us deal wisely with them, lest they multiply, and it come to pass, that, when there befalleth us any way war, they also join themselves unto our enemies, and fight against us, and so get them up out of the land.")

In the African/Kemetic/Anu birth-myth of Heru, once the evil Seth finds out the goddess Isis is pregnant with a male child, he plans to kill her baby. In the birth-myth of Krishna, before Krishna is born, a voice came from the sky during the wedding of Devaki and Vasudeva and announced to all that their eighth child would kill King Kamsa and restore peace, love, and harmony to India. King Kamsa finds out and proceeds to kill the first six babies born to Devaki and Vasudeva, with plans on killing the seventh and final prophesized eighth newborn. The seventh newborn named Balarama was taken to safety in the far away city of Gokula. After the prophesized birth of Krishna, King Kamsa ordered his soldiers to kill all the newborn babies they found, and to search for and kill the prophesized eighth newborn child of Vasudeva and Devaki.

Exodus 2:1–2

1. And there went a man of the house of Levi, and took to wife a daughter of Levi. 2. And the woman conceived, and bare a son: and when she saw him that he was a goodly child, she hid him three months.

Critique: Moses at birth is protected by his mother and hidden for three months because of the decree of the king that all the Hebrew male children at birth are to be thrown into the river and killed (Exodus 1:22). In the African/Kemetic/Anu birth-myth of Heru (Horus), his mother, the goddess Isis, hides him in the Nile Delta marshlands at birth to protect him from the evil ruler Seth, who is looking for the newborn Heru to kill him.

In the birth-myth of Krishna, the parents of Krishna are locked up in a prison so that King Kamsa can kill the eighth child when he is born. Once Krishna is born, a voice from the sky tells Vasudeva to take the newborn child to the city of Gokula and hide him for safety and protection. The voice puts the guards into a deep sleep, releases the chains, and opens the doors to allow the father and child to escape to safety.

Exodus 2:3–10

> 3. And when she could not longer hide him, she took for him an ark of bulrushes, and daubed it with slime and with pitch, and put the child therein; and she laid it in the flags by the river's brink. 4. And his sister stood afar off, to wit what would be done to him. 5. And the daughter of Pharaoh came down to wash herself at the river; and her maidens walked along by the river's side; and when she saw the ark among the flags, she sent her maid to fetch it. 6. And when she opened it, she saw the child: and, behold, the babe wept. And she had compassion on him, and said, This is one of the Hebrews' children. 7. Then said his sister to Pharaoh's daughter, Shall I go and call to thee a nurse of the Hebrew women, that she may nurse the child for thee? 8. And Pharaoh's daughter said to her, Go. And the maid went and called the child's mother. 9. And Pharaoh's daughter said unto her, Take this child away, and nurse it for me, and I will give thee thy wages. And the women took the child, and nursed it. 10. And the child grew, and she brought him unto Pharaoh's daughter, and he became her son. And she called his name Moses: and she said, Because I drew him out of the water.

Critique: Moses is placed in a small ark and placed in the flags by the river's edge for his own protection. (Note: the likely river in the geographical region of this myth is the Nile River in Egypt.) Moses is found and eventually raised by his foster mother, the pharaoh's daughter.

At birth Krishna is taken to the city of Gokula for protection from being killed, where he is raised by his foster parents, Nanda and Yashoda.

In the birth-myth of Buddha, seven days after he is born, his mother dies and he is raised by his foster mother and aunt, Queen Pajapati.

The Ten Commandments of Judaism and Christianity

Half of the Ten Commandments (6 through 10, with one containing slavery guidelines) are African/Kemetic/Anu negative confessions (have not's) and are taken right out of the well-known African/Kemetic/Anu Declarations of Innocence/Negative Confessions, found in the Papyrus of Nu and Ani, *Book of Coming Forth by Day.*

Four of the other commandments (1, 2, 3, and 5) are just a reworking of the numerous Declarations of Innocence, negative (have not's) and positive (do's or have done) and writings from scriptures like the Papyrus of Sutimes. The 4th Commandment is unique, referring to the Sabbath day being holy, and is yet another guideline for how slave owners should treat their slaves.

The myth of these Ten Commandments is that they are supposed to be the direct word of God given to Moses and the Hebrew people.

Ten Commandments: Exodus 20:3–17

1. Thou shalt have no other gods before me.

2. Thou shalt not make unto thee any graven image, or any likeness of anything that is in heaven above, or that is in the earth beneath, or that is in the water under the earth: Thou shalt not bow down thyself to them, nor serve them: for I the Lord thy God am a jealous God, visiting the iniquity of the fathers upon the children unto the third and fourth generation of them that hate me; And shewing mercy unto thousands of them that love me, and keep my commandments.

3. Thou shalt not take the name of the lord thy God in vain; for the lord will not hold him guiltless that taketh his name in vain.

4. Remember the Sabbath day, to keep it holy. Six days shalt thou labour, and do all thy work: but the seventh day is the Sabbath of the

lord thy God: in it thou shalt not do any work, thou nor thy son, nor thy daughter, thy manservant, nor thy maidservant, nor thy cattle, nor thy stranger that is within the gates: for in six days the lord made heaven and earth, the sea, and all that in them is, and rested the seventh day: wherefore the lord blessed the Sabbath day, and hallowed it.

5. Honour thy father and thy mother. That thy days may be long upon the land which the lord thy God giveth thee.

6. Thou shalt not kill.

7. Thou shalt not commit adultery.

8. Thou shalt not steal.

9. Thou shalt not bear false witness against thy neighbor.

10. Thou shalt not covet thy neighbor's house; thou shalt not covet thy neighbor's wife, or his manservant, or his maidservant, or his ox, or his ass, or anything that is thy neighbor's.

Critique: Earlier in the book, I covered the subject of the instructional and operational guidelines for slavery found in the Bibles of Judaism and Christianity. In the 4th and 10th Commandments, we again see rules laid out by the mythical God of Judaism and Christianity regarding slaves, referring to them as manservant or a maidservant.

There are so many Declarations of Innocence, Negative and Positive Confessions found within the *Book of Coming Forth by Day* that I have compiled a list of declarations found in several chapters of the book.

The use of negative and positive confessions and writing style are similar, while some are almost word for word the same as the Ten Commandments, as well as the Hebrew (not Christian) 613 Mitzvot: 248 Positive commandments and 365 Negative commandments contained in the Hebrew Torah, specified by Maimonides. The Ten Commandments (worded differently) are found within the broader commandments of the Hebrew Mitzvot.

Compilation of Negative and Positive Confessions found within the *Book of Coming Forth by Day.*

Note: The Papyrus of Nu and Papyrus of Ani are also referred to as the *Book of Coming Forth by Day.*

Declarations of Innocence/Negative Confessions
Papyrus of Ani

1. I have not committed sin. 2. I have not committed robbery with violence. 3. I have not stolen. 4. I have not slain men and women. 5. I have not slain the cattle belonging to the gods. 6. I have not snatched away the bread of a child, nor treated with contempt the god of my city. 7. I have not cursed god. 8. I have not stolen the bread of the gods. 9. I have not blasphemed. 10. I have not shut my ears to the words of truth. 11. I am not a man of violence. 12. I have not debauched the wife of any man. 13. I have not polluted myself. 14. I have terrorized none. 15. I have not committed adultery; I have not lain with men. 16. I have not stolen cultivated land. 17. I have not stolen grain. 18. I have not purloined (stolen in violation of trust) offerings. 19. I have not stolen any property of god. 20. I have not been a stirrer up of strife. 21. I am not a man of deceit. 22. I have slandered no man. 23. I have not uttered lies. 24. I have made none to weep. 25. I have not transgressed the law. 26. I have not acted or judged with undue haste. 27. I have never raised my voice spoken arrogantly, or in anger. 28. I have not acted with arrogance.

Papyrus of Nu
The Introduction of Maat

1. I have not defrauded the humble man of his property. 2. I have not committed sins against men. 3. I have not acted fraudulently or deceitfully in the seat of truth. 4. I have not wrought evil. 5. I have not attempted to direct servants. 6. I have not vilified a slave to his master. 7. I have not belittled god. 8. I have not plundered the offerings in the temples. 9. I have not inflicted pain. 10. I have not committed murder. 11. I have not given the order to commit murder. 12. I have not caused calamities to befall men and women. 13. I have not committed fornication or had intercourse with men. 14. I have not masturbated in

124

the sanctuaries of the god of my city. 15. I have not filched land from my neighbor's estate and added it to my own acre. 16. I have not encroached upon the fields of others. 17. I have not opposed my family and kinsfolk. 18. I have not turned back the god [or god] at his appearances. 19. I have not [belittled god] or thought scorn of god. 20. I have not brought forth my name for exaltation.

Critique: Several of these negative confessions state what some mythical African/Kemetic/Anu god thinks is the correct sexual orientation. Found within the Papyrus of Nebseni is another anti-LGBT Negative Confession which states: "I have not committed acts of sexual impurity, or lain with men." This judgmental and discriminatory projection of anti-LGBT sexual beliefs is similar to writings found within Judaism, Christianity, and Islam.

Positive Confessions

The Chapter of Changing into a Swallow: The Chapters of Making Transformations
Papyrus of Ani

> 1. I am purified at the Great Uart [the meaning of this phrase is unclear; it may mean: a place of washing or cleansing, or separating sin from the soul]. 2. I have done away with my wickedness. 3. I have put away utterly all my offenses of sins. 4. I have put away utterly all the taints of evil which appear tainted to me upon the earth. 5. I have purified myself. 6. I have made myself to be like a god. 7. I have come forth by day. 8. I have gained the mastery over my footsteps.

Chapter of Making the Transformation into a Divine Hawk
Papyrus of Ani

> 1. I have labored, I have made myself perfect. 2. I come forth daily into the house of the Twin Lion-gods [yesterday and today]. 3. I come forth therefrom into the House of Isis. 4. I look upon the holy things which are hidden. 5.

I have risen up like the divine hawk. 6. I make them to know concerning his victories. 7. I have stablished their fortresses for Osiris. 8. I have prepared the ways for him. 9. I have performed the things which he hath commanded. 10. I have forced a way through the Tuat [Otherworld]. 11. I have opened the roads which appertain to heaven, and those which appertain to the earth. 12. I have exalted thy face, O Lord of Eternity.

Address to the Gods of the Tuat/ Positive Confessions
Papyrus of Nu

1. I have performed the ordinances of men, and the things which gratify the gods. 2. I have propitiated the god by doing his will; I have given bread to the hungry man and water to him that was athirst and apparel to the naked man. 3. I have made propitiatory offerings and given cakes to the gods, and the things which appear at the word to the Spirits. 4. I am pure in respect of my mouth, and I am clean in respect of my hands. 5. My breast is purified by libations. 6. I have washed myself clean in the Lake of the South.

Negative Confessions

1. I have not committed sin. 2. I have done no act of deceit. 3. I have done no evil thing. 4. I have not borne false witness.

Critique: The 1st Commandment states, "Thou shalt have no other gods before me." The 2nd Commandment states, "Thou shalt not make unto thee any graven image, or any likeness of anything that is in heaven above…. Thou shalt not bow down thyself to them, nor serve them: for I the Lord thy God am a jealous God, visiting the iniquity of the fathers upon the children….And shewing mercy unto thousands of them that love me, and keep my commandments."

These commandments are about appeasement, placation, devotion, and conciliation. They are about exalting, glorifying, lauding, and satisfying the vindictive, egotistical, and pseudorighteousness of a mythical God in order to avoid punishment and attain a reward (mercy) from that God. The following excerpt is from the Papyrus of Sutimes and contains similarities to the 1st and 2nd Commandments.

Excerpt from the Papyrus of Sutimes

> Homage to thee, O thou Holy God, thou mighty and beneficent being, thou Prince of Eternity … peoples and nations exalt thee, and the awe of thy terror is in the hearts of men, and Spirit-souls and the dead … Thou settest the visible emblems [image] of thyself in Anu, and the majesty of thy transformations in the holy place.

Critique: The 3rd Commandment states, "Thou shalt not take the name of the lord thy God in vain; for the lord will not hold him guiltless that taketh his name in vain." Found within the Papyrus of Ani and Papyrus of Nu: "I have not [belittled god] or thought scorn of god"; "I have not cursed god"; "I have not snatched away the bread of a child, nor treated with contempt the god of my city"; "I have not stolen the bread of the gods"; "I have not stolen any property of god"; "I have not plundered the offerings in the temples"; "I have not blasphemed"; "I have not turned back the god [or god] at his appearances"; "I have not acted with arrogance"; "I have not brought forth my name for exaltation."

The 5th Commandment states, "Honor thy father and mother. That thy days may be long upon the land which the lord thy God giveth thee." Found within the Papyrus of Nu and Papyrus of Nebseni (Sheet 17) respectively: "I have not opposed my family and kinsfolk." Papyrus of Nebseni (Sheet 17): "I have seen the Osiris [my father]"; "I have saluted my mother or gazed upon my mother."

The 6th Commandment states, "Thou shalt not kill." Found within the Papyrus of Ani and Papyrus of Nu: "I have not slain men and women"; "I have not committed murder"; "I have not given the order to commit murder"; "I am not a man of violence"; "I have not slain the cattle belonging to the gods."

The 7th Commandment states, "Thou shalt not commit adultery." Found within the Papyrus of Ani and Papyrus of Nu: "I have not committed adultery; I have not lain with men"; "I have not committed fornication or had intercourse with men"; "I have not debauched the wife of any man."

The 8th Commandment states, "Thou shalt not steal." Found within the Papyrus of Ani and Papyrus of Nu: "I have not committed robbery with violence"; "I have not stolen"; "I have not stolen grain"; "I have not stolen cultivated land"; "I have not plundered the offerings in the temples"; "I have not filched land from my neighbor's estate and added it to my own acre"; "I have not encroached upon the fields of others."

The 9th Commandment states, "Thou shalt not bear false witness against thy neighbor." Found within the Papyrus of Ani and Papyrus of Nu: "I have not borne false witness"; "I am not a man of deceit"; "I have slandered no man"; "I have not uttered lies"; "I have not acted or judged with undue haste"; "I have not vilified a slave to his master."

The 10th Commandment states, "Thou shalt not covet thy neighbor's house; thou shalt not covet thy neighbor's wife, or his manservant, or his maidservant, or his ox, or his ass, or anything that is thy neighbor's." Found within the Papyrus of Ani and Papyrus of Nu: "I have not filched land from my neighbor's estate and added it to my own acre"; "I have not encroached upon the fields of others"; "I have not debauched the wife of any man"; "I have not attempted to direct servants"; "I have not defrauded the humble man of his property."

The 4th Commandment is unique—"Remember the Sabbath day, to keep it holy." However, it contains more details about the treatment of slaves. Rest your manservant (male slave), maidservant (female slave), stranger (another slave), and cattle on the "Holy Sabbath Day," and then you can go back to working your slaves like cattle, twelve to fourteen hours a day, beginning Sunday and continuing through Friday.

As stated before, these man-made religions are in no credible position to make moral value judgments about the LGBT community. Slavery has ended (or has it?), but this type of immoral writing is still present throughout the scriptures of Judaism, Islam, and Christianity.

Birth-Myth of Jesus of Christianity
Matthew 1:18, 20–21, and 23–25

> 18. Now the birth of Jesus Christ was on this wise: When as his mother Mary was espoused to Joseph, before they came together, she was found with child of the Holy Ghost.... 20. But while he thought on these things, be-hold, the angel of the LORD appeared unto him in a dream, saying, Joseph, thou son of David, fear not to take

unto thee Mary thy wife: for that which is conceived in her is of the Holy Ghost. 21. And she shall bring forth a son, and thou shalt call his name JESUS: for he shall save his people from their sins.… 23. Behold, a virgin shall be with child, and shall bring forth a son, and they shall call his name Emmanuel, which being interpreted is, God with us. 24. Then Joseph being raised from sleep did as the angel of the Lord had bidden him, and took unto him his wife: 25. And knew her not till she had brought forth her firstborn son: and he called his name JESUS.

Matthew 2:13–16

13. And when they were departed, behold, the angel of the Lord appeareth to Joseph in a dream, saying, Arise, and take the young child and his mother, and flee into Egypt, and be thou there until I bring thee word: for Herod will seek the young child to destroy him. 14. When he arose, he took the young child and his mother by night, and departed into Egypt: 15. And was there until the death of Herod: that it might be fulfilled which was spoken of the Lord by the prophet, saying, Out of Egypt have I called my son. 16. Then Herod, when he saw that he was mocked of the wise men, was exceeding wroth, and sent forth, and slew all the children that were in Bethlehem, and in all the coasts thereof, from two years old and under, according to the time which he had diligently inquired of the wise men.

Luke 1:30–31 and 35–37

30. And the angel said unto her, Fear not, Mary: for thou hast found favour with God. 31. And, behold, thou shalt conceive in thy womb, and bring forth a son, and shalt call his name JESUS.… 35. And the angel answered and said unto her, The Holy Ghost shall come upon thee, and the power of the Highest shall overshadow thee: therefore also that holy thing which shall be born of thee shall be called the Son of God. 36. And, behold, thy cousin Elisabeth,

she hath also conceived a son in her old age: and this is the sixth month with her, who was called barren. 37. For with God nothing shall be impossible.

Luke 2:6–7

6. And so it was, that, while they were there, the days were accomplished that she should be delivered. 7. And she brought forth her firstborn son, and wrapped him in swaddling clothes, and laid him in a manger; because there was no room for them in the inn.

Critique: We again find in the birth-myth of Jesus similarities to other birth-myths that are older than Christianity. There is an announcement by an angel of the impending birth of a divine Son of God. This announcement is made to Joseph in the form of a dream in Matthew 1:20-21.

An angel announces to Mary, who is favored by God, in Luke 1:30, "Thou hast found favour with God." Also in Luke 1:11-25, an angel announces to Zacharias that his wife Elisabeth, the cousin of Mary, who is old and barren, will also conceive of a child from God (John the Baptist).

In the African/Kemetic/Anu Annunciation, Conception, Birth, and Adoration of the Child, the first vignette depicts the mythical god Tehuti, the heart, mind, and tongue of the creator, announcing to the royal mother the impending birth of her son, descended from the creator god Amun (Amen).

In the birth-myth of Buddha, the celestial being Buddha decides to enter the womb of Queen Maya in the form of an elephant. Queen Maya is chosen by Buddha after consultation with the celestial gods, monks, and Bodhisattvas because she possesses the strength of ten thousand elephants. She is favored because she is perfect in her beauty and chastity. Queen Maya has a dream of a white elephant (symbolic of fertility and wisdom), a sign that she would give birth to a great leader.

In the birth-myth of Krishna of Hinduism, before he was born, a voice from heaven during the wedding of Devaki and Vasudeva announces to all that their eighth child would kill King Kamsa and restore peace, love, and harmony to India.

In the birth-myths of Jesus and John the Baptist, Mary and Elisabeth are impregnated by God, with Jesus being referred to as the "Son of God."

In the African/Kemetic/Anu birth-myth of Osiris, Nut, the sky goddess, is impregnated by the earth god Geb. In the birth-myth of Heru, the goddess Isis is impregnated through magic by the essence of a fashioned phallus of the deceased god Osiris.

In the Annunciation, Conception, Birth, and Adoration of the Child, the second vignette depicts the creator god Khnum (or Kneph) and the goddess Isis (or Hathor) holding the ankh, the symbol of life, up to the mouth of the royal mother, indicating that she is conceiving a son descended from the creator god Amun (Amen).

In the birth-myth of Krishna of Hinduism, the god Vishnu grows inside the womb of Devaki and is born as a god in human form, manifested as Krishna. In the birth-myth of Buddha, he enters the womb of Queen Maya in the form of a white elephant (symbol of fertility and wisdom) with the assistance of the gods. To avoid contamination, the gods placed Buddha in a jeweled box for protection while inside his mother's womb.

Jesus was born in an unusual place: a manger, because his parents were told there was no room in the inn. Heru was born in the Nile Delta marshlands. Krishna was born in a prison cell. Buddha was born in a garden under a sala tree.

Jesus was born during chaotic times, when the evil King Herod ruled. In the African/Kemetic/Anu birth-myth, Heru was born during chaotic times, when the evil Seth ruled the earth. Krishna was also born during chaotic times, when the evil King Kamsa ruled India.

Buddha's birth came about because something was happening on earth that required the intervention of celestial spirits. The gods implored Buddha to go down to earth and reveal the teachings of the Vaipulya Sutras for the blessings and salvation of the world.

Jesus was born to save his people from their sins (Matthew 1:21). He was prophesized to be conceived "in thy womb, and bring forth a son, and shalt call his name Jesus. He shall be great, and shall be called the son of the highest: and the Lord God shall give unto him the throne of his father David: And he shall reign over the house of Jacob for ever; and of his kingdom there shall be no end" (Luke 1:31–33).

Heru (Horus) was born and hailed as the avenger of his father, Osiris, who was murdered by the evil Seth. He retook the throne as ruler of earth, with the ever present threat of the evil Seth looming. Krishna was born with the prophecy of killing the evil King Kamsa. He eventually fulfilled the prophecy and restored the father of King Kamsa (King Ugrasena) to the throne, who had been overthrown and jailed by his evil son.

In the birth-myth of Jesus, Joseph, the stepfather of Jesus, had a dream where an angel tells him to take the newborn Jesus and his mother into Egypt and hide because King Herod sought to destroy the young child.

In the birth-myth of Krishna, King Kamsa planned to kill the newborn Krishna. A voice from heaven told the father, Vasudeva, to take the newborn Krishna to Gokula and hide him for safety.

In the African/Kemetic/Anu birth-myth of Heru, when the evil ruler of earth Seth finds out that Isis is pregnant with the child of Osiris, he wants to kill the infant. For the protection of the unborn child, Isis flees to the Nile Delta marshlands to give birth to Heru (Horus) and hide the newborn from Seth.

The myth of Jesus is similar to the myths of Krishna and Buddha because he is raised by someone who is not his biological parent. In the birth-myth of Jesus, he was raised by his stepfather Joseph. In the birth-myth of Krishna, he is raised in the city of Gokula by his foster parents, Nanda and Yashoda. In the birth-myth of Buddha, seven days after giving birth to Buddha, Queen Maya died and the newborn child was raised by his foster mother and aunt, Queen Pajapati.

Final Critique: All of the characters mentioned in this chapter, whether they are the son of God, divine savior, enlightened one, a god manifested on earth in human form, a charismatic leader descended from royalty, or a prophet, have similar attributes, and there are many common concepts connected to their myths.

The attributes and concepts are devotion; punishment; forgiveness; compassion; salvation; truth; morality; judgment; heroism; messianism; birth, death, and rebirth; resurrection; reincarnation; eternity; everlastingness; and enlightenment. The birth of these characters bring to earth hope, goodness, peace, love, harmony, and tranquility.

Growing up, I was told many times in Sunday school that Jesus spoke in the crib as an infant. However, there is no mention of Jesus speaking in the crib in the Christian Bible. Found within the birth-myth of Isa, the Islamic version of Jesus, are writings of him speaking as a newborn.

This is similar to the birth-myth of Buddha, who spoke as a newborn infant. Sura 19:24–33: "Then the child called out to her from beneath her: Grieve not; surely your Lord has made a stream to flow beneath you. And shake towards you the trunk of the palm tree; it will drop on you fresh ripe dates.… But she pointed to him. They said: How should we speak to one who was a child in the cradle? He said: Surely I am a servant of Allah; He has given me the book and made me a prophet. And he has made me blessed wherever I may be, and he has enjoined on me prayer and poor-rate so long as I live. And dutiful to my mother, and he has not made me insolent, unblessed. And peace on me the day I was born and on the day I die, and on the day I am raised to life."

At birth, the newborn Buddha stood up and began to walk, taking seven steps; as he did, lotus flowers appeared at each step. On the seventh step he stopped and said, "I am the chief of the world, eldest am I in the world. Foremost am I in the world. This is the last birth. There is now no more coming to be."

Within the birth-myths described in this chapter are similar emotional reactions to the birth of these divine babies. Luke 1:39–58: When Elisabeth, the cousin of Mary, finds out she is pregnant, Mary comes to visit her and gives salutation. When Elisabeth gives birth to John the Baptist, her friends rejoice with her. When Jesus is born, the shepherds glorify and praise the birth.

In the final vignette of the African/Kemetic/Anu birth-myth, the Annunciation, Conception, Birth, and Adoration of the Child, we find the gods praising and giving adoration to the newborn child of the royal mother.

In the birth-myth of Buddha, symbolic lotus flowers are mentioned. In Buddhism, the lotus flower symbolizes enlightenment and purity. After his birth, Buddha takes seven steps, and after each step lotus flowers appear. He is born an exalted being and a great spirit. Once the newborn and his mother return home, there is a celebration throughout the entire kingdom.

In the birth-myth of Krishna of Hinduism, Vishnu grows inside the womb of Devaki and is born a god in human form, manifested as Krishna. The birth of Krishna was accompanied by celebration among the gods. Heavy rains, lightning, and thunder accompanied the birth (and some myths say the rivers overflowed with joy).

In the African/Kemetic/Anu birth-myth of Heru, he is hailed as the coming avenger of the murder of his father, Osiris, who would retake the throne from his evil uncle, Seth.

The mythical divine saviors, sons of god, enlightened one, or prophets in this chapter all come to earth with a purpose: to save the earth from its sins; to provide a pathway for everlastingness, salvation, and eternity; to bring enlightenment, blessings and salvation to the world; to save the earth from the clutches of evil and brutal rulers; or to restore civil order, social organization, and monotheism.

At birth, these characters were praised, adored, and saluted; they were celebrated and exalted; they were born to the delight of the gods, to celestial music, or events and extreme weather conditions like lightning, thunder, rain, and flooding.

In the end, they all have in common the same redeeming qualities associated with their myths: justice, morality, peace, love, harmony, compassion, and tranquility.

Chapter 5

Other Similar Myths

One can find many myths within the scriptures of the world's dominant religions that are very similar to African/Kemetic/Anu myths. These include judgment day myths, the destruction of mankind, the concept of a holy trinity, and fratricide (the killing of a brother).

Judgment Day Myths

The myth of a day of judgment, where souls stand before god and the angels to be judged and a decision is rendered whether that soul goes to heaven or hell, is one of the oldest and most well-known religious myths.

I will critique the judgment day myth of Christianity, which is similar in concept to a Judgment Day myth in several dominant world religions; where a God or messiah comes to judge souls, and then the souls go to a fiery hell (a dark, foreboding place); wander aimlessly in despair; are endlessly recycled; go to heaven (a land of paradise); or rest in peace as one with the universe.

I will also critique for criticism certain African/Kemetic/Anu religious texts for similarities to the judgment day myth of Christianity. The order of the topics covered in this section on Judgment Day myths will be Judgment Day; concept of a god being a shepherd and stewarding souls to heaven; concept of fire and hell; and standing beside god in heaven.

Judgment Day Myth
Revelation 20:11–15

> 11. And I saw a great white throne, and him that sat on it, from whose face the earth and the heaven fled away;

and there was found no place for them. 12. And I saw the dead, small and great, stand before God; and the books were opened: and another book was opened, which is the book of life: and the dead were judged out of those things which were written in the books, according to their works. 13. And the sea gave up the dead which were in it; and death and hell delivered up the dead which were in them: and they were judged every man according to their works. 14. And death and hell were cast into the lake of fire. This is the second death. 15. And whosoever was not found written in the book of life was cast into the lake of fire.

Matthew 25:33–34

33. And he shall set the sheep on his right hand, but the goats on the left. 34. Then shall the King say unto them on his right hand, Come, ye blessed of my Father, inherit the kingdom prepared for you from the foundation of the world:

Matthew 25:41 and 46

41. Then shall he say also unto them on the left hand, Depart from me, ye cursed, into everlasting fire, prepared for the devil and his angels:… 46. And these shall go away into everlasting punishment: but the righteous into life eternal.

Critique: The belief in an afterlife and a judgment day can be found in the writings of the oldest African/Kemetic/Anu religious texts, known as the pyramid texts and coffin texts. The first artistic depictions of Osiris and a Judgment Scene date from between 1600-1250 BCE and can be found in the Papyrus of Nebseni, Papyrus of Nu, Papyrus of Iuau, Papyrus of Hunefer, and the Papyrus of Ani.

The African/Kemetic/Anu myth of Osiris on judgment day, sitting on his throne in the Hall of Judgment, where the deceased appears before the Company of Gods to have his or her soul weighed on the Scale of Truth or Justice, is depicted in great detail in the Papyrus of Hunefer and the

Papyrus of Ani (which I will summarize). The African/Kemetic/Anu myths are similar to the Christian judgment day.

The Judgment Scene of Ani

The Judgment Scene from the Papyrus of Ani depicts Ani, who is deceased but in human form, being followed by his wife, who is holding an ankh, the symbol of life, in her right hand as they enter the Hall of Judgment.

Osiris, the Lord of the Underworld (where departed souls go on their path to heaven or to be devoured/hell), sits on his throne, which is inside a shrine at the other end of the hall. Once the deceased souls reach Osiris, they have been deemed worthy of going into heaven.

Osiris is holding three items: a flail, a scepter, and a shepherd's crook. The flail and crook are shepherd's tools and symbolize Osiris shepherding, protecting and leading souls to heaven; the scepter represents power, dominion, and royal authority.

His color is green (after the evergreen tree), the symbolic color of everlastingness and eternity. He is wearing the distinctive African/Kemetic/Anu predynastic Atef crown. The feathers of the Atef crown symbolize truth, justice, morality, and balance. He is wrapped like a mummy, with his hands and head exposed. Hanging down from his chin is a long braided punt beard, another symbol of a predynastic mythical god.

Standing behind Osiris on the throne are Isis, his wife, and Nephthys, their sister. They are reaching out with their hands, holding the arms of Osiris and supporting him.

In front of Osiris, the four sons of Heru are standing on top of a lotus plant. They are wrapped like mummies, each with a different type of head. The four sons represent the canopic jars, which contained the organs of the deceased Osiris and accompanied him into the afterlife. They also represent the cardinal points. Their names are Imsety/Human (South), Hapy/Baboon (North), Duamutef/Jackal (East), and Qebehsenuef/Falcon (West). As mentioned earlier in chapter four, the blue and white lotus flowers are day blooming and night blooming flowers, respectively, and represent birth, death, and rebirth.

On top of the shrine of Osiris, one can find the head of a hawk or falcon, representing Heru, the divine child of Isis and Osiris. The falcon or hawk head sits between twelve cobra snakes, six on each side.

Remember, animals in African/Kemetic/Anu culture are not wor-shipped but represent attributes and characteristics of the gods and goddesses. The cobra looks like any other snake on the ground, but when it is disturbed or feels threatened, it can rise up on the forward portion of its body and flatten its neck, which looks like a hood.

The hawk and falcon are birds of prey; they hunt various types of prey, including other birds that they can catch in the air. The cobra, hawk, and falcon on top of the shrine symbolize ascension or rising up into heaven, royal power and protection. (Note: the hawk, falcon, and cobra as mentioned in chapter 2, are also the symbols of the solar creator god Ra. The hawk or falcon, and cobra on top of the shrine could also represent Ra, with the same symbolic meaning of ascension or rising up into heaven, royal power and protection.)

Once inside the Hall of Judgment, we find the "Company of Gods" sitting in a row of chairs. These twelve gods and goddesses were selected because they were popular, revered, ancient, and predynastic. They oversee the weighing of the heart or deeds of the deceased against the "Feather of Truth" on the "Scale of Truth or Justice."

The gods and goddesses all hold scepters, the symbol of power, dominion, and royal authority; they are the gods Sa (Sia) and Hu sitting together; the goddess Hathor; the god Heru; the goddesses Isis and Nephthys sitting together; the goddess Nut; the god Geb; the goddess Tefnut; the god Shu; the god Atum; and the god Ra-Harmachis (Ra manifested as Horus, called "Horus of the Horizon").

Below the Company of Gods is the Scale of Truth or Justice. It is two beams resembling a balancing scale; the heart or deeds of the deceased are placed on the left scale, and the Feather of Truth is placed on the right scale. The scale is balanced in the middle by "The Tongue of the Balance."

The tongue is symbolic of the Declarations of Innocence/Negative Confessions ("I have not stolen," "I have not committed sin," etc.) that the deceased must proclaim when entering the Hall of Judgment and standing before the Company of Gods and Osiris.

The white Feather of Truth is the artistic symbol of Maat, the African/Kemetic/Anu goddess of truth and justice. The Hall of Judgment is also referred to as "The Hall of Maat."

Some Egyptologists and scholars claim that the name "Maat" means "truth." She also represented the primal laws of the universe that supported creation and prevented it from falling into chaos. In this capacity, Maat represented balance and harmony. She was worshipped and revered by the pharaohs, who believed they had to uphold her laws of truth, justice, balance, and harmony. Some scholars believe the myth of the Feather of Truth is derived from the feathers in the Atef crown of Osiris, which represent truth, justice, morality, and balance.

The Scale of Truth or Justice is operated by the African/Kemetic/ Anu god Anubis, who can be seen kneeling down at the scale, testing the "Tongue of the Balance" to make sure that the top beam is horizontal. Anubis is depicted as a black-headed jackal with the body of a man. He is associated with mummification and assisting the dead on their way through the Underworld.

The jackal is an opportunistic animal that will eat both animals they have killed and vegetation; they will also eat carrion. They will pick over the remains left by large predators like lions and will bury as much meat as they can if they see other predators like hyenas coming.

Anubis is represented by a jackal because it symbolizes working with dead, decaying bodies while in the process of mummification, burial, and differentiating between good and bad at the Scale of Truth or Justice. His head is black because black symbolizes death and the darkness of the Underworld.

Some scholars say the myth of Anubis predates that of Osiris. Anubis is the son of Nephthys, the sister of Isis. His father was either Seth or Ra (a later myth has Osiris as his father). Anubis is associated with Osiris and was ruler of the Underworld before him. His myth is similar to the Christian myth of John the Baptist, who was the second cousin of Jesus and came before Jesus. I will examine this similar myth later in the chapter.

On the left side of the Scale of Truth or Justice are the goddesses of birth, Renenet and Khenet. Also on the left is the soul of Ani, represented as a bird with the head of Ani; the embryo of Ani, represented as a sarcophagus with the head of Ani; and Ani in human form, representing his destiny, standing before Anubis, awaiting the decision of the weighing of his heart or deeds.

On the right of the Scale of Truth or Justice stands the god Tehuti, who is depicted in African/Kemetic/Anu art as a man with the head of an ibis bird. The beak of the ibis was associated with a writing pen. Tehuti (Thoth) was considered the heart, mind, and tongue of the creator. He is also considered a writer, so we find him in the Judgment Scene recording the result.

Behind Tehuti sits the "Devourer of the Unjustified." This animal is depicted as having the head of a crocodile and the body of a hippopotamus. These two animals were selected because the hippopotamus is the dominant animal in the rivers, with the crocodile being second in line. People fear the predator crocodile with just cause, but the hippopotamus, a vegetarian (like the elephant and rhinoceros, two of Africa's other large animals), kills more people each year because of feeling threatened, defending territory, or defending newborns.

A hippopotamus, with its long and large teeth, can bite a crocodile in half, and any human being attacked by a hippo usually dies or is badly mangled. The Devourer has the head of the crocodile, because it devours the soul if it is found to be unjustified, and the body of the hippopotamus, because it rules the Underworld, where the unjustified souls are sent.

Once the heart or deeds and Declaration of Innocence/Negative Confessions are weighed against the Feather of Truth of Maat, a decision is made by the Company of Gods as to the fate of the deceased soul. If the Scale of Truth or Justice balances in favor of the deceased, then the Company of Gods justifies the soul and the deceased soul is passed on to Osiris, where it will remain for eternity with the gods and goddesses. If the Scale of Truth or Justice balances against the deceased, then the Company of Gods finds the soul to be unjustified, and it is devoured.

Ani's soul was found to be justified; in the Judgment Scene of Ani, he is depicted being led to the throne and shrine of Osiris by Heru, who presents him to Osiris.

Ani then kneels down and places offerings before the shrine and throne of Osiris, who accepts the offerings and welcomes Ani into everlastingness and a place with the gods and goddesses.

This myth is similar to many courtrooms in the United States and in some countries around the world. There are twelve members of the "Company of Gods" who sit in judgment, similar to the number of jurors in most US courtrooms.

Ani is similar to a defendant in a legal proceeding; Maat's Feather of Truth and the Scale of Truth or Justice is the origin of the symbol of the legal system in the United States: a woman holding a scale.

Tehuti is similar to a court reporter; Anubis weighs the deeds of the deceased against the Feather of Truth (for innocence), similar to a defense attorney; The Feather of Truth of Maat or Osiris is like a prosecutor who tests a defendant's declaration of innocence.

Heru is similar to an attorney as he presents Ani to Osiris; when the deceased soul is found justified by the Company of Gods, it is similar to an acquittal by a jury; when it is found unjustified, it is similar to a conviction and being sent to jail (or for capital crimes, being given the death penalty).

Osiris sitting on his throne is similar to a judge presiding over a courtroom, sitting in a chair up above the other characters in the courtroom; Isis and Nephthys who found, protected and resurrected Osiris are standing behind Osiris on his throne, reaching out with their hands holding his arms and supporting him. They are similar to bailiffs (court officers who protect, support, and provide security for a judge during a trial).

The scepter in the hands of Osiris represents power, dominion, and royal authority, the gavel and sound block of a judge is the symbol of authority, order, power, and dominion over the courtroom.

Concept of God as a Shepherd and Stewarding Souls to Heaven

Of the many African/Kemetic/Anu symbols for Osiris, two of his most sacred are the shepherd's crook and flail. Osiris is depicted in art holding a crook and flail; they are shepherd's tools and symbolize Osiris as a shepherd, leading and protecting the deceased souls on their journey through the Underworld. Sometimes Osiris is depicted with just the shepherd's crook and flail; other times, he also holds the scepter, symbolizing dominion, royal power, and authority.

Of all the symbols used in African/Kemetic/Anu culture, the shepherd's tools are two of the most prevalent. The shepherd's tools are usually seen with depictions of Osiris but also with other gods and goddesses. The crook and flail can also be found in the artistic depictions of many of the pharaohs (like the sarcophagus of Tutankhamen), who considered themselves to be descended from gods. The deceased in Africa/Kemet/Anu were often buried with the crook and flail to symbolize transforming the outward appearance of the deceased into the image of Osiris, the central and most important African/Kemetic/Anu deity, and the original diety to have risen from the dead.

The crook and flail are symbols of African/Kemetic/Anu religion, the same way the cross, crescent moon and star, and Star of David are the symbols of Christianity, Islam, and Judaism, respectively. These shepherd's tools also symbolizes the pharaohs protecting and leading the people of Africa/Kemet/Anu.

The candy-caned curve of the crook can fit around the neck of a sheep, and the long handle of the crook can help the shepherd hold them in place; it can also be used as a weapon.

The flail is a rod with three attached leathery (other fabrics are also used) beaded threads. The beads can vary in size, and the length and space between them can vary. Some flails are like a whip on steroids and can be used for threshing crops like wheat, to separate grains from their husks, but they can also be used as a weapon to ward off predators.

The crook and flail symbolize Osiris shepherding souls to heaven; however, the shepherds tools can also symbolize being meek like a sheep or represent power and punishment.

Jesus of Christianity is symbolically associated with being a Shepherd and leading sheep. In the Book of John, Jesus is called "The Good Shepherd" and is often depicted in Christian art holding a shepherd's crook, while also holding or directing sheep. The following parable of Jesus is about him protecting and leading humans down the righteous path to heaven, using the words shepherd and sheep as symbolic metaphors.

John 10:1–16

1. Verily, verily, I say unto you, He that entereth not by the door into the sheepfold, but climbeth up some other way, the same is a thief and a robber. 2. But he that entereth in by the door is the shepherd of the sheep. 3. To him the porter openeth; and the sheep hear his voice: and he calleth his own sheep by name, and leadeth them out. 4. And when he putteth forth his own sheep, he goeth before them, and the sheep follow him: for they know his voice. 5. And a stranger will they not follow, but will flee from him: for they know not the voice of strangers. 6. This parable spake Jesus unto them: but they understood not what things they were which he spake unto them. 7. Then said Jesus unto them again, Verily, verily, I say unto you, I am the door of the sheep. 8. All that ever came before me are thieves and robbers: but the sheep did not hear them. 9. I am the door: by me if any man enter in, he shall be saved, and shall go in and out, and find pasture. 10. The thief cometh not, but for to steal, and to kill, and to destroy: I am come that they might have life, and that they might have it more abundantly. 11. I am the good shepherd: the good shepherd giveth his life for the sheep. 12. But he that is an hireling, and not the shepherd, whose own the sheep are not, seeth the wolf coming, and leaveth the sheep, and fleeth: and the wolf catcheth them,

and scattereth the sheep. 13. The hireling fleeth, because he is an hireling, and careth not for the sheep. 14. I am the good shepherd, and know my sheep, and am known of mine. 15. As the Father knoweth me, even so know I the Father: and I lay down my life for the sheep. 16. And other sheep I have, which are not of this fold: them also I must bring, and they shall hear my voice; and there shall be one fold, and one shepherd.

Papyrus of Hunefer
Hymn to Osiris

I have given unto thee the sovereignty of thy father Geb, and the goddess Nut, thy mother, who gave birth to the gods, brought thee forth as the first born of the five gods, and created thy beauties and fashioned thy members. Thou art established as king, the white crown is upon thy head, and thou hast grasped in thy hands the crook and the whip [flail]; whilst thou were in the womb, thou were crowned lord of the two lands, and the Atef crown of Ra was upon thy brow.

Fire and Hell

Osiris is lord of the Underworld, which is associated with fire, hell, evil demons, and darkness; as well as a place for departed souls to go on their path to eternity, everlastingness, and heaven (or to be devoured). After he was murdered and dismembered, Isis and their sister, Nephthys, resurrected him.

In the Heliopolis Ennead myth, Osiris is the great-grandson of the god Atum. Atum, a solar creator god, is associated with fire.

In the excerpts below, "she" can refer to several African/Kemetic/Anu goddesses. Sekhmet is the African/Kemetic/Anu goddess of the west; she is known as the "Mighty-Mighty Lady of Flame." The goddess Bast (or Bastet) is her opposite, the goddess of the east.

Uatchet is the goddess of the north; she is referred to as the "Lady of Flame," and her opposite is Nekhebet, the goddess of the south. All of these goddesses are associated with truth, justice, and protection; they were all avengers of evil. They have many of the same attributes as the goddess Hathor, one of the most revered and popular deities in ancient Africa/Kemet/Anu. Hathor is a war goddess and a goddess of love, fertility, motherhood, truth, justice, and protection; she is also an avenger of evil. The myth of the Destruction of Mankind (see below) describes Hathor's destructive and avenging powers. Note: Lake of Neserser can refer to "Lake of Fire" – For comparison – Revelation 20:14-15 states: 14. "And death and hell were cast into the lake of fire. This is the second death." 15. "And whosoever was not found written in the book of life was cast into the lake of fire."

The following excerpts are taken from the Pylons (gateways) of the House of Osiris and the papyri of Ani, Nebseni, and Nu.

Papyrus of Ani
The Chapter of Not Letting the Head be Cut Off

> I am a Great One, the son of a Great One. I am Fire, the son of Fire, to whom was given his head after it had been cut off. The head of Osiris was not removed from his body, and the head of Osiris shall not be removed from his body. I have knitted myself together; I have made myself whole and complete. I shall renew my youth. I am Osiris Himself, the Lord of Eternity.

Papyrus of Nebseni
The Praises and Glorifying of Coming Out from and Going into Glorious Khert-Neter

> Deliver thou the scribe Nebseni, whose word is truth, from the god whose face is like unto that of a greyhound, whose brows are like those of a man, who feedeth upon the dead, who watcheth at the Bend of the Lake of Fire, who devoureth the bodies of the dead, and swalloweth hearts, and who voideth filth, but who himself remaineth unseen. His name is Everlasting Devourer and he liveth in the Domain of Fire, the Lake of Unt.

Papyrus of Nebseni

Thou hast created that which is in Kher-aha and that which is in Anu (Heliopolis). Every god feareth thee, for thou art exceedingly great and terrible; thou avenges every god or the man who curseth him, thou shootest arrows at him. Thou livest according to thy will. Thou art Uatchet, the Lady of Flame; evil befalleth those who set themselves up against thee.

Papyrus of Ani
The Praises and Glorifying of Coming Out from and Going into Glorious Khert-Neter

The goddess Hetepsekhus is the Eye of Ra. Others, however, say it is the flame which accompanieth Osiris to burn up the souls of his enemies.

The Pylons of the House of Osiris: The 8th Pylon

Blazing fire, unquenchable, with far-reaching tongues of flame, irresistible slaughter, which one may not pass through fear of its deadly attack.

The Pylons of the House of Osiris: The 18th Pylon

"Fire-lover, pure one, lover of slaughterings, cutter off of heads, devoted one, lady of the Great House, slaughterer of the fiends at eventide" is thy name. She inspecteth the swathing of the helpless one.

The Pylons of the House of Osiris: The 11th pylon

I have made my way, I know you, and I know thy name, and I know the name of her who is within thee: She who slayeth always, consumer of the fiends by fire, mistress of every pylon, the lady who acclaimed on the day of darkness.

The Pylons of the House of Osiris: The 21ˢᵗ Pylon

> Knife which cutteth when is uttered, slayer of those who approach thy flame is thy name. She possesseth hidden plans.

Papyrus of Nebseni (Sheet 17)

> When he setteth in life like crystal he performeth everything therein, and these things are like unto the things which are done in the Lake of Neserser, wherein there is none that rejoiceth, and wherein are all manner of evil things.

Papyrus of Nu (Sheet 10)

> Hail, ye gods whose scent is sweet. I—Hail—Flame, which cometh forth from the horizon! Hail thou art in the city. I have brought the Warden of his blight therein. Oh, stretch out unto me thy hand so that I may be able to pass my days in the Pool of Double Fire, and let me advance with my message.

Standing Beside God in Heaven

The following excerpts are taken from the Pyramid of Unas and the Pyramid of Pepi I: Doctrine of Eternal Life; and the Pyramid of Pepi I: Chapter of the Ladder to Heaven.

In the *Book of Gates*, the second section of the Tuat (Tuat, Duat, Amenta, Otherworld, and Underworld are associated with the land of the dead), Afu-Ra weighs the words and deeds of the deceased; the good stand on the right side of Afu-Ra and give offerings and praise, which are rewarded with good outcome, and the wicked stand to the left of Afu-Ra and are tortured, sacrificed, and destroyed.

Note: Phrases that refer to being on the right hand of God for protection as God destroys the enemies of God; or standing or sitting on the right hand of God in heaven, in a position of honor can be found written and expressed in several ways in the Torah/Tanakh of Judaism and Bible of Christianity.

Written as: "At the right hand of God"; "standing on the right hand of God"; "being by the right hand of God exalted"; "is on the right hand of God"; "Sit thou on my right hand, till I make thine enemies thy footstool?"; "sitting on the right hand of power"; "sat on the right hand of God"; and "sit on the right hand of the power of God."

Additional phrases as mentioned earlier in chapter three: "He is at my right hand"; "thou that savest by thy right hand"; "thy right hand hath holden me up"; "the saving strength of his right hand"; "thy right hand upholdeth me"; "Sit thou on my right hand, until I make thine enemies thy footstool"; and "thy right hand, O Lord, hath dashed in pieces the enemy."

The above variations of references about being at the right hand of God can be found in the Bible of Christianity in the books of: Romans 8:34, Acts 7:55-56, Acts 2:33, I Peter 3:22, Matthew 22:44, Matthew 26:64, Mark 16:19, and Luke 22:69 respectively.

The additional phrases mentioned earlier in chapter three can be found in the Bible of Christianity and Torah/Tanakh of Judaism in the books of: Psalms 16:8, 17:7, 18:35-36, 20:6-7, 63:8-9, Psalms 110:1, and Exodus 15:6 respectively.

Critique: Psalms 110:1 found in the Christian Bible's Old Testament and the Tanakh of Judaism is the same identical verse as Matthew 22:44 of the Christian Bible's New Testament —"The Lord (Christianity) or HaShem (Judaism) said unto my Lord, Sit thou at my right hand, until (til) I make thine enemies thy footstool."

The mythical God (male writers) of Christianity is or are, not only repeating the same verse in the Old and New Testament, but also repeating the same verse in the religious books of Judaism's Tanakh and Christianity's New Testament. The New Testament is not a part of Judaism and the Old Testament was allegedly written hundreds of years before the New Testament. Many different versions of the Christian Bible end Matthew 22:44 with a punctuation (?) question mark.

Pyramid of Unas

> Ra setteth upright the ladder for Osiris, and Horus raiseth up the ladder for his father Osiris, when Osiris goeth to find his soul; one standeth on the one side, and the other standeth on the other, and Unas is betwixt them. Unas

standeth up and is Horus, he sitteth down and is Set [Seth].

Unas is equipped with powers against the spirit-souls thereof, and he rises up in the form of the mighty one, the lord of those who dwell in power. Unas hath taken his seat with his side turned towards Geb [god of the earth].

Pyramid of Pepi I
The Doctrine of Eternal Life

The place of the deceased in heaven is by the side of God. In the most holy place, and he becomes god and an angel of God; he himself is a speaker of the truth and his Ka [spirit] is triumphant, He sits on a great throne by the side of God. The throne is of iron, or alabaster.… He is clothed in the finest raiment, like unto the raiment of those who sit on the throne of living right and truth.… When the Osiris of a man has entered into heaven as a living soul he is regarded as one of those who have eaten the Eye of Horus; he walks among the living ones, he becomes "God, the son of God," and all the gods of heaven become his brethren. His bones are the gods and goddesses of heaven; his right side belongs to Horus and his left side to Set.

Pyramid of Pepi I
Chapter of the Ladder to Heaven

Give thou unto Pepi the Ladder of the god Horus, give thou unto him the Ladder of the god Set, whereby Pepi shall appear in heaven, when he hath made use of the words of power of Ra. Hail thou god of the Kau [doubles] who advance when the Eye of Horus soareth upon the wings of Thoth on the eastern side of the Ladder of the god. Hail ye who desire that your bodies shall go into heaven.

Destruction of Mankind
Noah's Ark: Genesis 6:1–2 and 4–8

1. And it came to pass, when men began to multiply on the face of the earth, and daughters were born unto them, 2. That the sons of God saw the daughters of men that they were fair; and they took them wives of all which they chose…. 4. There were giants in the earth in those days; and also after that, when the sons of God came in unto the daughters of men, and they bare children to them, the same became mighty men which were of old, men of renown. 5. And God saw that the wickedness of man was great in the earth, and that every imagination of the thoughts of his heart was only evil continually. 6. And it repented the LORD that he had made man on the earth, and it grieved him at his heart. 7. And the LORD said, I will destroy man whom I have created from the face of the earth; both man, and beast, and the creeping thing, and the fowls of the air; for it repenteth me that I have made them. 8. But Noah found grace in the eyes of the LORD.

Genesis 7:15, 17–18, and 20

15. And they went in unto Noah into the ark, two and two of all flesh, wherein is the breath of life. 17. And the flood was forty days upon the earth; and the waters increased, and bare up the ark, and it was lift up above the earth. 18. And the waters prevailed and were increased greatly upon the earth; and the ark went upon the face of the waters. 20. Fifteen cubits upward did the waters prevail; and the mountains were covered.

Genesis 8:4–5

4. And the Ark rested in the seventh month, on the seventeenth day of the month, upon the mountains of Ararat. 5. And the waters decreased continually until the

tenth month: in the tenth month, on the first day of the month, were the tops of the mountains seen.

Genesis 8:20–21

20. And Noah builded an altar unto the LORD; and took of every clean beast, and of every clean fowl, and offered burnt offerings on the altar. 21. And the LORD smelled a sweet savour; and the LORD said in his heart, I will not again curse the ground any more for man's sake; for the imagination of man's heart is evil from his youth; neither will I again smite any more every thing living, as I have done.

Critique: In these selected verses about the myth of Noah and the Ark taken from the Book of Genesis, the first book of the religions of Judaism and Christianity, one can find similarities to the Destruction of Mankind, an older African/Kemetic/Anu myth. The similarities are gods, goddesses, and humans interacting and living together on earth; a supreme god who is unhappy with being blasphemed and disrespected; evil and wickedness are present in humans, and the supreme god regrets that he has created mankind; a supreme god who decides to destroy mankind as punishment for their behavior; and either before or during the destruction of mankind, the supreme god finds grace for (or has compassion for) some humans and decides to save them.

At some point in these myths, before or after the flood, an ark (or boat) is constructed with some type of instructions about the way the craft should be built, accessorized and how the passengers should be placed in it; the ark is filled with humans, animals, or gods; after the flood an altar or shrine is constructed (altars are usually found within shrines).

At some point in the respective myths, the earth is flooded; a large percentage of mankind is destroyed by the flood or at the hands of a goddess; during or after the destruction of most of mankind, a sacrificial offering is performed by the remaining humans on earth, and the supreme god forgives them or vows not to destroy mankind again.

Even after the destruction, forgiveness, and promise not to destroy mankind again, the supreme god still has a pessimistic view of mankind and the future of humans on earth. One can find in the myths of Noah and the Ark, the African/Kemetic/Anu Destruction of Mankind, and the

Papyrus of Nu the use of the words gods, humans, destroy, mountain, cubit, boat (or ark), shrine (or altar), repent, sacrifice, offering, and flood.

Myth of the Destruction of Mankind
The Book of the Heavenly Cow

The Destruction of Mankind is an African/Kemetic/Anu myth that is older than the Hebrew and Christian myth of Noah and the Ark. Found within the Book of the Heavenly Cow, it has been handed down via inscriptions from the royal tombs of Tutankhamen, Seti I, Ramses II, Ramses III, Ramses VI, and the Ramesside Papyrus in Turin, Italy.

This well-known myth has been translated by many scholars. Like most translations, the interpretation can vary, but there are common parts of the myth that are consistent no matter what version you are reading. This is a summary of this myth for comparison to the similar myth of Noah and the Ark.

The myth is from a time when gods, goddesses, and humans are mingling with each other on earth. The earth is being ruled over by Ra, who is getting older and has ruled for a very long time; he is starting to hear rumors that his subjects are complaining that he is too old to rule any longer, and they are being disrespectful in their characterizations of him.

Ra, who created the gods, goddesses, and humans, cannot believe they are complaining about him. Ra hears rumors that "Behold, his Majesty (Life, Strength, and Health to Him) hath grown old, and his bones have become like silver, and his members have turned into gold and his hair is like unto real lapis-lazuli (blue stone)." He calls together all the gods and goddesses who had lived with him in the unknown creation force called Nu.

They assemble in the Great Temple or Great House; when Ra enters, the gods and goddesses bow down on each side of him, showing respect, reverence, and submission. The gods ask Ra to speak to them, for they have heard what the humans are saying.

Ra begins to explain that mankind, who he created from his Eye, are now speaking out against him. He wants to know what the gods and goddesses think he should do about mankind; he is thinking of destroying all of mankind but does not want to do so until he has received an opinion from the gods and goddesses.

The gods advise Ra to send forth his Eye and destroy the blasphemers. Ra agrees and sends forth his Eye, in the form of the goddess Hathor, to destroy mankind (in another interpretation of this myth, Ra has the goddess Sekhmet, mentioned earlier, take on the form of Hathor to carry out the destruction on mankind). The humans hear what is about to occur and flee into the mountains, afraid because of what they have said about Ra.

Hathor goes forth with the consent and power of the Eye of Ra and pursues the blaspheming rebels into the mountains, where she overtakes them and destroys almost all of mankind. After the slaughter, Hathor returns to Ra, who praises her for what she has done. Hathor rejoices and explains that she derived pleasure from slaying mankind with the power given to her by Ra. She so enjoyed destroying mankind that during the night of the slaughter, she danced, celebrated, and waded in the blood of the slaughtered humans.

Ra is concerned that she enjoyed slaughtering the humans too much. He has a change of heart and decides to spare the rest of mankind from the final and total destruction that Hathor plans for them the next day. Ra orders his messengers to run like the wind to the city of Elephantine in Kemet/Egypt and bring back great quantities of unknown fruit; some scholars say mandrakes; the roots are used as a narcotic. Using education again to help understand African/Kemetic/Anu religious myths; the roots of some mandrake plants eerily resemble human beings with a head, arms, and legs. So we find the mandrake plant and root being used symbolically in a religious myth about a goddess dancing, celebrating, and wading in the blood of humans she has slaughtered. Once the fruit of mandrakes are brought back to Ra, he gives them to the goddess Sekhmet to crush and grind up.

The crushed fruit was mixed with beer and then mixed with the blood of the slaughtered humans; the completed mixture looked like human blood. In total they made seven-thousand vessels of the reddish beer-intoxicant. Ra then approved the mixture and ordered it to be taken up river, to the Meadows of the Four Heavens, where Hathor was to continue her slaughter of mankind the next day.

The reddish beer-intoxicant was poured over the meadows, and they became filled. The next morning, Hathor finds the fields flooded and rejoices at the sight of what appears to be blood; she proceeds to drink it, which causes her to become intoxicated. In her drunken state, she forgets about the slaughter of mankind.

Ra welcomes Hathor back and refers to her as "the beautiful one," ordering humans from that day forward to celebrate the festival of Hathor by drinking large quantities of beer.

Soon after this, Ra complains that his heart is weary of being with the children of men. He concludes that what was left of mankind was worthless. He feels that the plan to destroy mankind had not gone well, and he wishes that the destruction of the blaspheming humans had been more widespread.

The gods and goddesses respond by telling Ra not to despair for his power was in proportion to his will. Ra, however, is not to be consoled and again states that he is tired as never before and is ready to leave mankind forever. Nu orders the gods to help Ra leave the earth. With the help of Shu, the god of air, and Nut, the goddess of the sky, Ra prepares to leave.

Nut changes herself into a heavenly cow, and Ra gets onto her back. Nut and Shu lift Ra up into the air; as Ra is about to leave, the humans begin to cry out with fear and repentance and beg Ra to remain on earth and slay the final humans who had blasphemed against him.

Ra, however, continues on his way and moves on to another town, from where he plans to leave earth. Darkness covers the land, and the next day, the humans who had repented attack and slay the enemies of Ra who were still left on earth. When Ra finds out what had happened, he is pleased and forgives those who had repented, telling them that their slaughter of the enemies of Ra is above the slaughter of sacrifice. Ra then proceeds to leave earth and ascend into the heavens, where he prepares a place for all to come and join him.

The following excerpt of the Destruction of Mankind is called the Chapter of the Cow. The cow (boat) is Nut, the African/Kemetic/Anu sky goddess:

> The supporters [called] Heh-enti shall be by her shoulder. The supporters [called] Heh-enti shall be at her side, and one cubit and four spans of hers shall be in colours, and nine stars shall be on her belly, and Set shall be on her two thighs and shall keep watch before her two legs, and before her two legs shall be Shu, under her belly, and he shall be made [painted] in green genat colour. His two arms shall be under the stars and his name shall be made [written] in the middle of them, namely Shu himself.

A boat with a rudder and a double shrine shall be therein, and Aten shall be above it, and Ra shall be in it, in front of Shu, near his hand, or as another reading hath, behind him near his hand.... And the two flanks, towards the middle of the legs, shall be done in writing [the words] "The exterior heaven," and "I am what is in me," and "I will not permit them to make her to turn." That which is written under the boat which is in front shall read, "Thou shalt not be motionless, my son"; and the words which are written in an opposite direction shall read, "Thy support is like life," and "The word is as the word there," and "Thy son is with me," and "Life, strength, and health be to thy nostrils!"

Genesis 6:15–16 and 19

15. And this is the fashion which thou shalt make it of: The length of the ark shall be three hundred cubits, the breadth of it fifty cubits, and the height of it thirty cubits. 16. A window shalt thou make to the ark, and in a cubit shalt thou finish it above; and the door of the ark shalt thou set in the side thereof; with lower, second, and third stories shalt thou make it.... 19. And of every living thing of all flesh, two of every sort shalt thou bring into the ark, to keep them alive with thee; they shall be male and female.

From the Papyrus of Nu: The Chapter of Knowing the Souls of the East

"Khus" or "Khu" means the human spirit, soul, or shining spiritual entity encasing the human body, similar to a glowing aura.

"Sektet-Aarru" refers to a heavenly divine city.

I am he who is concerned with the tackle [?], which is in the divine bark, I am the sailor who ceaseth not on the boat of Ra. I, even I, know the two sycamore of turquoise between which Ra showed himself when he strideth forward over the supports of Shu toward the gate of the lord of the east through which Ra cometh forth. I, even I, know the Sektet-Aarru of Ra, the walls of which are of iron. The height of the wheat therein is five cubits, of the ears thereof two cubits, and the stalks thereof three cubits. The barley therein is in height seven cubits, the ears thereof are three cubits, and the stalks thereof are four cubits. And behold, the Khus or Khu, each one of whom therein is nine cubits in height, reaps near the divine souls of the east.

Critique: These excerpts refer to how to build an ark, how to accessorize a boat, and how the vessels should be staffed, and the last excerpt describes the divine city where Ra lives in heaven.

The presence of a double shrine in the boat of Ra and the presence of an altar in the myth of Noah (Genesis 8:20) are similar; altars are usually found within shrines as mentioned earlier.

Holy Trinities

A number of aboriginal religions around the world believe in some type of religious Holy Trinity. Mesopotamian and Mediterranean cultures like Babylon and Samaria recorded religious myths about Holy Trinities. It is nothing new for religions to present the abstract, confusing, and nonsensical concept of a supreme god combining with another god (or two other gods) to form one god that is really two (or three) gods.

In Hinduism, we find the Holy Trinity of Brahma, Shiva, and Vishnu. They are the creator, destroyer, and protector of creation, respectively. They are manifestations of the supreme god Brahman. Brahma, the creator of all things in the world, is referred to as the "Cosmic God." Shiva, the second god in the Hindu trinity, is the god of transformation, destruction, extinction, and darkness: he is called the Lord of Destruction. He is one of the most feared gods in Hinduism because he is a a god of retribution.

Vishnu is the protector, sustainer, and preserver of creation and life on earth. His attributes are truth, justice, righteousness, and order. When the balance between good and evil on earth tilts too much in the direction of evil, Vishnu is manifested on earth through birth in either human or animal form to restore order. One of his manifestations was that of Krishna.

These male gods also have a trinity of female counterparts. For Brahma, Saraswati, the goddess of knowledge, music, and the arts, is referred to as the "Queen of the Vedas." For Shiva, the consort is Kali, the goddess of divine motherhood, energy, time, power, destruction, death, and transformation. Kali means the "Black One"; she is also one of the most feared goddesses in Hinduism. Vishnu's consort is Lakshmi, the goddess of love, prosperity, wealth, beauty, and delight.

I will summarize four different African/Kemetic/Anu holy trinity myths: Amun, Ra, and Ptah; Khepri, Shu, and Tefnut; Khepri, Ra, and Atum; and Osiris, Isis, and Heru. There are other trinities, like the creation trinity of Hu, Sia, and Heke mentioned in chapter 2.

Within the religious myths of Africa/Kemet/Anu, there are also supreme gods who combine with one other god to form one god; for example, Ra combines with Heru (Horus) to become Ra-Harmachis and Amun combines with Ra to become Amun-Ra.

Amun, Ra, and Ptah

Amun, Ra, and Ptah, individual gods from Thebes, Heliopolis, and Memphis, were combined to form one of the more popular trinities in African/Kemetic/Anu culture.

Amun (Amen) from Thebes, originally was the god of air and wind, one of the elements of the primordial universe. His name signifies "the hidden one," since air and wind are invisible. His name became associated with the "breath of life," and his color became associated with the color blue, the color of the sky.

He is depicted in art as a man seated on a throne or standing holding an ankh, the symbol of life, in one hand, and a was-scepter, the symbol of dominion, royal power, and authority in the other hand, while wearing the double plumed feathered crown of Africa/Kemet/Anu, which looks exactly like the Tablets of Stone, which contained the Ten Commandments given to Moses.

Ra, a creator sun god, was considered to be the creator of everything and every living soul. He was worshipped all over Africa/Kemet/Anu, with his main center of followers located in Heliopolis, Egypt.

He is depicted in art as a man with the head of a hawk or falcon, holding an ankh, the symbol of life, in one hand and a was-scepter, the symbol of dominion, royal power, and authority, in the other hand. On top of the hawk or falcon's head, sits either an Atef crown or a solar disk encircled by a cobra.

Ra was the conqueror of evil, destruction, and death; he symbolized death and rebirth. It was Ra who sailed through the sky in a boat in the Barque of a Million Years, fighting the evil serpent Apep and his cohorts above the horizon for the twelve hours of day, and below the horizon for the twelve hours of night. While below the horizon Ra, the good sun god would bring light and comfort to the tortured souls below the horizon. He would reappear in the east, reborn and ready for battle again.

Ptah was a predynastic creator god worshipped throughout Kemet/Egypt (but mainly in Memphis and Heliopolis). The Apis bull was used in art to represent his soul on earth; he gave fertility and rebirth to the people. Ptah represented the three aspects of the universe: creation, stability, and death. He was an intellectual god, using thought, harmonics, and words to bring about the creation of the universe, earth, and all that are in it.

He was self-created but not created; he is depicted as a man with a punt beard wearing a skull cap. He is wrapped like a mummy with his hands free, holding a sacred staff (was-scepter) connected to a djed with an ankh on top—symbols of power, dominion, royal authority, stability, and life, respectively. When these three gods were combined, they were referred to as "Him." Amun was the hidden identity, the principle of unity; Ra was the outer face, the principle of filiations or ancestry; and Ptah was the outer body, the principle of manifestations.

The following excerpt is taken from the Leiden (Layden) Hymns from the Papyrus Leiden I 350, dated to the fifty-second year of the reign of Ramesses (Ramses) II, who ruled for sixty-seven years (1279-1212 BCE).

Leiden Hymn to Amun

> All the gods are three: Amun, Re [Ra], and Ptah, without their seconds. His identity is hidden as Amun, He is Re as face, His body is Ptah. Their towns are on earth, fixed for the span of eternity: Thebes, Heliopolis, and Memphis are established perennially. When a message is sent from the sky, it is heard in Heliopolis and repeated in Memphis for the god with the beautiful face put in a report, in Thoth's writing directed to the town of Amun, bearing their concerns, and the matter is answered in Thebes by an oracle emerging, intended for Ennead [Heliopolis].

Everything that comes from his mouth, the gods are bound by it, according to what has been decreed. When a message is sent, it is for killing or for giving life. Life and death depend on Him for everyone, except Him, Amun together with Re, and Ptah total three.

Khepri, Shu, and Tefnut

Another version of the concept of three gods being one can be found in the myth of Khepri, Shu, and Tefnut. This myth illustrates how religion is constantly being reworked. This myth started off as the creation myth of Atum of the Heliopolis Ennead (described earlier in the book). Atum is one of the Company of Gods mentioned in the pyramid texts, the oldest scriptures of Africa/Kemet/Anu.

However, by 400–300 BCE, priests had reworked this creation myth many times; depending on which version one reads, Khepri had replaced Atum as the creator of the gods; Osiris had replaced Atum as the creator of the gods; or a god called Neb-er-tcher, a manifestation of Osiris, had replaced Atum as the creator of the gods.

This excerpt about three gods being one and part of a trinity is taken from one of the reworked versions of the Heliopolis Ennead. It is taken from a papyrus that was preserved in the British Museum. This excerpt is found in the Book of Knowing the Evolutions of Ra, and of Overthrowing Apep: The History of the Creation of the Gods.

The History of the Creation of the Gods

> I was alone, I laid a foundation in my heart, and I made the other things which came into being, the things of Khepera [Khepri] which were made were manifold, and their offspring came into existence from the things to which they gave birth. It was I, who emitted Shu, and it was I, who emitted Tefnut, and from being one god I became three, that is to say, the two other gods who came into being on this earth came from myself, and Shu and Tefnut were raised up from out of Nu wherein they had been.

Khepri, initially a minor god, became associated with the solar creator god Ra and became a major creator god and a manifestation of Ra. So you also have the myth of two gods being combined to form one new supreme god, manifested in the form of Khepri.

He was self-created, associated with self-renewal and self-generation. He is depicted in art as a scarab, a man wearing a scarab crown, or a man with the head of a scarab. The scarab (dung beetle) was used to symbolize the creation of humans on earth and death, metamorphosis, regeneration, birth, rebirth, and resurrection.

Khepri, along with Shu, the god of air, and Tefnut, the goddess of moisture, symbolize the four elements of creation: sun (fire), dung beetle (earth), wind (air), and moisture (water).

Khepri, Ra, and Atum

Another reference to the concept of a trinity, where one god is three and the three are one, can be found in the myth of Ra and Isis. The excerpt below is taken from the Papyrus de Turin and the Papyrus of Ani.

Legend of Ra and Isis
Chapter of the Divine God

> I am whose name the gods know not. I am the maker of the hours and the creator of the days. I inaugurate festivals. I make the water flood. I am the creator of the fire of life through which the products of the workshops came into being. I am Khepera [Khepri] in the morning, Ra at mid-day, and Temu [Atum] in the evening.

Khepri and Atum, at different periods in African/Kemetic/Anu history, were combined with Ra to form one supreme god; they were manifestations of Ra. In this trilogy, they are three gods who represent the personal characteristics of one supreme creator god: Ra. All three gods were worshipped individually at some point in the history of African/Kemetic/Anu culture.

Khepri represents Ra in the morning, rising in the east new and reborn. Ra represents himself at mid-day, when he is at his strongest and most powerful. Atum represents Ra in the evening, when he is setting in the west, old and dying. This continuous cycle represents the mythical concept of birth, death, and rebirth.

Osiris, Isis, and Heru

The African/Kemetic/Anu trilogy myth most widely known is that of Osiris, Isis, and the child Heru (Horus). They were father, mother, and son. Even though they have individual myths and were worshipped as individual gods, they were viewed as an inseparable family unit. There is no three-is-one and one-is-three concept with these gods.

Osiris and Isis were an inseparable pair: sister-brother, mother-father, and husband-wife. Osiris, a predynastic god, was also a lunar (moon) god and associated with the constellation Orion. His myth was the most written about and revised myth throughout the dynasties of Kemet/Egypt.

Isis, a predynastic goddess, was the goddess of motherhood, fertility, nature, and magic. The original "Madonna," she is depicted in art as a woman with a sun disk sitting inside of cow's horns on top of her head or with a throne on top of her head. She was worshipped in Africa, Greece, Rome, the Middle East, Spain, Portugal, Germany, Britain, France, and other European countries.

She was associated with Sirius, the brightest star in the sky, through her assimilation, manifestation, and association with the African/Kemetic/Anu goddess Sopdet, who was the deification of the Kemetic/Egyptian star Sothis. Sopdet is depicted as a woman with a five-pointed star on top of her head. Most Egyptologists view Sothis as the personification of Sirius.

The myth of Isis was also associated with Spica, the brightest star in the Virgo (virgin) constellation. In Virgo, Spica marks the ear of wheat in the virgin's left hand. Osiris and Isis symbolized fertility; their association with the moon (waning and waxing of water) and the stars Sirius (celestial sign of flooding) and Spica (wheat) were connected to the annual flooding of the Nile River and the harvesting of the crops each year.

The three stars in the belt of Orion point to Sirius, linking the constellation and the sky's brightest star. The mythical divine child of Isis and Osiris was Heru, a predynastic god who was a mighty warrior; he fought many vicious battles and defeated the evil Seth to avenge the murder of his father Osiris and retake the throne as ruler of earth, thus restoring peace, love, harmony, and tranquility to earth.

Orion is also called "The Hunter." Many Egyptologists suggest that Heru, because of his warrior myth, is associated with Orion. Finally, with this trinity of two gods and one goddess, we come to the end-of-the-year celebrations held by many cultures around the world.

According to my research, no divine savior was born on December 25: not Krishna, not Heru (Horus), not even Jesus. The origin of Christmas has nothing to do with Jesus or Christianity. There is no mention whatsoever in the Christian Bible of Jesus being born on December 25. Many early Catholic, Coptic (Egyptian), and other Christian churches did not even celebrate Christmas because end-of-year celebrations were considered to be pagan.

Christmas has more to do with end-of-year celebrations and the winter solstice. There was significant debate among Christian religious leaders about when this feast should be celebrated—it often depended on the particular calendar in use when the date for Christmas was selected. Some Catholic, Eastern Orthodox, Greek Orthodox, and Coptic churches celebrate Christmas on January 6, 7, or 19.

Some Christian churches celebrate the Twelve Days of Christmas (some Christians call this period "Christmastide"), starting on December 25 or 26 and ending on January 5 or 6. January 6 or 7 (the day called "the Epiphany") marks the climax of the Christmas festival season—the day commemorates the manifestation of Jesus as "the Son of God" to the Gentiles. The difference in these dates is because of the different calendars that were used by the varying Christian sects: Gregorian, Julian, revised Julian, and so on.

End-of-year celebrations have been practiced by various cultures for thousands of years. The African/Kemetic/Anu 360-day calendar had five festival days added to complete the year; these five extra days celebrated the births of Osiris, Heru (Horus), Seth, Isis and Nephthys (in this order—not by birth order).

The ancient African/Kemetic/Anu celebration of Seth is one reason why some early Christian churches considered end-of-year celebrations to be pagan and associated with evil and the devil.

Finally, Osiris in art was depicted as green; he was referred to as the "god of everlastingness." Evergreen trees are linked to Osiris. The stars Sirius and Spica are linked to Isis; the stars of Orion's belt point to Sirius. When one places a star on top of an evergreen Christmas tree, it is symbolic of the myth of Osiris and Isis; and represents the inseparable bond between Isis and Osiris: mother-father, sister-brother, and husband-wife.

The African/Kemetic/Anu birth-myth of Heru was a time of celebration; the end of the year was a time of harvest and giving thanks for a good crop, year, and prosperity. Osiris, Isis, and Heru were celebrated throughout African/Kemetic/Anu culture: during the end-of-year celebrations; on individual days; and as a family unit of three (a trilogy): the father, mother, and divine son of a god and goddess.

Christian Communion (or Eucharist) and Sacrifice

Many religions depict the mythical concept of sacrifice. Gods and goddesses exert authority, dominion, and control over humans. Humans offer sacrifices to satisfy and appease a god or goddess, avoid the wrath and vengeance of that god or goddess, and receive the reward of everlastingness and eternity alongside that god or goddess in heaven.

The symbolic or real cannibalistic act of eating the flesh or drinking the blood of a human, god, or goddess in remembrance or celebration or to attain the power and essence of those humans, gods, or goddesses is found throughout human history.

The purpose of this act is to become like the gods or goddesses; absorb the power and soul of conquered humans; attain, remember, or celebrate the gift of salvation and resurrection into some afterlife where celestial beings exist; or attain power derived from the symbolic consumption of the flesh and blood of a god or goddess.

The Last Supper of Jesus

The Christian sacrament of the Eucharist or Communion is defined as a formal ceremony that confers a specific grace on those who receive it. It is a rite in which God is uniquely active and as a visible sign of an invisible reality. It commemorates the Last Supper of Jesus; believers consume consecrated bread and wine, which symbolize the body and blood of Jesus.

The Eucharist is an individual's solemn act of thanksgiving and rememberance of the ultimate pain, suffering, and sacrifice that Jesus, the mythical Son of God, endured so that all of mankind can have the opportunity to have their sins forgiven, be saved, and appear in heaven alongside of the Christian trinity of the Father, Son, and Holy Ghost.

Luke 22:16–20

16. For I say unto you, I will not any more eat thereof, until it be fulfilled in the kingdom of God. 17. And he took the cup, and gave thanks, and said, Take this, and divide it among yourselves: 18. For I say unto you, I will not drink of the fruit of the vine, until the kingdom of God shall come. 19. And he took bread, and gave thanks, and brake it, and gave unto them, saying, This is my body which is given for you: this do in remembrance of me. 20. Likewise also the cup after supper, saying, This cup is the new testament in my blood, which is shed for you.

In the excerpt below from John 6:50–59, Jesus refers to the word, manna. The definition of the word manna can be found in the Tanakh of Judaism and Bible of Christianity in the books of Numbers and Exodus.

Numbers 11: 7–8

7. And the manna was as coriander seed, and the colour thereof as the colour of bdellium. 8. And the people went about, and gathered it, and ground it in mills, or beat it in a mortar, and baked it in pans, and made cakes of it: and the taste of it was as the taste of fresh oil.

Exodus 16:33–35

33. And Moses said unto Aaron, Take a pot, and put an omer full of manna therein, and lay it up before the LORD, to be kept for your generations. 34. As the LORD commanded Moses, so Aaron laid it up before the Testimony, to be kept. 35. And the children of Israel did eat manna forty years, until they came to a land inhabited; they did eat manna, until they came unto the borders of the land of Canaan.

John 6:50–59

> 50. This is the bread which cometh down from heaven, that a man may eat thereof, and not die. 51. I am the living bread which came down from heaven: if any man eat of this bread, he shall live for ever: and the bread that I will give is my flesh, which I will give for the life of the world. 52. The Jews therefore strove among themselves, saying, How can this man give us his flesh to eat? 53. Then Jesus said unto them, Verily, verily, I say unto you, Except ye eat the flesh of the Son of man, and drink his blood, ye have no life in you. 54. Whoso eateth my flesh, and drinketh my blood, hath eternal life; and I will raise him up at the last day. 55. For my flesh is meat indeed, and my blood is drink indeed. 56. He that eateth my flesh, and drinketh my blood, dwelleth in me, and I in him. 57. As the living Father hath sent me, and I live by the Father: so he that eateth me, even he shall live by me. 58. This is that bread which came down from heaven: not as your fathers did eat manna, and are dead: he that eateth of this bread shall live for ever. 59. These things said he in the synagogue, as he taught in Capernaum.

King Unas

King Unas was a fifth-dynasty African/Kemetic/Anu ruler from the Old Kingdom between 2375 and 2345 BCE. Some of the oldest African/Kemetic/Anu myths are found in the pyramid texts located in the Pyramid of Unas at Saqqara, Egypt. The following excerpts are taken from the Pyramid of Unas.

The entire text can easily be referred to as the "Cannibal Hymns"; it is much more graphic than the excerpts which follow. It describes cutting up and boiling the body parts of firstborns and women in blazing caldrons; cutting off the scalps of gods; cutting the throats and taking out the intestines of gods for slaughter; eating the hearts and intestines of gods; and so on.

Pyramid of Unas

> Unas is the lord of offerings, the untier of the knot, and he himself maketh abundant the offerings of meat and drink.... Unas eats their magical powers, and he swallows their spirit-souls; the great ones among them serve for his meal at daybreak, the lesser serve for his meal at eventide, and the least among them serve for his meal at night. The old gods and goddesses become fuel for his furnace.... Unas is the Great Power, the Power of Powers. Unas is the Chief of the gods in visible form. Whatever he findeth upon his path he eats forthwith, and the magical might of Unas is before that of all the Spirit-bodies who dwell in the horizon. Unas is the firstborn of the firstborn gods. Unas is surrounded by thousands, and oblations are made unto him by hundreds; he is made manifest as the Great Power by Sah [Orion] the father of the gods. Unas repeats his rising in heaven and he is crowned lord of the horizon.... Unas hath eaten the whole of the knowledge of every god, and the period of his life is eternity, and the duration of his existence is everlastingness in the form of one who does what he wishes and does not do what he hates, and he abides in the horizon for ever and ever and ever.... offerings made unto him are more than those which are made unto the gods.... the seat of the heart of Unas is among those who live upon this earth for ever and ever and ever.

Critique: Sah is another African/Kemetic/Anu god associated with the constellation Orion. He was the mythical consort of the goddess Sopdet, who was associated with the star Sirius.

Unas was manifest as the Great Power by Sah (Orion), the father of the gods. He sacrificed, consumed the flesh, and drank the blood of gods and goddesses. He specifically targeted the older gods for fuel, to absorb their magical powers, to become the first of the spirit-bodies, to attain their knowledge, to rise up and attain eternity and everlastingness, and to reside in heaven as a lord of the horizon alongside Sah.

Thousands of gods and goddesses made oblations to satisfy or appease him ("oblations" are a solemn offering or presentation to a deity).

Jesus, the mythical Son of God, was sacrificed by his father (God). As the Son of God, Jesus knew the will of his father, the ultimate fate that awaited him, and the reason behind the sacrificial action. In order to appease his father, Jesus chose to sacrifice himself on behalf of humans, in what is called substitutionary atonement or vicarious atonement.

Christians who repent of their sins and seek forgiveness can be saved. Before his sacrifice, Jesus expressed a willingness to back away from the sacrificial action (Luke 22:42–44) but was given strength by his father; before he died, he felt abandoned by his father (Matthew 27:46).

Luke 22:42–44

42. Saying, Father, if thou be willing, remove this cup from me: nevertheless not my will, but thine, be done. 43. And there appeared an angel unto him from heaven, strengthening him. 44. And being in an agony he prayed more earnestly: and his sweat was as it were drops of blood falling down to the ground.

Matthew 27:46 and 50

46. And about the ninth hour Jesus cried with a loud voice saying, Eli, Eli, lama sabachthani? That is to say, My God, my God, why hast thou forsaken me?… 50. Jesus, when he had cried again with a loud voice, yielded up the ghost.

After Jesus died, God caused earthquakes, graves to open up, and the bodies of saints to rise. The resurrected saints went into the cities for people to see, causing people to finally believe that Jesus was the Son of God (Matthew 27:51–54).

Jesus, by submitting and sacrificing his life, took humanity's imperfections and penalty for sin upon himself, allowing them to be imperfect, sin, repent (seek forgiveness), and still be saved.

The violent, painful sacrifice of Jesus satisfied and appeased God, allowing him to provide a path for mankind to rise up to heaven and avoid his wrath, which would otherwise be brought to bear on an imperfect and sinful mankind.

Christians give thanks for the ultimate sacrifice of Jesus on their behalf with the symbolic eating and drinking of his flesh and blood in the sacrament of Communion, or the Eucharist.

Oblations were made to appease and satisfy Unas by the gods and goddesses. Unas made offerings of meat and drink to appease and satisfy the supreme god Sah. The goal of the sacrifices, offerings, and oblations was to rise up and live with Unas or Sah, the father of the gods in heaven. Unas consumed the flesh and drank the blood of gods and goddesses to become god-like, attain power, and live in heaven with Sah. Jesus is quoted in the above excerpt from the Book of John saying, "Whoso eateth my flesh, and drinketh my blood, hath eternal life."

Osiris and Seth; Cain and Abel

I will briefly critique the Christian and Jewish myth of Cain and Abel, and the African/Kemetic/Anu myth of Osiris and Seth. Osiris, the son of Geb and Nut, became the beloved ruler of earth, and under his reign, earth was a prosperous place, and humans and gods lived in peace.

Seth was also the son of Geb and Nut. He was presented in his earliest myths as a good god who, along with Heru, the son of Osiris, represented peace and harmony. He battled the evil serpent Apep to protect the gods and humans from harm. The myth of Seth was reworked by men over the years; in later African/Kemetic/Anu myths, he became evil incarnate and the adversary of Osiris and Heru.

Seth was jealous of his brother Osiris, who was the ruler of earth. He tricked him during a celebration into getting into a chest and lying down inside it; then he and his cohorts closed the chest, locking Osiris inside, and cast it into the Nile River, killing his brother.

When Isis, the wife of Osiris, found out what happened, she found the chest safely lodged among the branches of a tamarisk tree. The tree had grown quite large and had enclosed the chest.

The king of the country saw the tree and admired it, not knowing what was encased inside of it. He had it cut down and placed on top of his roof as a pillar. Isis went to the home of the king and queen, where she confided in the queen and asked to take the chest from the tree. The queen allowed her to do so, and Isis took the chest from the tree and hid it in Africa/Kemet/Anu.

Seth was out hunting one night, found the chest, and recognized it. He opened it and removed the body of Osiris, ripped it into fourteen pieces, and scattered them all over Africa/Kemet/Anu. Osiris is a lunar god—his body was found by Seth at night, under the moon—the fourteen pieces are symbolic of the number of days 14 to 16 (average 14 to about 15), between the new moon and full moon during the calendar year. Isis and her sister Nephthys found the pieces of Osiris's body and resurrected him, using magic and incantations. (Note: she found all the body parts except Osiris's phallus, so she fashioned one and mated with it to produce the divine child Heru.) Osiris cannot return to earth as ruler, so he became ruler of the Underworld, where departed souls go to have their heart or deeds weighed and either go to heaven or are devoured.

Seth, the murderer of his brother, became the evil ruler of the earth, while Heru (Horus), the son of Osiris, eventually grew up, waged war against Seth, and avenged the murder of his father by retaking the throne. A negotiated settlement by the god Tehuti was reached, stopping the brutal, bloody war Heru was waging against Seth. Seth turned into a snake, hid in a hole in the ground, and was driven out (or off the face) of the land by Heru (with the ever present danger of returning), restoring peace, harmony, and prosperity to Africa/Kemet/Anu.

Genesis 4:2–8

> 2. And she again bare his brother Abel. And Abel was a keeper of sheep, but Cain was a tiller of the ground. 3. And in process of time it came to pass, that Cain brought of the fruit of the ground an offering unto the LORD. 4. And Abel, he also brought of the firstlings of his flock and of the fat thereof. And the LORD had respect unto Abel and to his offering: 5. But unto Cain and to his offering he had not respect. And Cain was very wroth, and his countenance fell. 6. And the LORD said unto Cain, Why art thou wroth? and why is thy countenance fallen? 7. If thou doest well, shalt thou not be accepted? and if thou doest not well, sin lieth at the door. And unto thee shall be his desire, and thou shalt rule over him. 8. And Cain talked with Abel his brother: and it came to pass, when they were in the field, that Cain rose up against Abel his brother, and slew him.

Genesis 4:11–12

11. And now art thou cursed from the earth, which hath opened her mouth to receive thy brother's blood from thy hand. 12. When thou tillest the ground, it shall not henceforth yield unto thee her strength; a fugitive and a vagabond shalt thou be in the earth.

Genesis 4:14–16

14. Behold, thou hast driven me out this day from the face of the earth; and from thy face shall I be hid; and I shall be a fugitive and a vagabond in the earth; and it shall come to pass, that every one that findeth me shall slay me. 15. And the LORD said unto him, Therefore whosoever slayeth Cain, vengeance shall be taken on him sevenfold. And the LORD set a mark upon Cain, lest any finding him should kill him. 16. And Cain went out from the presence of the LORD, and dwelt in the land of Nod, on the east of Eden.

Critique: Cain and Abel were the sons of Adam and Eve in the religions of Christianity and Judaism. They lived outside the boundaries of the mythical Garden of Eden but were still close by Eden and interacted and conversed with God.

Cain was a tiller of the earth, Osiris was the ruler of the earth; Abel was a shepherd, Osiris's symbols were the crook and flail, the tools of the shepherd; Cain was not happy with the rejection by God of his offering, and Seth was not happy that Osiris was beloved by the gods, goddesses, and humans as the ruler of the earth.

Cain murdered his brother, Abel; Seth murdered his brother, Osiris. Cain was cursed from the earth, he was called a vagabond and fugitive of the earth, and he was worried that men would slay him. God placed a mark on Cain so that any man who slayed him would receive vengeance sevenfold. The mythical god Tehuti intervened in the war Heru was waging against Seth to avenge the murder of his father, Osiris, and negotiated a settlement that stopped the war.

Seth was then driven out (in one myth, he turned into a snake, and hid in a hole in the ground) and replaced as ruler of the earth by Heru. Cain was driven out from the face of the earth and hidden from the face of God, he fled east of Eden to the land of Nod. Once Osiris was resurrected by Isis and Nephthys, he cannot return to earth as ruler, so he departed earth and became ruler in the Underworld.

John the Baptist and Anubis

The African/Kemetic/Anu myth of the god Anubis is similar to the Christian myth of John the Baptist; this is yet another example of a Christian myth that reworked an older African/Kemetic/Anu myth.

John the Baptist was born to a mother (Elisabeth) who was impregnated by God, and Anubis was born to a goddess, Nephthys, who was impregnated by a god (either Osiris, Seth, or Ra). Elisabeth is the cousin of Mary, the mother of Jesus, which makes Jesus the second cousin of John the Baptist—Anubis was born to Nephthys, the sister of Osiris and Isis, which makes Anubis and Osiris father and son or uncle and nephew. (Depending on who the mythical father was.)

John the Baptist was at least three months older than Jesus, and Anubis was mythical ruler of the Underworld before Osiris. John the Baptist was a precursor and forerunner of Jesus; he was a prophet and preacher; and he performed baptisms, taught against sin, and encouraged repentance. John the Baptist taught the same religious philosophy as Jesus; he eventually was superseded by Jesus in popularity among the people. John the Baptist foretold of the coming of Jesus.

Anubis was Lord of the Underworld, caretaker, protector, and guide for departed souls on their path to heaven. When the myth of Osiris became more popular, Osiris superseded Anubis and became known as Lord of the Underworld and protector, caretaker, and guide of the deceased. In the Judgment Scene of Ani, Anubis assists Osiris in the Hall of Judgment by weighing the deceased deeds or heart against the Feather of Truth on the Scale of Truth or Justice.

Once a decision was rendered by the Company of Gods, who reviewed the weighing, the deceased was either devoured or sent to Osiris for entrance to heaven.

In Matthew 3:13–17 and Mark 1:9, Jesus is baptized by John the Baptist. Anubis was associated with the Underworld, embalming, and mummification; Osiris is depicted in art as a god who has been embalmed and mummified. In the myth of Anubis, he was the god who performed the embalming and mummification of Osiris.

John the Baptist was beheaded; his head was placed on a charger and given to a damsel, who brought it to her mother. Disciples came to retrieve his headless body and bury him (Matthew 14:10–12). Anubis is depicted as a man whose head had been replaced with the head of a jackal. Anubis was associated with burial and death.

Chapter 6

Astronomy and Religious Symbols

Religions have always been influenced by astronomy and astrology. "Astrology" is defined as a pseudoscience claiming divination by the positions of the planets, sun, and moon; a system of beliefs that the relative positions of celestial bodies can provide information about personality, human affairs, and other terrestrial matters. Man-made religions have strong connections to the twelve Zodiac constellations. The constellations of the Zodiac are Aquarius, the water bearer; Capricorn, the goat; Sagittarius, the archer; Scorpio, the scorpion; Libra, the scales; Virgo, the virgin or maiden; Leo, the lion; Cancer, the crab; Gemini, the twins; Taurus, the bull; Aries, the ram; and Pisces, the fish.

African/Kemetic/Anu religions often used the constellations, as did other religions. Islam uses the crescent moon and star as its spiritual symbol and bases its holidays and festivals on the lunar calendar. The Jewish Passover begins on the first full moon, usually after the vernal (spring) equinox, and the Jewish festival Sukkot begins on a full moon.

The date selected for the Christian observance of Easter is based entirely on the movement and position of the sun. Scientifically, the earth spinning on its axis as it revolves around the sun is the reason for the perceived movement of the sun on the horizon and the appearance from earth of the sun being lower or higher in the sky. Easter is always celebrated on the first Sunday after the first full moon on or after March 20 or 21. This gives Easter an association with both the moon and sun. March 20 or 21 is the date (depending on the year) of the vernal (spring) equinox in the northern hemisphere, the date the sun crosses directly over the earth's equator. The position of the sun on the horizon facing east at sunrise is centered in the middle of the horizon.

The sun and horizon form a celestial cross, and the sun is crucified on the horizon; the sun then crosses over or passes over the point of celestial crucifixion and continues on its northern ascension or movement each morning (at sunrise) on the horizon to the summer solstice on June 20 or 21, the northern limit of the sun's movement on the horizon.

The sun is not only moving northward on the horizon, it is also moving higher up in the sky and is directly overhead at the Tropic of Cancer at noon on June 20 or 21, the day of the summer solstice. The point when the earth is the farthest (sun highest in the sky) from the sun is called the "aphelion." The "aphelion" occurs in the first week of July (the date depends on the year). These predictable celestial events follow the same pattern year after year and are similar to the myth of the crucifixion and ascension of Jesus. The sun gives us life and light, and Jesus is often associated with the word "light" in the Christian Bible.

John 12:46

> 46. I am come a light into the world, that whosoever believeth on me should not abide in darkness.

John 8:12

> 12. Then spake Jesus again unto them, saying, I am the light of the world: he that followeth me shall not walk in darkness, but shall have the light of life.

John 9:5

> 5. As long as I am in the world, I am the light of the world.

Matthew 5:14

> 14. Ye are the light of the world. A city that is set on an hill cannot be hid.

The solar system's motion around a central sun is the basis for the Hindu concept of the great four ages of the Yuga system. A complete Yuga cycle, which is one full day in the life of the Hindu creator god Brahma, lasts millions of years. According to the myth, there are four ages of life on earth: Krita or Satya-Yuga, 1,728,000 years; Treta-Yuga, 1,296,000 years; Dvapara-Yuga, 864,000 years; and Kali-Yuga, 432,000 years.

Each cycle represents a leg of the Dharma bull, and the years of each cycle are derived by subtracting 432,000 years from each age, starting with the oldest. The first cycle, which was 1,728,000 years ago, was a time of peace, harmony, love, longevity, and great accomplishments on earth, as the Dharma bull was standing on all four legs.

In each successive age of life, the Dharma bull stood on one fewer leg and mankind deteriorated. The shortest and last cycle, which we are in now, lasts 432,000 years, and the Dharma bull is standing on only one leg; as a result, this is a dark age of evil, corruption, hate, greed, death, destruction, war, famine, and disease.

Hinduism describes Dharma as a natural, universal law whose observance enables humans to be contented and happy, and to avoid degradation and suffering. Dharma is the moral law combined with spiritual discipline that guides one's life. Dharma is considered the very foundation of life.

The bull and cow are sacred animals and symbols in the mythical religions of Africa/Kemet/Anu, Hinduism, and Buddhism.

The Great Year and the Zodiac

The Great Year is a term in astronomy used to describe the precession of the spring and autumn equinoxes. It takes about 25,765 years for the vernal (spring) equinox to pass through all twelve of the Zodiac constellations.

Think of the earth as a clock, and the equinoxes as two long hands on a clock that are moving counterclockwise and the Zodiac constellations as the hours on a clock.

The earth wobbles on its axis like a spinning top winding down as it spins on the floor. As the earth wobbles on its axis, the Zodiac constellations appear from earth to move and change slowly in the sky.

The vernal equinox in the northern hemisphere is on the verge of moving slowly out of the Zodiac constellation Pisces and into the Zodiac constellation of Aquarius—thus, "This is the Dawning of the Age of Aquarius."

The vernal equinox moves counterclockwise from one constellation to another about every two thousand years (about every 2,147.0833 years; the years can vary depending on the scientific source); currently we are in the constellation Pisces.

If you go backward 2,147.0833 years in order, starting from 2012 (which is close to the end of the current age of Pisces) to Aries, then Taurus, we would be at the end of the Zodiac Age of Taurus, around 2282 BCE. The Zodiac Age of Taurus was approximatley, 4429–2282 BCE, which places us in the era of the man-made religion of Africa/Kemet/Anu and close to the beginning of the religion of Hinduism.

Regardless of the Zodiac Age that a man lived in while writing the mythical religions of Africa/Kemet/Anu and Hinduism, one can find multiple Zodiac constellations overlapping and being associated with a particular myth.

The same is true of other religions like Judaism, Christianity, Islam, and Buddhism. Just like these religions reworked the religious myths of Africa/Kemet/Anu, they also used multiple and overlapping Zodiac signs connected to the twelve Zodiac Ages in their myths.

Buddhism arose out of Hinduism, and many sacred symbols (like the bull and cow) are similar in both religions. Cows often walk around untouched in India (where they are considered sacred), like you often see cats and dogs walking around in other countries.

The Dharma bull is a sacred animal in Hinduism. The cow is considered a sign of fertility and life; it is to be respected and cared for. The cow is considered the best source of milk for humans if the mother cannot provide it for her child; cows and bulls are slaughtered and meat is eaten, but vegetarianism is encouraged and abstention from eating meat brings spiritual rewards. The gestation period of a cow is 285 days (roughly nine months), close to that of a human female, and cows and bulls are believed to have healing powers.

Apis, the mythical bull in African/Kemetic/Anu religion, is associated with fertility, virility, strength, fighting spirit, and renewal of life. The bull is a symbol found in African/Kemetic/Anu hieroglyphics (Mdw-Ntr) and is associated with Ptah, who was worshipped in the cities of Memphis and Heliopolis in Kemet/Egypt. In later myths, Apis became associated with Osiris.

The sun disk located inside of a cow's horns is the artistic symbol of the crown worn by Hathor and Isis, the two most revered goddesses in African/Kemetic/Anu religion. Isis is sometimes depicted with a crown on her head in the shape of a throne; other times, she is shown with the sun disk between the cow's horns. At other times the goddess Hathor is depicted as a cow with the sun disk between its horns.

The ram, like the bull, was sacred in Africa/Kemet/Anu culture and in Hinduism. Khnum is depicted as having the body of a man and the head of a ram. Osiris is also depicted at times with a pair of ram horns attached to his Atef crown.

The African/Kemetic/Anu god Banebdjedet was a ram-headed god. His wife, the goddess Hatmehyt, was associated with fish, which were later considered a sacred animal associated with the Nile River.

One of the most visited tourist attractions in Luxor, Egypt, is the two processional rows of sphinxes, statues with the head of a ram and the body of a lion. They sit on either side of the long walkway leading up to the Temple of Ipet (called Temple of Luxor by the Arabs).

The use of "ram" within the names of people in Africa/Kemet/Anu was not uncommon; one of the more famous names used was Ramses or Ramesses. At least nine pharaohs chose some form of this name, including Ramses II, known as "Ramses the Great," who ruled for sixty-seven years.

The use of "ram" as part of a name is also common in India. In Hinduism, the god Ram or Rama is the seventh incarnation of Vishnu and the central character in the "Ramayana Epic." The Ramayana is referred to as the soul of India; it is a guide to god-realization and righteousness. The ideals presented in the Ramayana allow the individual believer to grow into an ideal citizen and human being.

In Judaism the names Ram and Ramah are associated with the words, high, tall, lofty, elevated, and sublime. The name Ram is associated with the Torah scholar, physician, and philosopher Rambam, Rabbi Moshe ben Maimon (Maimonides), author of the Jewish Thirteen Fundamental Principles of Faith mentioned in chapter four.

A relief of most of the Zodiac constellations, located in the Temple of Hathor at Dendera, Egypt, is dedicated to Osiris. This is one of the first known attempts to depict the movement of constellations visible at night over many years in Africa/Kemet/Anu; it also documents the twelve parts of the sky visible during the 25,765-year cycle of the Great Year.

African/Kemetic/Anu culture used many Zodiac constellations in their myths. Aries the ram is found at Luxor and associated with the creator god Khnum; Taurus the bull with the mythical bull Apis (in other versions of his myth and art, Apis is represented and depicted as a god, having the body of a man and the head of a bull); Leo the lion in the myth of The Sphinx, and the Twin Lion Gods of Yesterday and Today; Pisces the fish with the goddess Hatmehyt; Gemini the twins depicted in the Dendera Zodiac. Virgo the virgin is associated with the goddess Isis; Libra the scales with the Scale of Truth or Justice in the Judgment Scene of Ani; Capricorn the goat with fertility and used as a sacrificial animal; Aquarius the water bearer with the god Hapi (or Hapy), the god of the Nile River depicted in the Dendera Zodiac as a man pouring water from two vases. According to some scholars, a crab (Cancer the crab) ate the phallus of the dismembered Osiris and was considered sacred and forbidden from being eaten.

Astronomy, Christianity, and Judaism

The men who wrote the religious myths of Judaism and Christianity also used Zodiac signs in their symbolism. This section summarizes how conflicts have arisen over whether people are worshipping the correct Zodiac sign, how Zodiac signs were used to test the faith of a mythical character, and how one Zodiac sign slayed another over supremacy.

Christianity considers heaven to be up in the sky, where departed souls rise or ascend to be with God. The Christian Bible and Tanakh of Judaism states that God finished the creation in six days and rested on the seventh day, which he blessed and sanctified. The seventh day is the Sabbath day, which is to be remembered and kept holy. No work is to be done on this day, because it has been blessed by God.

However, despite these texts (Genesis 1:31, Genesis 2:1–3) and the 4th Commandment, most Christians around the world attend church on Sunday, the first day of the week, not the seventh day, which is Saturday. Sunday obviously gets its name from the sun, and many Christians unknowingly disobey their own Scriptures because Christianity is a solar (sun)-based religion. The men who wrote the myth of Jesus connected his myth with the sun. The "Son of God" rose in three days, on the first day of the week (Sunday). Because Jesus rose on the first day of the week (Sunday), most Christians attend church and celebrate the Sabbath on Sunday.

The verses in the Bible cited for Jesus rising on the first day of the week are: Matthew 28:1-6, Luke 24:1-8, and Mark 16:1-11. Mark 16:1-2 states: "And when the sabbath was past, Mary Magdalene, and Mary the mother of James, and Salome, had bought sweet spices, that they might come and anoint him. And very early in the morning the first day of the week, they came unto the sepulcher at the rising of the sun." Jesus is associated with the sun similar to African/Kemetic/Anu solar (sun) gods, Aten, Khepri, Atum, and Ra mentioned throughout this book.

Seventh-Day Adventists, however, follow the strict guidelines for the Sabbath day; they attend church to worship God on Saturday. Followers of Judaism and Seventh-Day Adventists observe the Sabbath day from sunset on Friday, when God finished his work of creation, to sunset on Saturday.

The Shofar, a ram's (Aries, the ram) horn, is blown in synagogues during certain Jewish holidays, such as Rosh Hashanah, the Jewish New Year. No work is permitted on Rosh Hashanah, and the biblical passage cited for that restriction is Leviticus 23:24–25.

According to some accounts, the ram's horn is to be blown in the synagogue a hundred times. This symbol reminds the Jewish people of the willingness of Abraham to sacrifice his son, Isaac, to fulfill God's command. The Shofar is in most cases made from the ram's (Aries) horn but can be made from the horn of a goat (Capricorn), a sheep (a male sheep is a ram), an antelope (one species of antelope is called goat-antelope), or a gazelle (both the gazelle and the antelope are in the same bovidae family as rams, goats, and sheep).

The one animal horn that is not used during the religious celebration of Rosh Hashanah is the bull (sign of Taurus), which was considered a sacred animal by the religions of Africa/Kemet/Anu and Hinduism. This may be partly because the African/Kemetic/Anu rulers oppressed the Jewish people.

Daniel 5:7–8 and 11–12

> 7. The king cried aloud to bring in the astrologers, the Chaldeans, and the soothsayers. And the king spake, and said to the wise men of Babylon, Whosoever shall read this writing, and shew me the interpretation thereof, shall be clothed with scarlet, and have a chain of gold about his neck, and shall be the third ruler in the kingdom. 8. Then came in all the king's wise men: but they could not read the writing, nor make known to the king the interpretation thereof.... 11. There is a man in thy kingdom, in whom is the spirit of the holy gods; and in the days of thy father light and understanding and wisdom, like the wisdom of the gods, was found in him; whom the king Nebuchadnezzar thy father, the king, I say, thy father, made master of the magicians, astrologers, Chaldeans, and soothsayers; 12. Forasmuch as an excellent spirit, and knowledge, and understanding, interpreting of

dreams, and shewing of hard sentences, and dissolving of doubts, were found in the same Daniel, whom the king named Belteshazzar: now let Daniel be called, and he will shew the interpretation.

Critique: There is little doubt in these Scriptures that astronomy and astrology play a major role as source material for the personal attributes associated with Daniel, one of the major characters in the religions of Judaism and Christianity. As mentioned, astrology is defined as a pseudoscience claming diviniation by the positions of the planets, sun, and moon; a system of beliefs that the relative positions of celestial bodies can provide information about personality, human affairs, and other terrestrial matters. A "Chaldean" is a wise man skilled in occult (knowledge of hidden supernatural forces). A "soothsayer" is someone who makes predictions of the future using magic, intuition, or intelligence.

Daniel 5:11 says he has the "spirit of the holy gods" in him (note: plural gods, similar to the polytheistic gods of Africa/Kemet/Anu and Hinduism, who are manifestations of a supreme god). Daniel is master of the magicians, astrologers, Chaldeans, and soothsayers.

Daniel in the Lions' Den

One of the major myths of Christianity and Judaism is the myth of Daniel in the Lions' Den (Daniel 6:1–28). Daniel is the favorite of the king, who has placed him above the other presidents and princes because of his excellent spirit. The other presidents and princes are jealous of Daniel and conspire to find a way to make him lose favor in the eyes of the king.

They devise a plan to use Daniel's faith against him, so they persuade the king to establish a royal statute, saying no other god for thirty days can be worshipped except him. Daniel still goes home and prays three times a day in the direction of Jerusalem, giving thanks to God.

The men who conspired against Daniel find him praying to God and tell the king, who becomes enraged that Daniel is worshipping another god and disobeying his decree. He has Daniel thrown in a lions den to see if his God will save him. The king seals up the den, goes home, and comes back the next day to find Daniel still alive.

Daniel tells the king that an angel of his God protected him from the lions by shutting the mouths of the lions overnight. Daniel is rewarded for his faith in his God, and the king orders the men who conspired against Daniel thrown into the lions' den along with their wives and children.

The same lions who were not allowed to harm Daniel kill his accusers and their families. The writers of the Christian Bible and the Tanakh of Judaism were living during the end of the Age of Aries, the ram or the Age of Pisces, the fish (Christianity) and middle to end of the Age of Aries, the ram (Judaism). The lion in this myth is symbolic of the old Zodiac constellation Leo (the lion).

This myth is a test of the loyalty and faith of Daniel to his God. The lion tests the protective powers, dominion, and supremacy of Daniel's God. Daniel's God reigns supreme over the Age of Leo, the lion—another religious symbol (The Sphinx and Twin Lion Gods of Yesterday and Today) of the African/Kemetic/Anu culture that oppressed the Jewish people.

Abraham and Isaac

Another test of loyalty and faith to God where a Zodiac constellation is used is the myth of Abraham and Isaac (Genesis 22:1–24). In this myth, God tests the faith and loyalty of Abraham by telling him to sacrifice his only son Isaac as a burnt offering. Abraham obeys God and goes to set up an altar and prepares to sacrifice his only son to God.

As Abraham prepares to kill Isaac, an angel of God stops him because he has passed the test. God knows that he fears him, has faith, and is loyal. Abraham then looks up and sees a ram with its horns stuck in a thicket. He takes the ram (from the Zodiac Age of Aries, the ram) and offers it up on the altar to God instead of his son. God is pleased with the offering and the loyalty and faith shown by Abraham in offering his only son for sacrifice, saying, "For now I know that thou fearest God, seeing thou hast not withheld thy son, thine only son for me.... I will bless thee, and in multiplying I will multiply thy seed as the stars of the heaven...."

The Ram versus the Goat

Sometimes the men writing these religious myths overlap Zodiac Ages; for example, we find Capricorn the goat and Aries the ram being used in the same myth, where the goat of Capricorn fights and slays the ram of Aries. We also find Jesus being associated with Pisces the fish and Aries, the ram. (A ram is a male sheep.)

One interesting religious myth where two Zodiac signs are fighting each other is found in Daniel 8:3–12, where Daniel is telling about one of his visions. Daniel is the master of the astrologers (Daniel 5:11), and in this myth the goat (Capricorn) is used as a sacrificial animal during the Zodiac Age of Aries the ram.

Daniel 8:3–12

> 3. Then I lifted up mine eyes, and saw, and, behold, there stood before the river a ram which had two horns: and the two horns were high; but one was higher than the other, and the higher came up last. 4. I saw the ram pushing westward, and northward, and southward; so that no beasts might stand before him, neither was there any that could deliver out of his hand; but he did according to his will, and became great. 5. And as I was considering, behold, an he goat came from the west on the face of the whole earth, and touched not the ground: and the goat had a notable horn between his eyes. 6. And he came to the ram that had two horns, which I had seen standing before the river, and ran unto him in the fury of his power. 7. And I saw him come close unto the ram, and he was moved with choler against him, and smote the ram, and brake his two horns: and there was no power in the ram to stand before him, but he cast him down to the ground, and stamped upon him: and there was none that could deliver the ram out of his hand. 8. Therefore the he goat waxed very great: and when he was strong, the great horn was broken; and for it came up four notable ones toward the four winds of heaven. 9. And out of one of them came forth a little horn, which waxed exceeding great, toward the south, and toward the east, and toward the pleasant land. 10. And it waxed great, even to the host of heaven; and it cast down some of the host and of the stars to the ground, and stamped upon them. 11. Yea, he magnified himself even to the prince of the host, and by him the daily sacrifice was taken away, and the place of a sanctuary was cast down. 12. And an host was given him against the

> daily sacrifice by reason of transgression, and it cast down
> the truth to the ground; and it practised, and prospered.

Critique: "Stamped" means stomp, walk heavily, destroy, or extinguish. The goat of Capricorn in this vision is literally pulling out of the sky the constellation Aries the ram: "some of the host and of the stars to the ground," where he "stamped upon them." This action ends the daily sacrificing of the goat of Capricorn (Daniel 8:11–12), which is from an older Zodiac Age and not the current Zodiac Age of Aries, the ram.

The religious books of Judaism and Christianity state in Daniel 8:20–21 that the use of the ram of Aries and the goat of Capricorn is symbolic of the mythical war between the kingdom of Grecia and the kingdoms of Media and Persia. The two horns of the ram represent the mythical kings of Media and Persia, and the "rough goat" is the mythical king of Grecia.

Moses and the Molten Calf

Exodus Chapter 12 describes the guidelines and instructions God gives to Moses and his brother Aaron about the Passover. They are to tell the congregation of Israel about the use of a lamb (a young sheep) as the animal to be eaten during the lord's Passover.

God is passing through Egypt that night to destroy the first-born in the land of Egypt and to destroy the gods of the Egyptians. The Jewish people in order to avoid the wrath of god are to mark with the blood of the slaughtered lamb the two side posts and the upper door post of the houses where they live and where they have eaten the lamb. Moses and the Jewish people of this mythical time are associated with the Zodiac Age of Aries, the ram. (A ram is a male sheep.)

The African/Kemetic/Anu mythical religion is associated with several Zodiac Ages, including Aquarius, Leo, Aries, Pisces, and Taurus. The Egyptian association with the bull and cow led to the conflict between Moses and the children of Israel over the molten calf.

Summary of Exodus 32:1–35

Moses had been up on the mountain for a very long time and the children of Israel feared he would not return. So the children of Israel complained and then convinced Aaron to make a molten calf for them to worship and pray to.

The molten calf represents Taurus the bull and is symbolic of the other gods and goddesses of Ancient Egypt that the children of Israel were familiar with but were not supposed to worship anymore (e.g., the goddesses Nut, associated with the Heavenly Cow or Cow of Heaven, and Hathor, represented at times as a Divine Cow).

Moses came down from the mountain, found the children of Israel worshipping the molten calf (the wrong god), and went ballistic; he smashed the Tablets of Stone that God had given him; broke apart the molten calf and burned it; then ground it up into powder and "strawed it upon the water, and made the children of Israel drink of it."

He then chewed out Aaron and made the children of Israel choose which god they were going to worship; he commanded them to take up arms and "slay every man his brother, and every man his companion, and every man his neighbour." Moses' orders were followed, and about three thousand men died that day.

Moses then ordered the people to consecrate themselves to God. He then went back up onto the mountain and asked God to forgive their sins. God told Moses that all who sinned against him would be removed from his book, and he was to go and lead the people to the Promised Land. God plagued the children of Israel because they worshipped the molten calf they had asked Aaron to make.

Jesus, the Equinoxes, and the Solstices in the Northern Hemisphere

The death of Jesus is a well-known Christian myth; he was crucified on a cross; placed in a sepulcher (burial chamber); rose after three days; then ascended up into heaven to live with God. This myth is almost identical to what happens during the autumnal equinox, winter solstice, vernal equinox, and summer solstice in the northern hemisphere.

Jesus is very similar to the African/Kemetic/Anu solar gods written about in this book. His personal attributes are associated with the sun; he is the son (sun) of God. As mentioned earlier in the chapter, the use of symbolic light as a means to illuminate the world from darkness is associated with Jesus in the Christian Bible (John 12:46, John 8:12, John 9:5, and Matthew 5:14).

In the northern hemisphere, the autumnal equinox arrives on September 22 or 23 (depending on the year), when the sun is centered on the earth's equator. When the sun rises in the east, it is in the middle of the horizon, and when the sun sets in the west, it is in the middle of the horizon; the sun forms a "celestial cross" and is "crucifying the horizon."

The sun's movement on the horizon during this time of year is from north to south as it crosses the earth's equator. The sun is also descending (or becoming lower) in the sky as seen from earth. The sun has crossed over or passed over the earth's equator by September 24.

As the sun sets each day in the west, it continues to move south and descend in the sky as seen from earth until the winter solstice, when it is directly overhead at the Tropic of Capricorn at noon on December 21 or 22 (depending on the year). The point when the earth is the closet (sun lowest in the sky) to the sun is called the "perihelion." The "perihelion" occurs in the first week of January (the date depends on the year).

At the winter solstice, the sun appears to stop its southern movement on the horizon and pauses for about three days, then it reverses and begins to move north on the horizon.

As mentioned earlier, scientifically, the reason for the movement of the sun on the horizon and the appearance from earth of being lower or higher in the sky is because of the movement of the earth as it revolves around the sun and spins on its axis.

Around three days after the winter solstice, December 25, the sun starts to rise up in the sky as seen from earth and begins to move from south to north on the horizon each morning at sunrise. The sun continues moving north on the horizon and up in the sky until March 20 or 21 (depending on the year), the vernal (spring) equinox. The sun crosses directly over the earth's equator and is centered in the middle of the horizon facing east at sunrise again, "crucifying the horizon" and forming a "celestial cross."

The sun then crosses over or passes over the point of the celestial crucifixion and continues on its northern ascension or movement each morning at sunrise until the summer solstice on June 20 or 21. The sun is directly overhead at the Tropic of Cancer at noon on the day of the summer solstice. As mentioned earlier, the point when the earth is the farthest (sun highest in the sky) from the sun is called the "aphelion." The "aphelion" occurs in the first week of July (the date depends on the year).

If you compare the mythical crucifixion, death, burial, resurrection in three days, and ascension into heaven of Jesus with the celestial solar events of the equinoxes and solstices, one can see similarities.

The sun in September and March in the northern hemisphere crucifies the horizon at sunset and sunrise, forming a celestial cross. After the autumnal equinox in September, the sun moves south on the horizon and reaches its most southern point on the horizon, where it stops on the day of the winter solstice.

Also after the autumnal equinox, the sun is moving lower and lower in the sky as seen from earth. It reaches its lowest point in the sky as viewed from earth and is the closest to earth on December 21 or 22 (the winter solstice) thru the first week in January (the "perihelion"). At the winter solstice the sun stops, pauses, dies, or is buried. About three days after the sun stops, pauses, dies, or is buried, it is resurrected or reborn and begins to rise up in the sky again as viewed from earth, as it starts moving northward on the horizon.

There is another crucifixion of the sun on the horizon during the vernal equinox, the time of year Easter is celebrated (the first Sunday after the first full moon on or after the vernal (spring) equinox, March 20 or 21).

The sun then continues northward on the horizon and crosses over or passes over the celestial point of crucifixion and ascends or rises to its highest point in the sky on June 20 or 21 (the summer solstice) thru the first week of July (the "aphelion"). The sun on the day of the summer solstice at sunrise reaches its most northern point on the horizon. The sun again pauses for about three days before reversing itself and heading south again on the horizon.

The myth of Jesus is man-made, but it follows the natural law of nature and the universe as it mimics the perceived movement of the sun, caused by the earth being tilted on its axis, spinning, and wobbling as it revolves around the sun.

Religious Symbols

The use of religious symbols has its origin in African/Kemetic/Anu culture. Islam uses the crescent moon and star as its religious symbol. Tehuti is associated with the moon and is depicted at times as a man with the head of an ibis bird.

The crown on top of his head is the curved beak of the ibis, which looks like the crescent moon with a full moon or sun inside of the crescent moon. Osiris was associated with the moon, and his wife, Isis, was associated with the star Sirius.

Osiris and Isis are the inseparable pair: sister-brother, husband-wife, and mother-father. Islam's use of the moon and star as a celestial pairing is similar. The African/Kemetic/Anu goddess Hathor is depicted wearing a crown with cow's horns shaped like a crescent moon with the sun inside the cow's horns. Isis is sometimes depicted with the same crown on top of her head.

The cross of Christianity has its origin in African/Kemetic/Anu culture. The African/Kemetic/Anu ankh, Christian cross, Latin-Christian cross, equilateral cross, and Christian patriarchal cross can be found in the hieroglyphics of Africa/Kemet/Anu. (Note: The African/Kemetic/Anu name for hieroglyphics is Mdw-Ntr.) The early Coptic (Egyptian) Christian ankh and crosses were derived from the African/Kemetic/Anu ankh. The Tau cross originated in Africa/Kemet/Anu and is nothing more than the bottom half of the ankh.

The shape of the Jewish Tablets of Stone, Stone Tablets, or Tablets of Testimony of Moses is identical to the double-plumed crown found sitting on top of the heads of numerous gods and goddesses of Africa/Kemet/Anu, including Amun, Mont-ra, Ankhnesneferibra, Min, Suchos, Ptah-Sokar-Osiris, and Sopdu. The shape of a stele or stela (a stone tablet), used by some to carve African/Kemetic/Anu hieroglyphics into, is in the exact same shape as the Hebrew Tablets of Stone of Moses.

The Tejen or Tekhen (obelisk) is another African/Kemetic/Anu religious symbol found in countries around the world (either stolen out of Africa or re-created). It is found in such places as the middle of St. Peter's Square at the Vatican in Rome; Central Park in New York City; Victoria (Thames) Embankment in London; Place de la Concorde in Paris; and recreated as the Washington Monument in Washington DC.

Tejens or Tekhens (obelisks) were used as grave markers in the United States and all around the world, especially in European countries, starting in the late seventeenth century and continuing into the nineteenth century. This African/Kemetic/Anu solar religious monument symbolizes protection, stability, the creative force, vivifying power, and resurrection.

The long shaft of the Tejen or Tekhen represents the sun's rays, which bring forth the power of life, and the pyramid on top of the long shaft represents eternity and everlastingness. It is designed to make the viewer look up and think of the deceased, who is resurrected and in heaven.

As a grave marker, it is designed to protect the deceased's spirit by perforating the sky so that accumulated negative forces built up on earth can be released from the grave area. It also symbolizes pointing, protecting, and leading the way for the deceased soul or spirit to ascend up into heaven.

The Tejen or Tekhen (obelisk) was always placed in an open area around the center of religious structures like the Grande Lodge of Wa-Set and around temples like the Temple of Ipet (called Temple of Luxor by the Arabs) and the Temple of Ipet-Isut, the Holiest of Places (called Temple of Karnak by the Arabs).

As mentioned earlier, the Tejen or Tekhen is associated with the sun, protection, stability, the creative force, vivifying power, and resurrection. When you see the Tejen (obelisk) sitting in the middle of St. Peter's Square at the Vatican in Rome, it is evidence of the degree to which African/Kemetic/Anu culture has been used by the men who made up the religion of Christianity.

This African/Kemetic/Anu religious symbol was taken out of Africa in the first century CE, and erected in the Forum of Caesar; then moved to the Circus of Caligula (later Circus of Nero) in Rome. The Tejen was then moved to St. Peter's Square on the orders of Pope Sixtus V in 1586. Where in Africa/Kemet/Anu the Tejen was taken from is unclear and in dispute, but some historian's and scholars claim the Tejen or Tekhen (obelisk) was taken from one of the numerous African/ Kemetic/Anu temples dedicated to the numerous sun gods located in Heliopolis, Egypt. Some historian's and scholars say the Tejen or Tekhen in St. Peters Square was first erected in the African/Kemetic/Anu city of Philae or Alexandria by Gaius Cornelius Gallus, the Roman Prefect to Kemet/Egypt, memorializing his accomplishments in Africa/Kemet/Anu.

St. Peter's Basilica faces east. The sun rises in the east and the "Son of God" (Jesus) was born in the east (Jerusalem). Jesus as mentioned earlier is associated with the sun. The Tejen is a symbol of the sun, and is also associated with the east and the rising sun. At the funeral of Pope John Paul II when the Trapezoidal Coffin of Pope John Paul II was placed down on the ground in St. Peter's Square, it directly faced the Tejen or Tekhen (obelisk) in the direction of east, where the sun rises.

Also from an aerial view of the funeral of Pope John Paul II, the open space resulting from the arraignment of the seating in front of the Tejen or Tekhen (obelisk) was shaped like a Tejen with the top pointing east in the direction of the rising sun. Some historians and scholars have also claimed that the Tejen or Tekhen is a sun dial (or gnomon: the stationary arm that projects the shadow of a sundial), and that the Tejen or Tekhen is also aligned with the winter and summer solstices. Matthew 24:27 states: "For as the lightning cometh out of the east, and shineth even unto the west; so shall also the coming of the Son of man be." The men who designed the Vatican over the years could have chosen any Christian symbol for St. Peter's Square, but they chose the Tejen.

Vatican City is one of the holiest sites of the Catholic Christian church. The tomb of the mythical disciple of Jesus, Peter (of whom Jesus said in the Bible, "Thou art Peter and upon this rock I will build my church"), is according to some scholars and historians (not all) located on the site of St. Peter's Basilica. Many of the popes of the Catholic Church are buried in St. Peter's Basilica.

What is interesting is that when you look at an aerial view of Vatican City, the St. Peter's Basilica complex is shaped like a Christian cross, with Peter's tomb positioned in the center, where the two arms of the cross intersect.

If you follow a straight line from the tomb of Peter, it leads straight to the African/Kemetic/Anu Tejen or Tekhen with a cross on top, positioned in the middle of St. Peter's Square. St. Peter's Square and the buildings that flank the square are shaped like an African/Kemetic/Anu ankh.

The two sites are connected, and the Tejen or Tekhen (obelisk) has the same symbolic meaning for the tombs of the deceased popes and Peter as it does for the deceased who are buried in cemeteries around the world: it is a solar symbol of protection, stability, the creative force, vivifying power, and resurrection.

The solar connection is also interesting because the top part of St. Peter's Square is shaped like an oval, similar to the elliptical orbit of the earth around the sun. The Tejen or Tekhen sits in the center of the oval, like the sun sits in the center of the planets that revolve around it. Another astronomy connection associated with St. Peter's Square can be seen from an aerial view: the lines on the ground inside of St. Peter's Square (see back cover) form a Chaos Star (if you draw an X and then draw a proportional straight horizontal line through the middle of the X and then draw a proportional vertical line through the middle of the X that is what a chaos star looks like. You can also look at the asterick above the number eight on your computer keyboard and just draw a proportional horizontal line through the middle of the asterick. The Tejen or Tekhen sits in the middle of the Chaos Star, which is referred to as a sun, like the star we call our sun.

The numerous columns that line St. Peter's Square and the front of the Basilica are also of African/Kemetic/Anu origin. Columns were used in the Grande Lodge of Wa-Set and sites like the Temple of Queen Hatshepsut and temple sites at Edfu, Medinet, Thebes, Denderah, and Philae.

Columns were used for religious temples in Africa/Kemet/Anu long before Greece or Rome ever existed. Millions of Christians visit Vatican City, St. Peter's Square, and St. Peter's Basilica each year. They stand around the Tejen or Tekhen in the middle of St. Peter's Square to pray and listen to their religious and spiritual leader, the pope.

The Interlacing Triangles, Six-Pointed Star, or Hexagram

One of the most popular religious symbols is the two interlacing triangles, which form a hexagram; their use has often been debated and theorized by scholars. The ancient origins and the history of this symbol have been mysteriously (and conveniently) lost, and there are many theories about its meaning.

Hexagrams are found in Hinduism; "mandala" means sacred circle and symbolizes the womb of creation. Mandalas translate complex mathematical expressions into simple shapes and forms. They are geometric designs that are made through the uniform division of the circle.

The shapes that are derived from this division of the circle are symbolic of the mathematical principles of creation. They are symbolic of how nature works and are representative of the order of the universe; they are symbols of heaven and earth.

Yantras are a particular field of Mandala imagery. A Yantra is a three dimensional Mandala, it is a series of geometrical diagrams using even-sided interlacing triangles, isosceles triangles (a triangle having two sides of equal length), or both. They represent the universe and are used in Hindu meditation and worship. The Yantra symbolizes the origin, history, dynamics, and development of the universe and the material world.

The best-known Yantra diagram is the Sri Yantra Mandala; it is a meditation and concentration diagram. When you concentrate and look into the center of the diagram, it begins to play tricks on your eyes. The longer you look at the diagram, you begin to see triangles in a row pointing up; triangles in a row pointing down; hexagrams or interlaced triangles; both even-sided triangles and isosceles triangles; triangles that are touching at the top point; triangles that are starting to interlace at their top points; diamond shapes; circles; squares; rectangles; and other geometric shapes.

Jewish people refer to this symbol as the Star of David. It is not mentioned in any ancient Jewish scriptures. Depending on which source you are using, the Star of David does not appear to be associated with the Jewish people until the Middle Ages, and then it does not have any great religious significance. The symbol is more a part of Jewish tradition, culture, and identity than it is a religious symbol. It has become the most closely associated symbol with the Jewish people.

During World War II, Nazis in Germany forced Jewish people to wear the interlaced triangles as a means of identifying and persecuting them. Their property and homes were marked with the interlaced triangles. When the war ended, the Star of David became a unifying symbol in the ongoing struggle of the Jewish people seeking a homeland.

On May 14, 1948, Israel declared its independence, and the Star of David was solidified as the symbol of the Jewish people when it was chosen as the emblem for the national flag of the State of Israel. Throughout history, it has not only been associated with David but also King Solomon, and it is sometimes referred to as "Magen David," which means "Shield of David."

The hexagram, six-pointed star, or interlaced triangles can be found among different religions. The symbol can be found on the windows of Christian churches as a symbol of identifying with the Jewish people of the Christian Bible. Some Christians refer to the hexagram as the "Star of Creation" (see later text). It is found among the Rastafarians of Jamaica and some African-American churches, who view King David, King Solomon, and the Star of David as African. It can also be found in mosques and on Islamic artifacts. Islam associates the hexagram with both King David and King Solomon, who are viewed as great prophets and are revered characters within Islam.

There are many theories about the meaning of the interlaced triangles or hexagram; some say it represents the shield of King David, or the seal of King Solomon. Some view it as the satanic symbol of the devil. Some believe it represents the six domains of God: east, west, north, south, heaven, and earth. One theory is that the interlacing triangles or hexagram represents good and evil; and others theorize the twelve sides of the star represent the twelve tribes of Israel. Some say it symbolizes "as above so as below."

In addition to being a religious symbol, the hexagram is also used by a variety of individuals, cultures, and organizations. The smaller stars in the center of the five-pointed star of the United States Presidential Medal of Freedom form a six-pointed star or hexagram; some sheriff's badges in the United States are shaped like a hexagram.

The hexagram is associated with the Star of Saturn; it was associated with magicians like the French occult author Eliphas Levi (1810–1875); it is also used as part of the seal of the Theosophical Society, founded in 1875.

The hexagram, interlaced triangles, or six-pointed star is one of the symbols of Freemasons, who derive many of their symbols and emblems from ancient African/Kemetic/Anu culture. It is also found on the back of the US dollar in the arrangement of the stars above the eagle's head.

On the left side of the back of the US dollar, when you interlace a triangle over the pyramid (starting with a horizontal line at the base of where the separation is at the top of the pyramid, where the Eye of Horus is, and draw a line straight across to the lettering on either side), the lines (points) will connect with the letters "A" on the left and "S" on the right. Then draw a line down on each side, closing the interlaced triangle or hexagram to "O," the last letter of the word "Ordo" at the bottom of the pyramid. Then if you look horizontal on the base of the pyramid (now a hexagram) to the left, the point of the pyramid or hexagram points to the letter "N," and the right point of the hexagram or pyramid (going horizontal) points to the letter "M."

These letters spell the word "Mason." Some of the founding fathers of America were associated with the Freemasons. There are many other Masonic symbols on the dollar bill and in the government and culture of the United States of America, which another whole book could be written about.

Note: One of the most respected members of the founding fathers of America was Thomas Paine. The readers of this book will find his 1793 book *The Age of Reason* interesting. In it he promotes deism, reason, and freethinking and argues against institutionalized religion and Christian doctrines. An author, pamphleteer, radical, intellectual, and revolutionary, Paine was involved in the French Revolution, where he was thrown in jail. In America his writings called for independence from Great Britain. He authored a series of pro-revolutionary pamphlets that helped ignite and spark the American Revolution.

The Star of Creation

Some scholars of African/Kemetic/Anu history refer to the hexagram as the "Star of Creation." Some Christian denominations also refer to the hexagram by the same name. The African/Kemetic/Anu meaning of the hexagram is hard to find, but it has been written about by several African/Kemetic/Anu scholars.

Through education, one can try and understand what these scholars and historians think the hexagram means. The hexagram is really two interlacing pyramids that represent the fusion of heaven and earth. In addition it represents the descent and ascent of spirit and matter.

The triangle (pyramid) pointing down represents descent; when we are born, we come from an everlasting, eternal, and heavenly spiritual form, and our spirit is manifested in our body, a temporary and mortal physical form on earth. The triangle pointing up represents ascent; when we die, our spirit leaves our temporary and mortal physical bodies and returns back to heaven in the form of an everlasting and eternal spirit.

The hexagram also represents the phrase "as above so as below," meaning the same laws in the heavens are also present in both humans and the earth we live on. How old are the atoms that make up our bodies? They are billions of years old—as old as the Big Bang Theory of the origin and beginning of the universe—with hydrogen being the oldest at around 13.7 to 14 billion years old. The other atoms that make up our bodies are at least 4 billion years old. Which are older, the atoms of a baby or an elderly person? It does not matter; the atoms of a baby are the same age as that of an elderly person: 4 to 14 billion years old.

Earth and the solar system we live in were created out of a stellar nursery (a molecular cloud with stars forming inside) at least 4.5 billion years ago. The earth, other planets, numerous moons, asteroids, meteoroids, and comets revolve around the sun, which is the star at the center of our solar system.

Asteroids, meteoroids, and comets come in different sizes and shapes; their orbital paths can be influenced by the gravitational pull of planets and the sun. This causes their orbital paths to be altered, which can result in collisions, releasing energy (and in the case of earth, this can cause destruction).

Atoms, on the other hand, are composed of three types of particles: protons, neutrons, and electrons. Protons (positive charge) and neutrons (neutral charge) are inside the nucleus, located in the center of the atom. Electrons (negative charge) swarm, zip, and revolve around the space between the outer edges of the atom and the nucleus.

The characteristics of the atom are similar to the gravitational pull of the planets and sun, which can cause collisions and annihilation. As electrons swarm, zip, and revolve around an atom and its nucleus, the negative electrons are drawn to the positive protons in the nucleus, and electrons can be knocked loose from the atom, taking their negative charge. This changes a neutral atom, leaving behind a atom with a net positive charge.

Free electrons can be accelerated, and if it collides with the opposite anti-particle of the electron, called a positron (an elementary particle with a positive charge), both particles may scatter, causing annihilation.

Precession is a comparatively slow gyration of the rotation axis of a spinning body about another line intersecting it so as to describe a cone. Precession of the earth's equinoxes is due to: the earth wobbling on it's axis like a spinning top winding down as it spins on the floor; as well as the westward motion of the equinoxes along the ecliptic; nonspherical shape of the earth; and the gravitational tidal forces of the moon and sun applying torque to the equatorial bulge of the earth.

Planets like mercury that orbit the sun experience precession. Atoms experience precession due to magnetic fields, type of isotope, chemical bonds, nearby atoms and molecules in its neighborhood, and nearby atoms and organization of molecules in tissue.

All things are composed of cells; bacteria and protozoa are single celled and consists of atoms. Humans, animals, plants, and fungi are multicellular and consist of millions, billions, and trillions of cells, which consist of millions, billions, and trillions of atoms.

Cells come in different types, sizes, and shapes; similarly, planets, stars, comets, meteors, and asteroids come in all types, sizes, and shapes. Cells carry out thousands of biochemical reactions each minute and reproduce new cells that perpetuate life.

After the Big Bang, space or the universe inflated, expanded, and began to cool. It continues to expand to this day. The stellar nursery (or molecular cloud) produced stars and planets because of its lowering temperatures, high density, gravitational force, and internal forces. Stars were produced like the sun at the center of our solar system, which produces, perpetuates, and gives us life on earth.

The atoms that make up our bodies come from the beginning of the universe. When you look into the sky at night or the sun in the daytime, you are looking at where you came from, what created you, and what gives you life in the present moment.

One day when we die and are cremated or buried in the ground, our cremated atoms will rise into in the sky; and our buried bodies will decay and be absorbed back into the earth—as a result—over time our atoms will return back into the sky and the heavens, where we originally came from.

African/Kemetic/Anu culture says the Star of Creation means "as above so as below." The same laws of nature are present in atoms, the solar system, and biological cells. They are all related, the same age atomically, and function in a similar way. We come from a spiritual form in the heavens and return to a spiritual form in the heavens when we die.

Chapter 7

The LGBT Animal Community

Genesis is the first book in the Bible of Christianity and the Tanakh of Judaism. Genesis chapters 1 and 2 state that God created the great whales, fish, and every living creature that moves, which the waters brought forth abundantly. God created every winged fowl, the beast of the earth, and the cattle after their kind, and every living thing that creeps upon the earth.

God saw that the creation was good and blessed the creatures that walk on the earth, fly in the air, and live in the waters. The creatures were told to be fruitful and multiply. God saw that everything he had made was "very good." He then sanctified his creation and rested on the seventh day.

Christianity and Judaism's scriptures and belief, that LGBT sexual preference and orientation is against the word of god, have its origins in the man-made religious writings of Africa/Kemet/Anu. This is not the word of God, just the word of the men who were influenced by African/Kemetic/Anu religion.

There are varying interpretations of the Declarations of Innocence/Negative Confessions found in the Papyrus of Ani, Papyrus of Nu, and Papyrus of Nebseni: "I have not committed adultery, I have not lain with men," "I have not committed fornication or had intercourse with men," and "I have not committed acts of sexual impurity, or lain with men."

These Declarations of Innocence are the source for the verses in Leviticus, the third book in the Bible of Christianity and the Tanakh of Judaism. Leviticus 18:22 says, "Thou shalt not lie with mankind, as with womankind: it is abomination." Leviticus 20:13 says, "If a man also lie with mankind, as he lieth with a woman, both of them have committed an abomination: they shall surely be put to death; their blood shall be upon them."

These scriptures in Leviticus were written by the same men who wrote in Leviticus 25:44–46 that God sanctions the buying and selling of slaves (and more unbelievable, the buying and selling of children as slaves).

Instead of referring to these texts as the "Book of Leviticus," it should be called the "Book of Discrimination, Violence, Ignorance, and Pathologically Insane Crackpots." The writers (and followers) of these scriptures were indeed mentally disturbed.

Any LGBT teenager or adult should ignore these man-made idiotic scriptures. How would you feel if someone wrote a religious book saying Santa Claus—or Bigfoot, or Tinkerbell, or the Tooth Fairy—said the LGBT lifestyle was an abomination? It wouldn't bother you, would it?

Any god that would enslave children is not a god, it's just a man with a sick mind writing a myth attributing his belief to a god. If Genesis chapters 1 and 2 are the word and work of God, then all animals have been blessed and sanctified by God, even those animals that display some form of LGBT behavior.

LGBT behavior in animals has been cited in court cases brought against anti-LGBT states in America. The information on LGBT animals is easy to research, so if you are interested, you can easily find it.

There are several animals that I will briefly mention. One animal who's sexual behavior is similar to humans is the bonobo ape. The bonobo, a great ape, is also called a pygmy chimpanzee/monkey or dwarf or gracile chimpanzee/monkey. Bonobos are some of the most nonviolent and peaceful animals on earth.

They have been referred to as the "free love primate" or "make love not war primate." Research and studies suggest that they are much more like humans, because a large percentage of their sexual activity has nothing to do with reproduction and more to do with pleasure. They are bisexual —and unfortunately, like humans, some adults have sex with adolescents. When bonobos are upset or agitated, they use sex to resolve the conflict instead of fighting.

Male giraffes also engage in courtship and mounting. They will rub their long necks together, and then one male will mount the other. Some studies have reported that males mounting each other is as common as heterosexual activity.

Studies have also shown that male bottlenose dolphins engage in same-sex activity at the same rate as heterosexual activity. One dolphin will use his snout to stimulate the penis of another, and they will rub their erect penises up against the body of another dolphin. One study reported that sometimes dolphins will engage in sexual activity with a trainer, getting an erection and trying to rub up against the trainer's body.

Studies have shown that it is common for male gray whales to roll around, splash, and rub their bellies together, allowing their genitals to touch.

The American bison have been observed engaging in same-sex mounting more than male-female copulation. The females only mate about once a year, and the males engage in same-sex behavior several times a day.

A well-known LGBT bird is the male Guianan Cock-of-the-Rock: this bird is said to engage in LGBT behavior about 40 percent of the time. A small percentage of these male birds never copulate with a female.

Both the black swan and the penguin are well-documented as engaging in same-sex pairing and child rearing. Observations of male black swans have shown that some same-sex males will use a female to mate with, then chase her away after she lays her egg; the male and his same-sex partner will hatch and raise the baby swan. Same-sex males will also drive away heterosexual couples from their egg and then hatch and raise the baby.

Roy and Silo, two famous chinstrap penguins of the Central Park Zoo in New York City, were same-sex partners for six years; they even hatched an egg that was given to them by zookeepers. The name of the baby penguin was Tango, and a book was written about them: *And Tango Makes Three*. Another famous same-sex pair of penguins who hatched and raised a baby were Harry and Pepper of the San Francisco Zoo.

Like Roy and Silo, Harry and Pepper broke up after six years. New studies from the Center for Functional and Evolutionary Ecology in Montpellier, France, suggest that the only reason penguins engage in same-sex pairings is because there is a shortage of mates from the opposite sex, and they are lonely. The study found that all same-sex couples eventually broke up and found an opposite-sex partner to pair with, and female same-sex pairs would split up to raise an egg with a male.

The problem with this study is that the relationships between Roy and Silo, and Harry and Pepper, lasted for six years. What difference does it make if they paired because of loneliness or attraction? The fact is they were in same-sex relationships, which lasted for years.

Over a six-year period, wasn't there ever the opportunity to form a heterosexual relationship? They are obviously bisexual, and if the opposite sex is not around, they have no problem being in a same-sex relationship when the need for affection, love, and bonding is required.

I am sure that not all penguins engage in same-sex pairings when there is a lack of members available from the opposite sex. The ones who do are bisexual, and their sexual preference is biologically predetermined at birth.

In an all-female or all-male prison, there is a lack of opposite-sex partners to have sex with. Despite this fact, the majority of people incarcerated in same-sex prisons do not engage in same-sex intercourse. There are people in prison who were LGBT before they went to prison and will be that way inside of prison.

However, inside prison there are always individuals who do engage in same-sex relationships because they are lonely and require love, affection, and bonding. They have no problem whatsoever forming a same-sex relationship.

Most inmates in prison do not form same-sex relationships because they are heterosexual and prefer sexual relationships with members of the opposite sex. Individuals who engage in same-sex relationships see nothing wrong with their choice, because their sexual views, beliefs, and preferences are biologically predetermined at birth.

Penguins (or human beings) do not choose a same-sex relationship simply and only because they are lonely. If that were the case, can you imagine the number of LGBT penguins (and people) that would populate the earth? I mean there are a lot of lonely people in this world and probably penguins too.

I am sure, just like in prison, there are lonely women and men in the world who choose same-sex relationships for love, affection, and bonding. However, biologically predetermined beliefs, views, and bisexual preferences, in my opinion, carry more weight in this debate.

In closing, I hope this book will help someone not feel guilty or have low spiritual self-esteem because of religion. Religion is not the word of any god, just the judgmental beliefs of the men who wrote the religious myths. If someone wants to follow a particular religion, then that is good for them (if it helps them make it through life). If a person tries to impose their religious beliefs onto others, then people should be aware that religions are nothing more than a man-made mythological belief; readers can use the material in this book to tell them so, and then tell them to go have a seat in a corner. With religion, I beg to differ. Ameen. Amun. AMEN.

BIBLIOGRAPHY

Amen, Nur Ankh. The Ankh: African Origin of Electromagnetism. Jamaica, NY: Nur Ankh Amen Co., 1993.

Asante, Molefi Kete. Classical Africa. Maywood, NJ: The Peoples Publishing Group, Inc., 1994.

Bagemihl, Bruce. Biological Exuberance: Animal Homosexuality and Natural Diversity. New, York, NY: St. Martin's Press, 1999.

Bauval, Robert and Gilbert, Adrian. The Orion Mystery. New York, NY: Three Rivers Press, 1994.

Ben-Jochannan, Yosef A.A., We the Black Jews: volumes I and II. Baltimore, MD: Black Classic Press, 1993.

Brugsch-Bey, Heinrich Karl. A History of Egypt Under the Pharaohs. Whitefish, MT: Kessinger Publishing, 1891.

Brugsch-Bey, Heireich, Karl and Underwood, Francis Henry (edited by, with introduction). The True Story of the Exodus of Israel. Boston, MA, and New York, NY: Lee and Shepard Publishers (MA) and Charles T. Dillingham (NY), 1880.

Budge, Wallis E.A., The Gods of the Egyptians: volumes I and II. New York, NY: Dover Publications, 1969.

Budge, Wallis E.A., Egyptian Religion. New York, NY: Carol Publishing Group, 1991.

Budge, Wallis E.A. The Book of the Dead. New York, NY: Carol Publishing Group, 1994.

Cann, Rebecca L., Stoneking, Mark, and Wilson, Allan C. "Mitochondrial DNA and Human Evolution, 1987," Nature Journal 325, (2010): 31–36.

Coppens, Yves. "Biography: Yves Coppens." Anthropoligist, http://yvescoppens.co.tv/

Davidson, Basil. A Guide to African History: revised and edited by Haskel Frankel, Garden City New York: Zenith Books, 1965.

Diop, Cheikh Anta. The African Origin of Civilization. Chicago, IL: Lawerence Hill Books, 1974.

Freud, Sigmund. Moses and Monotheism. New York, NY: Alfred A. Knopf Inc. and Random House, 1939.

Franklin, John Hope. Black Americans. New York, NY: Time-Life Books, 1973.

Franklin, John Hope and Moss Jr., Alfred A. From Slavery to Freedom. New York, NY: Alfred A. Knopf, Inc., 1988.

Hoagland, Richard, and Bara, Mike. Coast to Coast AM with Ian Punnett. Premiere Radio Networks Program # 001221C., 2000.

Hoyle, Fred. The Nature of the Universe. New York, NY: The New American Library, 1995.

James, George G.M. Stolen Legacy. Trenton, NJ: Africa World Press, 1992.

Jewish Virtual Library. The Holy Scriptures: The Tanakh. Jewish Publication Society, 1917, from the Jewish Bible, http://www.jewishvirtuallibrary.org/jsource/Bible/jpstoc.html.

Johanson, Donald. "Biographies: Donald Johanson." Paleoanthropologist, http://www.talkorigins.org/faqs/homs/djohanson.html.

Katz, Loren William. Eyewitness: The Negro in American History. Belmont, CA: David S. Lake Publishers, 1974.

Kunjufu, Jawanza. Lessons from History: A Celebration in Blackness. Sauk Village, IL: African American Images, 1988.

Lalitavistara (Life of Buddha). "Lalitavistara, East Wall, Panel I, Bodhisattva in Tusita Heaven amongst the Gods, 1/159," http://www.photodharma.net/Indonesia/05-Lalitavistara/05 - Lalitavistara.htm.

Lalitavistara. "The Birth of Buddha (Lalitavistara): Borobudur reliefs: Episode 1 (panels 1–15) and Episode 2 (panels 16–45)," hppt://www.srilankanewsweb.com/wiki-Lalitavistara.

Leakey, Louis and Leakey, Mary. "Louis and Mary Leakey: Famous Biologists." Biography, http://www.macroevolution.net/mary-leakey-2.html.

Leakey, Richard. "Leakey.com: One Hundred Years of the Leakey Family in East Africa.," http://www.leakey.com/richard_leakey.htm.

Life of Buddha. "The Birth of the Prince," Buddhist Studies, http://www.buddhanet.net/e-learning/buddhism/lifebuddha/2lbud.htm.

Lurker, Manfred. The Gods and Symbols of Ancient Egypt. New York, NY: Thames and Hudson Inc., 1982.

Massey, Gerald. Ancient Egypt: The Light of the World. Sioux Falls, SD: NuVision Publications, 2008.

Paine, Thomas. The Age of Reason: Being An Investigation of True and Fabulous Theology. London, (U.K.): Printed by Barrois, 1794.

Quirke, Stephen. Ancient Egyptian Religion. London, (U.K.): British Museum Press, 1992.

Rogers, J.A., Africa's Gift to America. St. Petersburg, FL: Helga M. Rogers, 1989.

Roughgarden, Joan. Evolution's Rainbow: Diversity, Gender and Sexuality in Nature and People. Brekeley and Los Angeles, CA. and London, (U.K.): University of California Press, 2004.

Sacred Texts. Hinduism, http://www.sacred-texts.com/hin.

Seely, Rod R., Stephens, Trent D. and Tate, Phillip. Anatomy and Physiology. New York, NY: McGraw-Hill Companies, Inc, 2006.

Sertima, Ivan Van. Nile Valley Civilizations. New Brunswick, NJ: Journal of African Civilizations, 1985.

Sertima, Ivan Van. Golden Age of the Moor. New Brunswick, NJ, and London (U.K.): Transaction Publishers, 1993.

Sertima, Ivan Van. The African Presence in Ancient America: They Came Before Columbus. New York, NY: Random House, 1976.

Sertima, Ivan Van. Egypt Revisited. New Brunswick, NJ, and London (U.K.): Transaction Publishers, 1989.

Singh, Nagendra Kr. Encylopaedic Dictionary of Sanskrit Literature Vol I A-Dh, edited by J.N. Bhattacharya and Nilanjana Sarkar. Lalitavistara: Biography of Buddha, pp. 772–773. Enclave, Delhi 110093 (India): published by N.K. Singh for Global Vision Publishing House, 2004.

Taieb, Maurice. "Paleoanthropology: The history man.," Article: Nature, http://www.nature.com/nature/journal/v443/n7109/full/443268a.html.

The Agganna Sutta. "On Knowledge of Beginnings of Humankind: The Buddhist Cosmology." http://www.urbandharma.org/pdf/AggannaSutta.pdf.

The Bradshaw Foundation in association with Stephen Oppenheimer. "Journey of Mankind the Peopling of the World." http://www.bradshawfoundation.com/journey/timeline.swf.

The Buddha. "The Birth of the Buddha: Translated from the Introduction to the Jataka" (i. 4721): Buddhist Writings. The Harvard Classics 1909–1914, http://www.bartleby.com/45/3/102.html

The Holy Bible: The Gideons International. Nashville, TN: National Publishing Company, 1983.

The Qur'an: Translated by M.H. Shakir. Elmhurst, NY: Tahrike Tarsile Qur'an Inc., 1991.

Timberlake, Karen C., Chemistry: An Introduction to General, Organic, and Biological Chemistry. San Francisco, CA: Benjamin Cummings, 2003.

Welsing, Frances Cress. The Isis Papers: The Keys to the Colors. Chicago, IL: Third World Press, 1992.

White, Timothy. "The Emergence of Modern Humans." University of California at Berkeley, http://www.isepp.org/Pages/03-04%20 Pages/White.html.

Williams, Bruce. "The Lost Pharaohs of Nubia." Archaeology 33, no.5: Discover Magazine, 1980, pp. 12–21.

Williams, Bruce. "The Nubian Salvage Project: An Early Kingdom in the Land of Bow: The A-Group Royal Cemetary at Qustul." The Oriental Institute of the University of Chicago, http://www .oi.uchicago.edu/museum/special/nubia/.

Zuk, Marlene. Sexual Selections: What We Can and Can't Learn about Sex From Animals. Berkeley and Los Angeles, CA, and London, (U.K.): University of California Press, 2002.

Index

standing beside God in heaven, 135,
146–47
Star of Creation, 117, 118, 190,
191–94
Star of David, 117–18, 141, 189–90
Star of Saturn, 190
stars, xii, xviii, 27–29, 31, 41,
51–52, 55, 66–67, 69–70, 98–99,
153, 192–93. *See also specific stars*
stele (stela) (stone tablet), 186
Stone Tablets, 13, 117, 156, 183,
186
Suchos, 186
Sudra, 55–56
Sudras, 79
Sukkot, 172
summer solstice, 173, 183–85, 187
sun
Aten associated with, 177
Atum associated with, 177
crucifixion of, 185
earth's orbit around, 188
and Hathor, 185
Jesus associated with, 177, 187
as marking passing of daytime
hours, 31
movement of, 172–73, 183–85
and myth of Khepri, 15, 70, 177
and myth of Ra, 16, 177
as one of "two lights" (eyes of
Ra), 30–31
sun dial, 187
sun disk, 175
supreme god
Allah as, 109
Amen-Ra as, 18–19
Aten as, 1, 110
Brahma as, 108
Brahman as, 50, 80, 155
in combination with other god(s),
155–56, 159

as element of creation myth, 20,
46, 67, 150
in Islamic creation myth, 64
man-made belief in, 97
personal attributes ascribed to, 97
Ra as, 56
Sah as, 167
as self-created, 20, 63
Sura
4:24–25, 77
4:92, 78
7:189, 64
15:26, 63, 64
15:26–30, 59–60
15:31–40, 60–61
15:41–46, 61–63
19:5–15, 104
19:16–25, 106
19:24–33, 132
19:29–36, 107
21:30–33, 65–66
23:6, 77
24:31, 78
24:32, 77
24:40–45, 66–67
24:58, 78
32:7–9, 63, 64
33:50, 77
33:55, 78
71:13–17, 65
Suti (Seth), 39, 90
Sutta Pitaka, 50

T
Tablets of Stone, 13, 117, 156, 183,
186
Tablets of Testimony, 13, 117, 156,
183, 186
Tanakh (Tenakh or Tenak)
as acronym, 118
as based on hearsay, 28